# ADOLESCENCE

# ADOLESCENCE

## An Anthropological Inquiry

Alice Schlegel
Herbert Barry III

THE FREE PRESS
*A Division of Macmillan, Inc.*
NEW YORK

Collier Macmillan Canada
TORONTO

Maxwell Macmillan International
NEW YORK   OXFORD   SINGAPORE   SYDNEY

The Free Press
A Division of Macmillan, Inc.
866 Third Avenue, New York, N.Y. 10022

Collier Macmillan Canada, Inc.
1200 Eglinton Avenue East
Suite 200
Don Mills, Ontario M3C 3N1

Printed in the United States of America

printing number
1  2  3  4  5  6  7  8  9  10

**Library of Congress Cataloging-in-Publication Data**

Schlegel, Alice.
    Adolescence : an anthropological inquiry / Alice Schlegel, Herbert
Barry III.
      p.  cm.
    Includes bibliographical references and index.
    ISBN 0-02-927895-3
    1. Adolescence—Cross-cultural studies.   I. Barry, Herbert.
II. Title.
HQ796.S4139   1991
305.23′5—dc20
                                     90–25216
                                       CIP

# Contents

# Preface

In spite of years of anthropological research on child socialization, adolescence has received little attention from anthropologists. (Margaret Mead's work described in *Coming of Age in Samoa* is one of the few exceptions to such a generalization.) The study on which we draw in this book is a response to the previous neglect. At the time we collected our data, we had to rely for the most part on brief, or even incidental, mention of the treatment and behavior of adolescents in reports devoted to other issues. It is not unusual for an ethnographic monograph to contain three or four pages about weddings and only a couple of paragraphs or a few scattered sentences about adolescent life. Nevertheless, we were able to retrieve a good deal of information about a number of issues. An increasing number of reports are being published to fill this gap in the socialization literature.

Our work is unique, we believe, because of its scope. A broad range of measures of adolescent behavior and treatment were coded and assessed in a worldwide representative sample of preindustrial societies. With few exceptions, studies of adolescence by psychologists and sociologists have been conducted in modern, industrial (or modernizing, industrializing) societies. There is no way of knowing how widely applicable their findings are. We take a cross-cultural approach and treat adolescence as a universal social and cultural phenomenon. Single-society studies, whatever the culture under investigation, can be assessed vis-à-vis the general patterns we have traced.

This is an anthropological inquiry. We have looked for regularities in behavior in societies across the world; at the same time, we have searched for cultural differences and their concomitants. While our concern is human behavior, we remember that Homo sapiens is a species of primates. Where appropriate, we have drawn from the research of ethologists and primatologists to enlarge our understanding of humankind.

Anthropologists have, over the years, been integrating the theoretical positions, methods, and research findings of other social scientists into their corpus of knowledge. We have drawn on the works of sociologists and psychologists in our development of hypotheses and our interpretations of the statistical analyses. We have looked to historians to provide case studies out of the European and American past to complement the ethnographic reports on non-Western peoples.

We came to this research project from different directions. The first author, an anthropologist, had written about traditional Hopi adolescence and was fresh from experiencing the adolescence of her son and daughter. The second author, a psychologist, had participated in a number of cross-cultural studies coding and analyzing data on infancy and childhood. Our work together began with a study of adolescent initiation ceremonies. A cross-cultural study of adolescence seemed to be the logical next step.

The code consists of 341 variables coded separately for girls and boys. Only a portion of the code was tested and used for this study. The variables that we selected were those related to our different theoretical interests.

Schlegel's research on kinship, social organization, and gender are most apparent in Chapters 2, 4, 5, 6, and 10. Barry's work on deviance and on personality constitute an important resource for the planning and writing of Chapters 8 and 9.

The coding for the study, under our joint direction, was done at the University of Pittsburgh. We were assisted by five coders: Ehsan M. Fahim, Gratia L. Meyer, Caterina Provost, Thomas C. H. Scott, and Janet Shuster. We are indebted to the National Institute of Mental Health for supporting this part of the project.

Barry arranged the data for statistical analysis, conducted analyses at the University of Pittsburgh, and prepared the tables. Schlegel wrote the text at the University of Arizona; she conducted additional analyses with the help of Rohn Eloul. Margaret St. John and Judith Werner provided references for Chapter 1 to works on adolescence in the fields of psychology and sociology, respectively. We are grateful to the National Science Foundation for its support of this phase of the project.

Colleagues and friends listened, read sections, provided references, and gave sound advice and criticism. Susan Milmoe, our editor at The Free Press, rescued us from many infelicitous phrases. Doris Sample prepared the manuscript. We thank all of these, and our able assistants, for their valuable contributions.

*Alice Schlegel*
Tucson, Arizona

*Herbert Barry III*
Pittsburgh, Pennsylvania

# 1

# The Anthropological Study of Adolescence

TODAY'S adolescent is easy to define as the teenager. The adolescent in preindustrial societies is more elusive. Does social adolescence even exist in societies or social strata in which children marry young, in some cases before puberty? Is adolescence extended when full adulthood is not achieved until the mid-twenties or even older? All peoples—and all families—have to deal with biological and social changes as their children transform into adults. In differences across cultures in the treatment and behavior of persons aged 11 to 17 or so, are there common features? If so, on what are they based? How can we account for the variability?

When G. S. Hall (1916) discovered adolescence, so to speak, he assumed that its age-specific features were behavioral consequences of physiological drives (Muus 1975). He emphasized the *Sturm und Drang* of adolescence, the emotional turbulence beginning at puberty that would inevitably be out-grown when the person moved into full adulthood in the early twenties. Be-cause the social and psychological characteristics of adolescence have a physiological basis, he argued, an adolescent stage is an inescapable feature of human development. Although this thesis has been countered by many, including Mead (1928) in her work on Samoan adolescents, and his theory that individual development recapitulates the cultural history of the species is no longer taken seriously, the issues he identified are still being debated. His work on the peer group prepared the ground for numerous studies of peer relationships (e.g., Hollingshead 1949; Coleman 1961); and his identification of adolescence as a period of emotional lability received further attention from psychologists (e.g., Kandel and Lesser 1972).

Whether or not adolescence is a universal *social* stage of life is another question. All peoples recognize the biological changes that occur with repro-ductive maturation, but is an adolescent social stage common across cultures or only a product of industrialization?

1

The view of life as comprising a series of stages has a long history in the West. It dates at least as far back as the 6th century B.C. and continues throughout the Middle Ages, as one element in those cosmos-ordering schemas that so engaged the attention of our ancestors. The concept was represented iconographically in many "Ages of Life" sculptures and paintings; later, it was diffused as a theme in popular art through widely distributed prints. Not until the late 19th century did the "Ages of Life" theme begin to seem provincial and out of date (cf. Ariès 1962, Chapter 1). In these classificatory representations, adolescence stood along with infancy, childhood, and the various stages of adulthood and senescence. The adolescent was often depicted at sport or in courtship, as Ariès (1962:24) wrote: "feasting, boys and girls walking together, a court of love, and the Maytime wedding festivities or hunt of the calendars." It may be that medieval adolescents entertained their elders through mock combat on the playing field as they still do in high school sports events, and that adults found as much amusement or annoyance in the romantic adventures of adolescents then as they do today.

This tradition seems to have been forgotten, so that it is now commonplace to assume that adolescence as a stage did not exist until extended schooling, which prolonged dependence upon parents, created it. Those who believe that adolescence is an artifact of contemporary conditions find support in Ariès (1962), whose comprehensive study of childhood was one of the first ripples in the new wave of intimate history of daily life. After discussing the variable terms applied to young people in French, Ariès (1962:29) concluded: "People had no idea of what we call adolescence, and the idea was a long time taking shape." (For a recent statement of this position, see Sebald 1984.)

We believe that Ariès misapplied contemporary usage and understanding to earlier historical periods. First, terms such as *adolescens* (L.) referred more to dependency status than to age, and thus were not restricted to people in the teenage years. Variability in the use of terms, therefore, does not imply that people had no concept of this stage of life. Second, most of Ariès's historical data come from the nobility, who married their children early for dynastic reasons, thus propelling them abruptly into adulthood. In this class, high social status overrode age status in determining how the child was treated. In other classes, young people were socially midway between childhood and adulthood. Other historians (Roubin 1977; Davis 1971) illuminated the age-specific customs of European adolescents and youths for the early modern period, some of them, such as the charivari or "rough music" (mocking of inappropriate marriages [cf. Chapter 5]), still practiced until fairly recent times. While adolescents as we know them—kept in the natal home under the authority of parents, attending school, and bedeviled by a bewildering array of occupational choices—are a modern phenomenon, adolescence as a social stage with its own activities and behaviors, expectations and rewards, is well recorded in the history and literature of earlier times.

Shakespeare's works alone give ample evidence that some of the behavioral dispositions we expect to find in contemporary adolescents were recognized in the 16th century: the rebellious "son" (Caliban) and dutiful daughter of *The Tempest,* the hell-raising Price Hal of *Falstaff,* and the hopelessly idealistic romantic lovers of *Romeo and Juliet* all have their present-day counterparts.

Social scientists generally agree that adolescence is a period intervening between childhood and full adulthood, during which preparation for adult occupational, marital, and social class statuses and roles is initiated or intensified. Coleman (1980) summed up adolescence as including biological and affective reorganization, severance of early emotional ties to parents, and experimentation with social roles. While anthropologists have made a few extended studies of adolescence in particular societies (Mead 1928; Elwin 1947), the great bulk of research on adolescence has been conducted by psychoanalysts and developmental psychologists, with sociologists contributing a fair amount.

Researchers in recent years have been examining adolescence in an updated "Ages of Man" framework, variously called life stages, the life span, or the life course (Bush and Simmons 1981). Emphasis is placed on the relation of proximate stages or the problems of stage transition somewhat more than on the stages themselves; when attention is paid to a particular stage, e.g., adolescence, it is often viewed explicitly as bearing the fruits of preceding stages and sowing the seed for following ones (cf. Erikson 1950; Newman and Newman 1976).

However, the approaches differ somewhat among disciplines. Psychoanalysts tend to look at adolescence as the time when childhood conflicts are resolved and the person learns to control sexual and aggressive impulses (cf. Blos 1979). Developmental psychologists also deal with the movement out of childhood, focusing on cognitive reorganization (cf. Petersen 1988). Sociologists, on the other hand, emphasize adolescence as a period of socialization for adult social roles (Bush and Simmons 1981). Putting it simplistically, sociologists view adolescence from the perspective of adulthood, whereas psychoanalysts and developmental psychologists treat it as part of child development.

These differing perspectives of the disciplines lead to somewhat different conclusions about the universality of an adolescent social stage. The developmental psychologist and psychoanalyst look for some period of transition between childhood and adulthood that allows affective resolution and cognitive restructuring to occur, making adolescence a psychological imperative.

To the sociologist, however, adolescence may appear unnecessary in societies in which adult social roles can be learned or anticipated in childhood. For example, Friedenberg (1973:110) averred that in most primitive cultures, "one is either a child or an adult and adolescence is absent" because "adolescence is conceived as a distinct stage of life in societies so complicated and differentiated that each individual's social role and function takes years to define and learn.'' In other words, adolescence is identified as a training period, which can be dispensed with when no special training is needed. However, most sociological studies of adolescence deal with modern society and do not concern themselves with the question of universality. The definition of adolescence given by Elder (1975a:3), for example, explicitly confines itself to contemporary adolescence:

> Despite a lack of consensus among social scientists on the social boundaries of contemporary adolescence, the clearest marker for entry into adolescence is the transition from primary to secondary school (from sixth to seventh grade). Entry into one or more adult roles (marriage, parenthood, full-time employment, financial independence) is commonly regarded as the upper boundary.

Another consequence of the differences among the sister disciplines influenced our thinking. Looking at adolescence as a time of preparation for adult life, to be studied through age norms, roles, and the context of roles, sociologists tend to emphasize sociogenic, or situational, causes of behavior. To the sociologist, for example, contentment or stress and their behavioral expressions are the consequences of environmental influences rather than of success or failure in resolving psychic conflict (cf. Pearlin 1975). The causes of disaffection in adolescence lie within frustrations associated with present or anticipated role failure rather than the adolescent's psyche (Stinchcombe 1964; Finestone 1976). The psychoanalyst and the developmental psychologist, however, are generally more concerned with psychogenic factors, such as the ways in which the conflicts of early development are reactivated by present conditions to affect self-image and behavior (cf. Howard 1982; Shweder 1979).

Until the 1970s, anthropologists, influenced by psychoanalytic and learning theory, tended to look at antecedent conditions of socialization as the determinants of adult behavior, the intervening variable being personality. Noteworthy exceptions are Nadel (1967, orig. 1952), who accounted for differences in witchcraft beliefs by sociogenic rather than psychogenic factors, and Young (1965). Although a social psychologist, Young dealt with a topic dear to the hearts of anthropologists, initiation ceremonies, as a response to situational needs of the society rather than to psychological needs of the initiates or the initiators—quite a departure from the psychogenic approaches of some other investigators (e.g., Whiting, Kluckhohn, and Anthony 1958).[1]

More recently, anthropologists have responded to the direction set by sociologists and psychologists of the interactionist or phenomenological approach (cf. LeVine 1973:46–48; Howard 1982) by including situational responses as determinants of behavior. The work of Roberts and his collaborators (e.g., Roberts and Sutton-Smith 1962) combined psychogenic and sociogenic theory in the conflict-enculturation theory of involvement in games; Schlegel and Barry (1989) utilized this theory in their study of adolescent games.

Much of the work of the last 20 years in anthropology assessing the behavior of children leans heavily on situational explanations. Ember (1973) reported that the "masculine" behavior of boys is modified when they perform tasks conventionally assigned to girls because the settings promote "feminine" behavior. Bolton et al. (1976) found that children who herd are more independent and self-reliant than children in the same community who do not. Howard (1982) cited his research among Hawaiian children as an example of the interactional approach. Munroe and Munroe's (1989) work on birth order and behavior of children was sensitive to the situational features of child experience. A strong assertion of the sociogenic position was made by B. Whiting. Drawing on the work of Whiting and Whiting (1975), she stated their conviction that parents' "greatest effect is in the assignment of the child to settings that have important socializing influences" (Whiting 1980:97).

Schlegel (1975) adduced both pychogenic and situational explanations of attitude and behavior in a study of girls' adolescence among the Hopi, a Pueblo Indian people of Arizona; her findings are summarized here:

> Conflict with the mother results from abrupt role changes, and anxiety over future marriage is attributed both to family structure and to childhood anxieties over relations with the father. At puberty, the girl who in childhood had few responsibilities and great freedom of movement is suddenly kept within the house most of the time, where she is expected to spend long hours grinding corn and learning cooking techniques in serious preparation for marriage. This is a tense time for mothers and daughters, exacerbated by parental pressures to find a good husband. The burden of attracting a spouse rests with girls, for in this society, men marry into their wives' homes. Fathers want the assistance a son-in-law gives in farming and herding; the girls' mothers and maternal uncles are eager for them to marry and bear children who will perpetuate the matrilineal clans; and the girls themselves look forward to the adult status that becomes theirs upon marriage. Boys, however, are not so eager to give up their carefree bachelor lives; and their reluctance to marry intensifies the anxiousness some girls may already feel about the prospect of marrying, in spite of the fact that every normal woman marries.

Schlegel located the origin of this anxiousness in the early relations with fathers who were loving but unpredictable. She maintained that neither present circumstances nor past events alone were sufficient to account for the strong emotion older women still exhibit when talking about these matters, or the parents' fear, which had little objective basis, that an adolescent daughter is liable to fall into depression and die if a hoped-for suitor rejects her.

In the study reported in this book, we rely on both antecedent and situational explanations of adolescent behavior. We relate various features of adolescence to the current situation and to parental socialization practices in infancy and early childhood. However, we cannot provide a clear answer to the question of which is primary, nor do we feel that it is necessary to try. We will attempt to outline complexes of related variables, antecedent and situational, that combine in meaningful ways. In some cases, personality (inferred from infant and early child-rearing techniques) may take precedence. In others, the influence of the social situation may appear stronger. In still others, the interaction of variables may make such an attempt meaningless as well as impossible.

———

The anthropological approach is distinctive in being holistic, placing its object of study within social and cultural systems (cf. Cohen 1964). Anthropologists study whole cultures, even when their particular interest is in one institution or a single cultural domain. For anthropologists, adolescence is not only a time for learning adult roles, as sociologists tend to see it, but also a time during which young people are often making important contributions to society: observations from many societies indicate that adolescents are *useful* to their families and communities, an impression one rarely gets if one studies only Western adolescence. Adolescence can be studied as a stage *sui generis* rather than as simply a marginal or transitional period.

In the light of comparative data that adolescence may be as short as one year, particularly for girls, the psychological view of adolescence as a time for resolution of earlier conflicts is called into question. When sexual gratification is delayed long past puberty and socially meaningful status is withheld, as it is in modern society, the revival of earlier conflicts may be a function of social adolescence rather than the reverse: these conflicts over authority and inappropriately directed sexual desires would be muted if not prevented by the elimination of an adolescent stage, if at puberty all young people were given the full sexual gratification and adult status of marriage. Sociologists and psychologists can tell us much about what happens to adolescents in modern society, but their models may not always be applicable across cultures.

Anthropologists study adolescence as a contributing part of a larger system of social organization. Whereas the sociologist or social psychologist might ask, "How does society affect the adolescent?" the anthropologist will ask, in addition, "How do adolescents affect society?" With social power vested in adults, particularly in adult males in most places, an anthro-

pological question would be, "How do adults use adolescents in the further-
ing of their own ends—as laborers, pawns in marriage negotiations, per-
formers in dance or sports, or other ways?" The uses to which adolescents
are put will, in turn, determine many of their activities.

Up to now, we have discussed anthropology as a human science and related it to other sciences of human behavior. One of the fruitful develop-
ments of recent years has been the incorporation of the research of
ethologists and primatologists into anthropological theories of human behavior. *Homo sapiens* is a unique species, the only one with language and
culture, but it belongs to the order of mammals and the family of primates.
Cross-species comparisons allow human behavior to be understood within
the broader spectrum of animal behavior generally, by testing for regularities
that go beyond culture. Such comparisons have expanded the meaning of
*holistic* for anthropology. The systems within which behaviors are located
can be extended beyond a single society and the domain of human societies
to the domain of primate or even mammalian social organization. We have
borne this in mind as we designed our questions and interpreted our analyses.

A sense of the relation of adolescence to larger systems is the major contribution anthropologists can offer here. Empirical field research requires
the anthropologist to be both a participant and an observer in a culture for a
limited period. The anthropologist observes and records behaviors and conversation, measuring as closely as possible the cultural features under investigation. These data are then recorded and analyzed to describe culture and
social organization at a particular point in time. The shortcoming of this
method is one well known to life-course sociologists, who have drawn attention to the cohort effect, or behavior due not to abiding norms or patterns
but rather to conditions specific to a particular time (Mannheim 1952; Riley
et al. 1972; Elder 1974). The observer often cannot separate the age effect—
being at a particular age or stage in life with its institutionalized norms—
from the cohort effect, particularly when behaviors rather than informant
generalizations about the culture are used as indicators of cultural features.
For example, if the anthropologist determines that delinquency is pervasive
among the adolescents of a particular society, is that a cultural norm related
to long-standing patterns of family structure or child socialization? Or is that
fact the consequence, say, of a random spurt in population growth, resulting
in a decline in anticipated access to resources and a realization that the path
to successful adulthood is blocked? In recognition of this possibility, anthropologists try to elicit the cultural interpretation of present behavior, in order
to disentangle traditional norms and patterns from behavior due to situational factors.[2] Nevertheless, cohort effect has to be considered in the analysis of data across cultures. It introduces an element of randomness that can
produce deviant cases, societies whose data are not in accord with the statistically significant pattern established for a set of variables.

## An Anthropological Definition of Adolescence

An anthropological definition of adolescence, in common with psychological and sociological definitions, recognizes adolescence as a social stage intervening between childhood and adulthood in the passage through life. (We will have more to say about a second stage, youth, in some but not all societies.) Adolescence can be seen as a period of social role learning and restructuring: not simply a period in which early learning is crystallized, but rather one in which unlearning and new learning take place. Along with training for specific roles, there is learning in the sense of cognitive and affective reorganization away from the behavioral modes of childhood and toward adult modes. The child is characterized by dependency, subordination, and social asexuality, even as these vary across cultures. As his social scope, responsibilities, and expectations enlarge, the adolescent assumes greater autonomy, more of a peer relationship with same-sex adults, and an interest in sexual activities. Such unlearning and relearning is unlikely to be without cost to adolescents or to their families, who must also undergo changes in the ways they respond to their maturing children.

To be successful, socialization must be both responsive and anticipatory, that is, it must help the individual both to operate in the present and to prepare for the future. Anticipatory socialization becomes accelerated sometime after about age 10, when major changes are propelling the individual toward biological adulthood; yet the young person is not a full adult and does not receive whatever respect and deference are due to adults of the same sex and social status. There is a certain ambiguity to the conflicting goals of adolescent socialization, which seek to maintain some of the subordination and dependency of childhood while moving the adolescent toward adulthood. Possibly this ambivalence accounts for the social awkwardness so typical of adolescents around the world. Much of their psychological discomfort and lack of social poise may result from these conflicting socialization goals.

Unlearning and relearning are necessary because of the particular biological and social characteristics of our species. One consequence of the long period of immaturity is that dependency, necessary for survival, is deeply engrained in the child. The child's strongest bonds are to the family, yet the incest taboo and customs that militate against incest direct the adolescent to consider or actively pursue the formation of an intimate bond with someone outside this close circle. The fact that human beings live in socially integrated communities rather than as social isolates or in isolated families means that, at some point before full adulthood, young people must prepare for an active role in the community. In anticipating the social and sexual relationships and responsibilities of adult life, the adolescent is shifting focus away from a predominant attention to the household and toward attention to both the household and the community, from members of the family to persons who will become in-laws or with whom there will be common interests in associations broader than the family—kin groups, sodalities, factions, networks, and other kinds of social groupings that adults form.

This shift of focus to the broader world does not go unaided. The process is facilitated by social structures intervening between the few and primary structures of childhood and the many and complex structures of adult life. One of these structures in the modern world is the secondary school, which, if it is to socialize effectively, cannot be merely a continuation of primary school but must take the particular needs and goals of adolescents into account. Universally, however, an important intervening structure is the peer group, comprising members of the same sex. Although it is true that younger children have peer groups, which assume greater importance as the child gets older, it is our contention that the position of the peer group becomes central to socialization in adolescence rather than ancillary to it (cf. Coleman 1980). By no means does the peer group supplant the family as a socializing agent; rather, it coexists with the family as a structure that allows for intense interaction outside the family, for the organization of activities that affect the community, and for jockeying for status in settings relatively free from adult intervention. Within the peer group, adolescents can try out the social activities and maneuverings of adulthood while still sheltered by their families. The peer group gives them the opportunity to experiment while their subordinate age status gives them license to do so without being taken too seriously.

It is the peer group, more than any other structure, that is critical to a holistic definition of adolescence, playing a role not only in the life of the individual but also in the social organization of the community. Children do not pose much of a problem to the community, as they are under the control of their families. Their play-group activities are unlikely to affect the community, even though considerable community resources may be allocated to children, particularly where the state has taken over such responsibilities as education. However, the rapid biological changes of puberty make adolescents a population within the community that requires more than simply familial attention.

The shift from nonreproductive capacity to reproductivity means that adolescent sexuality must be considered. Though an adolescent girl's sexuality may be an issue only for her family, who have to deal with any offspring she may produce outside of marriage, the sexuality of unmated boys can cause problems for the community, which must try to keep them from sexual relations with inappropriate girls or married women. Youthful energy must be channeled in socially constructive directions, and the potential aggressiveness of boys must be curbed. Peer groups, as extrafamilial structures that are less powerful than adult structures, are means through which adults can organize adolescent activities, motivating and rewarding them collectively for behavior that is beneficial to the community and punishing them for lapses.[3] We need to examine how adults use peer groups to structure the lives of adolescents until they are safely absorbed into the adult population and how the community, as well as the family, uses its adolescent children as a source of labor or for other social ends.

Taking an anthropological view of the passage through life, we assume that, though there may be some variability across cultures in the chronological age at which people enter and leave social stages, each stage is to some degree linked to important biological changes. Minimally, universally recognized social stages are infancy, childhood, adulthood, and, we contend, adolescence.[4] Transition from one stage to another, whether gradual or abrupt, is signified by differences in the kind or intensity of occupational and leisure activities and in familial and community roles and responsibilities. Treatment of the individual by the family and community will vary according to the life stage. Our concern is to examine the behavior and treatment of adolescents and the concomitant features of culture and social organization that account for variability across cultures.

Social adolescence is unlikely to begin much before age 11, when the physical and cognitive capacities of the child have matured to the point where children can be given social responsibilities. It usually ends at marriage, although marriage is not universally a marker of entry into full adulthood even though reproductive activities undergo marked changes at marriage.

Although the beginning of adolescence may be partially determined by biological development, the end is socially determined. Generally, however, if full social adulthood is delayed many years beyond puberty, there is a further stage between adolescence and adulthood. Following Keniston (1971), we call this *youth,* a stage during which one's behavior and treatment differ in important ways from those of adolescents and yet one is not fully adult. Youth is not an extension of adolescence but rather a stage with its own expectations and demands, during which various occupations and potential marriage partners may be given a trial or young men and women may have a special community role (see Chapter 3).

We are not the first to recognize the necessity of adolescence. Aberle et al. (1963:261) stated:

> There is such a gap [between the point at which young individuals are sexually mature and the point at which they can fend for themselves] in all known human groups—or least in no known human group does the onset of sexual maturity coincide with *full* assumption of adult economic and social responsibilities. Even where marriage occurs at a very early age—indeed, especially where it does—the youthful marital partner, or pair, remains under the direction of senior members of the kin group. (italics in the original)

Their position differs somewhat from ours, because we do not see any discrepancy between full social adulthood and some degree of subordination to senior members of the kin group. Such subordination is usual in societies in which residence is in an extended family and headship of the family household or estate may not begin until the head is well into middle age. As we and many others do, these authors recognize the disjuncture between biological and social maturity. Children do not usually assume adult status when first menstruation or first ejaculation is experienced or expected.

In certain societies adolescence for girls ends with marriage at or shortly after puberty, and it is instructive to examine them.[5] In some of these, it is parenthood, not marriage, that signals full adulthood for one or both sexes. In such cases, girls might become mothers, and thereby adults, anywhere from two to four years after puberty, in the middle or late teens. Some examples from our study are the Gheg of Albania, the Micmac of eastern Canada, and the Quiche of Guatemala. In other societies, such as the Aranda of Australia, the Copper Eskimo of Alaska, and the Yanomamo of Venezuela, childhood ends and social adolescence begins before puberty; even if a girl becomes an adult when she marries soon after menarche, there is a period of social adolescence preceding puberty. Among the Aranda, for example, the adolescent initiation ceremony occurs when the girl's breasts begin to develop.

When adolescence is very short and there is no youth stage, behavioral reorganization may continue into the early years of social adulthood. Long adolescence, i.e., delay in marriage and adulthood, is significantly associated with neolocal residence, the young couple living apart from either parental family (see Chapter 6). More typically in traditional societies, however, they live either with his family or, less commonly, with hers; and junior adults continue to defer to senior kin. Under these conditions, it is possible for quite young people to marry. While the *social* transition from adolescent to adult may be abrupt, the behavioral and psychological processes that the adolescent undergoes are unlikely to terminate rapidly. It may be necessary to think of adolescence as a time during which these processes of reorganization get underway rather than a time during which they are necessarily completed.

Finally, we must consider whether adolescence is equally important for the two sexes. When we examine the roles of adult women and men, we see that the subordination of children to adults continues in a new form for women in most places, as subordination to men; the girls' pattern of subordination need not undergo so much of a transformation as the boys' as they grow into adulthood. In such places, girls may not need as long a period of readjustment as boys do. In fact, we generally find that social adolescence for girls ends at an earlier age than for boys, about two or four years earlier in most cases (see Chapter 3). Similarly, the transition from childhood to adulthood is generally more continuous for girls than for boys. The greater degree of discontinuity for boys should be reflected in behavior that differs from that of girls. We will look at the relevant data later in the book.

## Premises of the Study

Our initial research was designed to collect information about issues related to adolescence and to discern patterns across cultures rather than to test specific hypotheses. The hypotheses that formed the basis for data collection are simple but by no means self-evident. The first one is that a universal or nearly universal stage of social adolescence exists between childhood and full adulthood, characterized by differences from the preceding and following stages in the ways that adolescents behave and are treated. The second hypothesis is that some measurable difference exists across cultures between the treatment of girls and that of boys, corresponding to a universal distinction between the sexes in social roles and cultural perception.

The issues emerged from two sources, the abundant literature on adolescence in Western society and ethnographic descriptions of adolescents. The empirical evidence is weighted on the side of commonalities across cultures. (It is these commonalities, in fact, that give rise to the model of adolescence offered in the following chapter.)

One issue that receives particular attention in the sociological and psychological literature is the adolescent's separating from the natal home while at the same time remaining in it. Not all societies inculcate independence and autonomy to the degree that Western ones do; however, as individuals become more involved with persons and social groups outside the family, dependency on the family is somewhat diluted, and the enlargement of the social world brings in its train an increase in responsibilities. Nevertheless, for all adolescents, even those most separated from the family (like the child in boarding school), the parental home is where the young person is socially and emotionally grounded. Therefore, we need information on household activities and the character of family relations.

A second issue, which has received more attention from ethnographers and social historians than from sociologists and psychologists, is the place of adolescents in the larger community and the their contributions to it.

As we indicated earlier, we regard the peer group as intervening between the child's heavy involvement in the family and the adult's dual involvement in family and community. This structured setting is where much of the social learning for adulthood takes place. The peer group as a social institution has been well studied by sociologists in particular, and their literature helped us frame our inquiry into the forms, activities, and relationships of that universal phenomenon.

A third issue, adolescent pathology, raises questions about the interplay of family, community, and peer group. We consider it unlikely that adolescence can be a stress-free time for young people or for their parents, as relationships in the family constellation are changing rapidly at the same time that the child's body is taking on new conformations and capabilities. With the accompanying internal stresses, both those originating in hormonal changes and those involving unlearning and relearning, it seems to us implausible that adolescence would be experienced without uncertainties, self-doubts, and ambiguities in family attachments. However, these reactions need not be of such magnitude as to result in physical or mental pathology, nor need they erupt into antisocial behavior. We are concerned with the conditions under which social pathology arises.

A fourth issue is adolescent sexuality, and we ask whether its management is as problematic elsewhere as our society finds it. The range in the ethnographic literature is very wide. At one extreme, a number of Middle Eastern peoples are known to kill girls who have dishonored their families by losing their virginity. At the other extreme are Asian and Pacific groups that maintain adolescent houses where young people are expected and encouraged to indulge in sexual intercourse with a number of partners. A similar range is seen for homosexuality, from general tolerance (and in a few societies, prescribed adolescent homosexual acts) to strict prohibition. It is not only the potential reproduction of the adolescent girl that must be regulated, even in very permissive societies. Just as important to those who control young people is the regulation of their sexual desires, channeling them in appropriate directions toward approved partners and preventing wayward passions from disrupting the social alliances of the elders.

The final issue is preparation for adult life. We wish to know what makes for success in adolescence and how adolescents prove their future worth to the community of adults. These questions do not necessarily elicit the same answers. The adolescent athlete in America may be a success among his peers and receive the praise of sports-minded adults, but he is not by reason of his athletic ability being groomed as a future professional or corporation executive. Nevertheless, although success in the present does not ensure success in the future, the character traits that underlie present-oriented and future-oriented activities may be similar for both the athlete and the corporation member. Competitiveness and cooperativeness are useful character traits in both settings. We examine the inculcation of character traits during adolescence, those just mentioned and others.

An important part of preparation for adult life is the training in productive activities that the adolescent receives. In many societies, such as those practicing foraging (hunting and gathering wild foods for subsistence) or simple horticulture, most of the specific training will have been given before adolescence. For example, it is not unusual among foragers for a boy's first kill of a large animal to mark the end of childhood and the beginning of adolescence. When productive activities are more elaborated, as in societies with advanced horticulture or agriculture, or when the management of private property is associated with adult status, as in pastoral or agricultural societies, adolescence is likely to be a time in which preparation for adult productive roles is more intensive.

Schooling is an important means of transmitting adult skills in industrial nations. Very few societies examined in this study send adolescents to school; schooling in preindustrial societies is usually restricted to the elite or, if more widely dispersed, to young children only. By adolescence, most children have left school and are engaged in some productive work. Even as recently as 1962, in a nation as economically advanced as the Federal Republic of Germany, only 19.8 percent of adolescents between 16 and 18 were in school, most of the remainder already working full time or as apprentices (Allerbeck and Hoag 1985). In this book, we shall give schooling limited attention.

## The Cross-Cultural Method

We followed the cross-cultural or hologeistic method, in which variables are coded for a large representative sample of societies. The data are then subjected to statistical analyses to find pairs or clusters of correlated variables. The ultimate goal is to demonstrate, or to provide the data to infer, causal relationships among variables (cf. Levinson and Malone 1980).

Our codes were constructed to elicit information on the issues of interest. Coding was done from ethnographic monographs, published accounts of a culture usually but not always written by anthropologists. Because the data were not originally collected for the study, many questions cannot be answered with available data in every case. The quantity and type of missing data vary considerably from one society to another; for some of the variables, there was information on fewer than 10 of 186 societies, while for others there were as many as 177 cases with information. This is a methodological difficulty of hologeistic research, for scattered missing data restrict the techniques of statistical analysis that can be used.

Another difficulty in this type of research is that the ethnographic accounts at times report observed behavior and at times recount what informants say about their culture. There is often some discrepancy between what people believe and say about their behavior and what the relatively unbiased observer witnesses. Even with observed data, interpretations can differ widely between observers. Coders must exercise judgment, based on wide knowledge of ethnographic cases, in resolving discrepancies. Anthropologists are trained observers who usually spend enough time in the field to make fairly accurate assessments of behavior. The descriptions they offer can generally be trusted, even if they may interpret them in idiosyncratic ways. Mead's (1928) study of Samoan girls is a case in point: the accounts included in her book, the data, contradict the sunny picture she painted of stress-free adolescence in her interpretation.

Still another difficulty with using ethnographies, which describe whole cultures or major segments such as castes or communities, is the scarcity of detailed information on intracultural variability. One form of such variability is often reported, differences between girls and boys in their settings and activities. Our study measures this intracultural variation.

These limitations of the hologeistic method are offset by some distinct advantages. First, it is the only method that systematically utilizes the breadth of the ethnographic record. Commonalities among cultures can be found that crosscut the usual typologies based on subsistence type, level of societal complexity, type of descent, regional placement, and the like.

Second, isolating culture traits and pulling them out of context eliminates "noise," the distracting effect of coterminous traits within that culture. When one is analyzing a single culture, it is easy to assume that the cause of x condition lies in y as the antecedent condition. Even if several cultures, all having x and y present, are under examination, for these conditions x and y, the several cultures can be seen simply as replicas of one another. Testing the proposition across a wide sample of societies, however, one might find that the coexistence of x and y is a deviant case. The clearest presentation of this problem known to us was given by Köbben (1973) in his lively article "Comparativists and Non-Comparativists in Anthropology." In demonstrating the pitfalls of generalizing on the basis of a single or very limited number of cases, he compiled a list of contradictory pairs of generalizations. One, relevant to this study, is as follows (Köbben 1973:589):

8a: a society, such as the Ibo, where a father allows his son autonomy, is likely to produce men high in achievement motivation; hence is open to modernization. . . .
    b: a society, such as the Hindustani's where the father is an authoritarian figure, produces aggression in the sons, who become, thereby, highly ambitious; hence is open to modernization. . . .

One of these pairs is likely to represent a deviant case, that is, to deviate from the statistically established correlation; or perhaps both do, if in fact there is no significant association between authority of the father and achievement motivation when tested worldwide.

Users of the hologeistic method are aware, sometimes painfully so, of the limitations of the method and make every effort to compensate for them. One such is to refine the procedural steps. Another, widely discussed among cross-culturalists, is triangulation, that is, using other methods to test propositions that have been tested by the hologeistic method. Single-case analyses, intracultural comparisons, tests of similar propositions conducted by social scientists of other disciplines, and hologeistic tests of different but related propositions are all ways in which cross-cultural researchers gain—or lose—confidence in their findings. We hope that the findings of this study will be retested by a variety of other methods.

## Methodological Procedures

The sample used is the Standard Cross-Cultural Sample (Murdock and White 1980), a sample of 186 preindustrial societies worldwide (listed in Appendix I), selected by Murdock to be representative of regional placement, level of sociocultural complexity, and major features of social organization. As some world regions have been reported on more fully than others, societies in the sample vary in the quantity of information on them. Wherever appropriate, Murdock selected representative societies with the largest amount of available data. Attempts were made to exclude societies known to have had close or continuous contact, thus avoiding the effects of diffusion as much as possible. (In cross-cultural research, this is called Galton's problem.) One feature of the sample is the pinpointing of each cultural unit to a specific time and to the smallest identifiable subgroup of the society, usually a community. This pinpointing by time and locale enhances the accuracy of correlations between traits, because their presence or absence must coexist temporally and spatially within a unit of interacting persons in order to be meaningful.

The coding manual is given in Appendix II. It contains variables related to the actions and personality of adolescents, features of their social settings, and the nature of their interpersonal relationships. It includes variables previously coded for infancy and childhood (Barry and Paxson 1980; Barry et al. 1980a). Five research assistants did the coding from the ethnographic documents, collected in the research library of the Cross-Cultural Cumulative Coding Center at the University of Pittsburgh. The coding was preceded by a three-month period of training, during which time the coders arrived at consensus about the meaning of the codes and the codes themselves were refined. Although resources did not permit every society to be coded twice independently, societies were randomly selected for recoding. In these cases, coder discrepancies were minimal, giving us confidence that consensus had been reached.[6]

Data analyses have been conducted at both the University of Pittsburgh and the University of Arizona. Given the random missing data problem, only bivariate statistics could be used. Details of the procedure are discussed in Appendix II.

Societies change over time, traditional ones no less than modern nation-states. A description accurate at one period may be inaccurate 50, or even 20, years later. To avoid confusion, anthropologists often use the "ethnographic present," referring in the present tense to cases as they were at one particular point in time. For example, the life of Hopi adolescents, used for illustration in several chapters, is referred to in this manner, even though the data come from the first author's historical reconstruction of adolescent life in the late 19th century and no Hopis experience adolescence in that way today.

All of the societies in the sample have been pinpointed by place and time, the latter usually being time of first contact or earliest reliable report-age. Details on the sample are given in Murdock and White (1980). When societies not in the sample are used for illustration, the time period is that of the ethnographer's fieldwork or historical reconstruction and can be obtained from the cited ethnography. Information on historical cases is given in the past tense except for historical societies in the sample, such as the Romans.

The use of the ethnographic present has been criticized as implying that tribal societies are changeless and that only the great civilizations and their descendants have a history. No such implication colors the use of the ethnographic present in cross-cultural research; it is a useful convention that facilitates the comparison of many cases from different times as well as places.

# 2

# An Ethological Approach to Human Social Organization[1]

OF the biological changes that adolescents undergo, the most critical to themselves and society is the transformation from a nonreproductive to a reproductive state. We have alluded before to the problem of fertile daughters and lusty sons; unless girls are married shortly after puberty, their fertility must be dealt with. The sexuality of adolescent boys is a matter of concern almost everywhere, for the marriage of boys at puberty is rare.

Why do societies not avoid these problems by marrying children at puberty? Even among foragers, hunting and gathering peoples who generally have no property and therefore have no economic reasons to delay marriage, boys do not get permanent mates until some time after puberty. Foraging societies generally allow sexual freedom; but this does not avoid the problem altogether, as boys still have to negotiate with girls for sex and cannot count on having a partner always available. Even in permissive societies, not all boys may find their sexual desires satisfied whenever they wish. In small foraging bands, no unrelated girls may be available during a boy's adolescence, and then adultery with a married woman can become a strong temptation.

The most likely answer to this question is that permanent mating is not appropriate until the boy has proven his ability to provide for a wife and children. The works of several anthropologists, Meillassoux (1981) and Collier and Rosaldo (1981), discussed the exchange nature—meat for domestic comforts—of marriage among foragers. Collier and Rosaldo, recognizing that the provisions go not only to the wife but also to her parents, labeled this category "bride service societies." They extended it to include some South American and other societies that practice very simple horticulture along with gathering and hunting and thus exhibit many of the features of true foragers. In such groups, women have considerable freedom to bestow themselves on mates, and the mating bond remains intact as long as the husband provides the wife and her parents with game. As women gather their own

18

vegetal food, it is the ability to contribute meat that determines whether a boy is ready to assume the roles of husband and of father to his wife's children. The wife provides the husband with cooked food and sex while he provides her with raw meat and sex. It is not a question of going hungry without a wife, for a female relative will happily allow an unmarried boy or man to eat at her hearth if he contributes meat. Rather, it is having the right to expect cooked food and sex, in contrast to having to ask or negotiate for them, that makes marriage attractive to men in foraging societies. Marriage also secures men the right to domestic comforts and the social support to uphold these rights. The benefits of fatherhood will be addressed in Chapter 6.

Rarely do boys in their early teens take on the full economic responsibility of adult men. It is not unusual among foragers for a boy to leave childhood, that is, to be recognized as a social adolescent, after his first successful kill of a large game animal around puberty. Some time may elapse, from one to several years, before he can convince a girl and her parents that he can be relied on for a steady supply of meat. In more complex societies in which goods are exchanged, it may take years for the boy and his father to accumulate or negotiate for goods to accompany the marriage or for his productive capacity and potential leadership qualities to be assessed as adequate for a son-in-law.

The exceptions to this, instances in which boys may be married at puberty, seem to be those in which neither wealth and productive capacity nor leadership position are at issue, that is, in some aristocratic families in which economic security and the boy's future role are assured by the status into which he was born. Furthermore, marriage in such cases provides an opportunity for the parents of the couple to cement a political or economic alliance; they are eager to contract it as soon as their children are minimally ready. Perhaps there are tribal or peasant societies in which marriage for boys at puberty is thought to be desirable by adults for other reasons, but we know of no such cases. Child betrothals occur, but such betrothals rarely if ever have the same binding quality as marriage and can usually be broken if one or the other party turns out to be unacceptable. Thus, while girls may marry as early as 13, boys are rarely deemed marriageable before their late teens. The subject of marriage is developed in Chapter 6.

Social adolescence, then, is a response to the disjuncture between sexual reproductivity and full social maturity. It appears to be universal for boys; for girls, in the majority of societies, at least a short period of social adolescence intervenes between puberty and the full assumption of adult roles, usually at marriage.

We focus on reproduction as a key issue for an understanding of adolescence and on the social systems of reproduction—for human society, the systems of kinship and marriage—as central to social organization. We consider both biological and social factors in the management of reproduction.

Ethologists have established beyond doubt that the social organization of most animals militates against close inbreeding, that is, mating between parents and children and between siblings. Various mechanisms accomplish this outbreeding. A common one is the dispersal of the young at puberty, the result being that the likelihood of close kin mating is reduced. Dispersal may serve other purposes as well, such as preventing a concentration of animals that would degrade the local habitat (cf. Dunbar 1988:82). Whatever the proximate cause, the result is a reduction of inbreeding. Another mechanism, well established for mice, who live as adults in close proximity to near kin, is the genetically programmed repulsion between parents and children and between siblings as mates (Beauchamp et al. 1985). These mechanisms may have evolved in response to genetic degradation caused by very close inbreeding and to the greater survival of offspring among those individuals who mate outside the parent-child-sibling sphere. First-cousin mating, however, is not close inbreeding; in some species, it may confer the advantage of preserving biologically adaptive features without concentrating maladaptive ones (cf. Lewin 1984).

We expect to find behaviors in human societies, as in societies of other animals, that reduce the likelihood of close inbreeding. In addition to the behaviors to be discussed later, there is the incest taboo, a cultural universal. With very few exceptions the taboo includes the nuclear family; beyond that, marriage rules may vary from permissive to highly restrictive of between-kin marriage. At the permissive end of the continuum, Aiyappan (1934) discussed uncle-niece marriage (between mother's brother and sister's daughter) among non-Aryan peoples of India and mentioned a few cases of grandfather-granddaughter marriage as well. First-cousin marriage is widespread among tribal peoples, and the marriage of the children of two brothers is a preferred form in many Moslem groups.

In contrast to these endogamous societies, there are those in which marriage between any known kin is incestuous. An extreme example is medieval Europe. Goody (1983) credited the changes toward extreme exogamy in early Christian European marriage rules to the increasing control of the Catholic Church over marriage; prohibition of marriages to kin was seen by Goody as one strategy by which the Church broke down the corporateness of kin groups. Neither social mechanisms nor the cultural taboo are sufficient to prevent incest altogether; however, they restrain it to the point that the offspring of incestuous unions comprise only a very small fraction of the total human population.

In a discussion of mating systems among foragers, Meillassoux (1981) dismissed the universality and importance of the incest taboo, citing several ethnographic or historical reports of tolerance toward the mating of father and daughter or sister and brother. With the exception of the curious and not well understood case of Roman Egypt, where there seem to have been some legal marriages between full siblings (Hopkins 1980), these are all instances of either social deviance reported by ethnographers or very specific exceptions to general incest prohibitions to mark unusual events or situations. Examples are the royal incestuous marriages of Egypt and Hawaii and some African noble clans to preserve the purity of the blood line. In no sense can incest be said to be inconsequential; the fact that it is not always publicly punished may simply be due to the widespread notion in stateless societies that what happens inside the family is no one's business but its own.

A requirement of the human family, which contains sexually mature but unmated members, is to be organized in such a way as to avoid incestuous matings. In addition, parents wish not only to avoid inappropriate matings but to encourage appropriate ones—marriages—from which they will derive some social or material benefit. The reproductive system of human society is the consequence of several factors: social mechanisms comparable to the social mechanisms of other species, the cultural rules that prohibit some matings and encourage others, the marital strategies individuals employ to secure economic and political advantage, and sometimes mutual attraction.

## The Avoidance of Incest

Chapter 6 will focus on certain features of marriage and how these mechanisms for regulating reproduction affect the lives of adolescents. At this point we wish to propose a general pattern of social organization by sex and age that characterizes *Homo sapiens* as distinct from other species. Our model, which we call a human ethogram,[2] is patterned after the diagrams of what Bischof (1975a) called "conjugal structures," or structures of mating relationships. Bischof's point is that social groupings have evolved to prevent close inbreeding. Our ethogram shows that outcome, as it diagrams the position of adolescents within the social structure. It is not our intention to imply that mating patterns have the same deterministic role for humans that they do for other species, but rather to suggest that reproductive patterns are an important component of human social organization. Reproduction as the point of departure will not explain everything about social organization, but it can raise to the fore some universal patterns not readily explicable in other terms. The social mechanisms that deter close inbreeding produce a pattern of social groupings that includes adolescents as a social category.

*Homo sapiens* is a species of primates, and it is instructive to examine the features of primate social organization even though there is no other primate species that replicates the social arrangements of our species, which includes both pair-bonded mates and community interaction. For example, although gibbons are like us in being pair-bonded, meaning that a male and female pair interact closely over time and cooperate in reproduction and early socialization of their young as humans do, gibbons do not have anything approaching a community life. In primate species in which troops of animals are found, there seem to be two basic structures. In one, exemplified by the hamadryas baboon, a male controls a "harem" of female mates, and most social activity at the troop level consists of interactions between males. In the other, the animals mate "promiscuously," as primatologists would have it. The chimpanzee, our closest primate relative, has this type of mating behavior. Males interact at the troop level with other males, as do females with other females, and closely related kin of opposite sex—mother and son, sister and brother—interact with one another throughout life.

In the "harem" species, close inbreeding is prevented by male control over females, that is, females are prevented by their mate, who is not a father or brother, from mating with close kin. The corresponding mechanisms in the "promiscuous" species are not all well understood. There appears to be a biological or social inhibition on mating with close kin (Bischof 1975a:53); at least, the frequency of observed mother-son and sibling matings is very low compared to other kinds. It is unclear whether there are mechanisms to inhibit matings of fathers and daughters or of half-siblings through the father, because the observer does not know who the father of any particular animal is. Among chimpanzees, females who leave the troop are not likely to mate with fathers or brothers. Simonds (1977) cogently summarized the vast body of literature on primate social organization; the preceding description draws upon his work.

Simonds (1977) and more specifically Chance and Jolly (1970) distinguished several kinds of social groupings that occur widely among monkeys and apes. Chance and Jolly (1970:157) stated: "Three main sub-groups are widely distributed amongst subhuman primate societies: assemblies of females and young, clusters of juveniles and cohorts of adult males." The female assembly consists of females of all ages along with infants. Juveniles come and go between the assembly, where they seek out their mothers, and the juvenile cluster, where young animals, those past infancy, play together. In some species, such as the savannah baboons, these juvenile clusters are mixed-sex groups, from which females split off as they approach puberty and join the female assemblies. In others, such as the hamadryas baboons, the play groups are almost entirely male, the females having been preempted by their future mate and incorporated into his harem, although he does not mate with them at this age (Chance and Jolly 1970:130). The play groups seem to provide the basis for attachment among males in primate societies, female attachments being formed and maintained throughout the lives of females through their involvement in the female assemblies. We can add to those widespread types of groups the "bachelor bands" (Chance and Jolly 1970), sexually mature but unmated males, who are found along with mated males in some species.

The variety of social dyads and clusters found in human society can also be found in the societies of other primates. The male-female pair bond of the monogamous and "harem" species are found in human mating relations, the monogamous or polygynous marriage. To our knowledge, no one has identified "polyandrous" clusters among primates. While polyandry, the marriage of one woman to two or more men, is rare as a preferred or frequent form of marriage in human societies (cf. Peter 1963; Levine and Sangree 1980), it is more widely found as a tolerated deviance than is commonly believed (cf. Schlegel 1972:50). Cecisbeism, or the institution of the married woman's legitimate lover, is another form of female pair-bonding with multiple males (Peter 1963). The tolerance that the gorilla alpha male shows toward the mating of subordinate males with the females of his band is somewhat analogous to polyandry or cecisbeism.

Female assemblies and male cohorts bring to mind the widespread tendency in human society for adults of the same sex to cluster together in occupational, ritual, or recreational groupings outside the family and to do so within the family in large, extended-family households. Play groups of juveniles, of course, are as universal in human communities as in primate troops. There is also a parallel between the bachelor band and the adolescent male peer group. Considering these elements of primate social organization from the point of view of the prevention of close inbreeding, we construct the ethogram shown in Figure 2.1 as a hypothesis of human social groupings. This, we believe, is applicable to all societies for boys and, for girls, to those

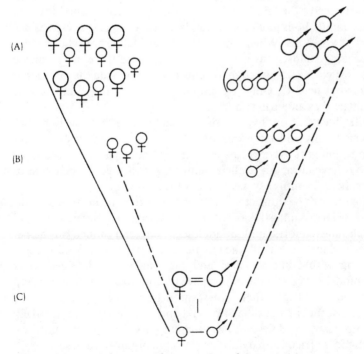

**Figure 2.1**   An Ethogram of Human Social Organization

societies in which girls have a social adolescence. The fact that there is no social adolescence for girls in one society of which we are aware, the Gros Ventre Indians of North America, in which girls are married before puberty, suggests that there may be others like it. Thus, while we postulate a universal social adolescence for boys and a nearly universal one for girls, our model accommodates societies that advance girls directly from childhood to adulthood, at or before puberty. These, however, are not represented in the diagram.

The model is divided into three levels. Level A represents the adult community structures, whatever their content may be, from few and generalized to many and specialized. As indicated previously, the majority of adult structures in most societies are for members of one sex only. Level B represents adolescent peer groups, from friendship dyads to informal groups to formal age sets. To take two examples for boys, peer groups among the Rwala Bedouins of Syria and Jordan are relatively unimportant but friendship dyads have great emotional salience (Rohn Eloul, personal communication); at the other extreme, among the Nyakyusa of Tanzania, adolescent boys are segregated into a boys' village peripheral to the adult community where they virtually govern themselves, and the peer group supersedes personal friendships in structuring boys' activities.

Level C represents the unit of biological and social reproduction that can loosely be termed "the family." In some societies such as ours, this will be the nuclear-family household where child socialization is the responsibility of primarily two adults. When groups of kin outside the household cooperate in socializing children, as is often the case where there are localized descent groups such as clans or cognatic clusters, kin outside the household will be included at level C. Only for simplicity's sake is the monogamous nuclear family used as an illustration.

The model illustrates our hypothesis that adolescents continue to be embedded in their family and kin group of origin, their participation in peer groupings and adult groups coexisting with strong family participation. Even Nyakyusa boys have close ties to their families, for they continue to eat at their mothers' hearths until they have wives of their own.

The ethogram can be translated into narrative form. It shows four principal kinds of social groupings: the dual-sex family that includes people of all ages; the adult male cohorts that put adolescent boys very much on the periphery if they include them at all; the female cohorts that include adolescent girls interacting with adult females; and the single-sex adolescent peer groups. The model recognizes the importance of both family and peer group to the adolescent; it indicates that adolescent girls are likely to spend more time with adults of the same sex than are boys and that peer groups are likely to be more important to adolescent boys than to girls. By "peer group" we mean anything from friendship dyads to very large organized age sets.

Our hypothesis states that human social organization, like the social organization of other primates, includes social mechanisms that prevent close inbreeding. One of these is the tendency toward sexual separation, at puberty if not before, when girls spend more time with other females and boys are more in contact with other males. Another is the redirection of the attention of the biological adolescent, especially the boy, away from the natal family toward other persons of the same age, the peer group.

The peer group has its foundation in the juvenile play group, in which the child begins to learn the social skills required to get along with age-mates. However, the adolescent peer group differs in two important respects. First, it involves the members' attention more than the play group; the increased maturity and self-direction of the adolescent make peer socialization of greater importance to adolescents than to younger children, who are more under the direction of their parents. As the adolescent moves out from the family, he or she looks more to the peer group for support (Coleman 1980:409). Petersen (1988) cited several studies showing that in contemporary society, peer groups become larger, more complex, and more salient than children's play groups. This tendency seems to be universal wherever communities contain enough children for the age-group to expand.

Second, it is a single-sex group. Although there is relatively little cross-cultural research on children's play groups, what has been done suggests a tendency for children to congregate with members of the same sex even though play does occur between boys and girls. Whiting and Whiting (1975:48), in their study of children in six cultures, referred to this apparent affinity of children for others of the same sex, but they did not distinguish between the younger group (ages three through six) and the older ones (ages seven through 11) (see also Whiting and Edwards 1988). Although Schlegel did not make systematic observations of Hopi play groups, her impressions, corroborated by information given by Hopis about the traditional culture, are that girls and boys under eight or nine sometimes played together, while older prepubertal ones more often (but not exclusively) played apart. This also can be inferred from Dennis (1940), who made his observations among the Hopi a generation earlier.

There may be a general human pattern to associate increasingly with members of the same sex until one reaches puberty, by which time single-sex peer groups predominate, although groups of girls and boys may get together for dancing or other special-purpose activities. The stage of heterosexual cliques, identified as characteristic of late adolescence in contemporary America (Dunphy 1963), is absent from preindustrial societies because, by late biological adolescence, girls at least tend to be married. When later marriages occur, as in early modern Europe (see Chapter 6), there is greater emphasis on segregating the sexes than in modern industrial society, in which gender is a less significant marker of social status than it is in traditional societies (cf. Schlegel and Barry 1980b).

The model depicts our assumption that the family plays a central role in the lives of adolescents, even in modern urban settings where a combination of factors—primarily nuclear-family residence and occupational opportunities that can take young people away from the home community—push the young person toward developing an extraordinary degree of independence from the family of origin. Attachment to the family is greater for girls than for boys, perpetuating a tendency found among children as well: Whiting and Whiting (1975:45) reported that in all of the six cultures they studied, including a community in the United States, girls remain closer to home; and they cited Nerlove (1969) and Nerlove, Munroe, and Munroe (1971) for corroborative studies.

We predict a difference in the involvement of girls and boys with adults of the same sex, a human pattern in many respects similar to that of some other primates. This pattern is manifest as follows. Adolescent girls, usually along with their mothers, spend more time with adult women of the "female assembly," to borrow the term from primatology, and are more actively engaged with them than boys are with men. Girls frequently accompany their mothers to gatherings of related or unrelated women, where they also interact with female peers. Boys less often accompany their fathers to adult men's gatherings. When in the company of men, they are often socially and spatially isolated from them, hanging about on the periphery of the "male cohort." Frequently, men and adolescent boys have little interaction outside the family; when it does occur, the boys as a group are subordinate to the authority of the men as a group. Here is just one example of this sex difference, quoted from Brandt's (1971:93) study of a Korean village:

> At important events where many people are present, several different age groups invariably form. In looking over hundreds of photographs that I took in the village with quite different objectives in mind, I later discovered that in an overwhelming majority the men included at random in any one picture were within a few years of each other. On the other hand, women's work groups, whether washing at the well, gathering oysters, or gardening, include people of all ages. Similarly, in domestic household work grandmother, daughter-in-law, and granddaughter all work together in the kitchen or courtyard.

The pattern can be seen most clearly during the leisure hours of evening, after the families' work is done. In society after society, adult men gather then to socialize and conduct the informal politics of small community life. It may be someone's home where they meet to drink beer, as do the Nyakyusa (Wilson 1963), or a commercial establishment like the local teahouse of the Far East, the coffeehouse of the Near East, and the European tavern. It may be the village men's house so common in the tribal world and well described for much of New Guinea, the Pacific, and tropical South America, or simply some customary place like a central plaza. Adolescent boys cluster along the peripheries of these men's gatherings or are off on business of their own. Meanwhile, adolescent girls and women are at home unless some ritual or community matter pertaining to women calls them out.

This pattern is not absolute; it does not, for example, characterize the !Kung of the Kalahari Desert, whose family campfires, around which family members sit, are close enough to permit free discussion back and forth among women and men. Some other foraging groups are also exceptions to this generalization, like the Eskimo, where an entire community of under 100 souls may collect in a single large structure for an evening's socializing. Not all foragers, however, are so flexible: Hart and Pilling (1960:36) described the evening hours of the Tiwi of Australia by telling of "men visiting from fire to fire as the women, who were not encouraged to walk about after dark, gossiped [*sic*] around their own fires." Nevertheless, this pattern appears to be extremely widespread, and we expect that adolescent socialization for adult life includes this aspect of gender difference.

This gender difference can be seen in the following observations of two formerly tribal societies and one traditional state that even today maintain some of the customs of earlier times. The first observation was made by Schlegel on a visit to the Ifugao in 1983.

> The Ifugao are a formerly tribal but rapidly modernizing people of Mountain Provinces, Philippines. Aboriginally, their subsistence economy depended upon the cultivation of rice in terraced fields along the mountain slopes and upon raising of pigs. While many today are Christian, pre-Christian elements can still be seen in such customs as burial practices.
>
> A murder had occurred a few days previous to my visit, and there would be a war dance in front of the victim's house and a pig sacrifice by its leaders to honor the victim. The dancers, all adult men, appeared, slowly dancing their way in front of the house where the body was laid out to a house yard close to where the pig would be sacrificed. My guide and I went along with the people who followed the dancers. When we got to the house yard, everyone except those actively involved in the pig sacrifice sat down under and around a shelter. I was the only adult woman present, but some adolescent girls huddled together, whispering and giggling, on a bench off to the side. Men and boys sat on the ground, mainly under the shelter. The boys, who looked to be between about 14 and 18, clustered together apart from the men. While the men sat upright and separate from one another, conversing in low tones, the boys were sprawled on the ground, arms and legs draped over one another, whispering and giggling like the girls. In this important public setting, there was clear separation by sex and age, and the solemn dignity of adult men contrasted sharply with the casual poses of the adolescent boys.

Schlegel also visited Malaysia in 1983, when the second observation took place in Kuala Trengganu, a traditional town on the east coast of Malaysia.

The people I associated with were of the upper class, nobility of the Trengganu Sultanate and elite commoners. The time was Hari Raya, the feast celebrating the end of Ramadan, when everyone goes visiting house to house of kin and friend. As I went about the rounds with my host family, I noticed that within the homes there was the same kind of informal mixing of the sexes—freedom in seating arrangements and in conversation—that one finds in urban European or American families. Adolescent girls were present along with adults and children, although they tended not to participate in the conversation unless directly addressed. On a few occasions, an adolescent son of the family was also present. However, during several of the visits, groups of adolescent boys, the children of neighbors or kin, came calling as a group. After giving formal greetings and eating heartily of the treats laid out at this time, they departed quickly.

This difference in the behavior of girls and boys was even more noticeable at a feast given to celebrate a young adolescent's circumcision. Except for the boy being honored and a few of his male cousins who helped serve, adolescent boys were conspicuously absent. They did come in at one point, however, as a group, seating themselves to the side of the large room where the men were being served, where they ate and soon took their leave.

In both of these instances the observed behavior occurred under ritual circumstances. The cohort clustering of the boys, not mixing with adult men but spatially peripheral to them, was striking. The last description is of a mundane setting. It is drawn from Schlegel's field notes on the Hopi, on whose culture she has conducted research since 1968.

Traditional Hopi make very clear statements about the spatial separation of the sexes. Houses belong to women, and that is the appropriate location for the activities of females of all ages and small boys. As boys reach age seven or so, they begin to spend time in the kivas, the ceremonial chambers that are used as men's clubhouses when not required for ritual purposes. While I have never entered a kiva when it was in use as a clubhouse, men have reported to me that in earlier times when men actually used the kivas in this way much of the time, male children and adolescents sat at one end, where they were supposed to keep quiet enough so that they would not disturb the men. They were expected to learn by listening to discussions and homilies. Before initiation into the men's societies at age 18 or so, which marked formal transition from boyhood to manhood, and marriage, usually a short time after, a young male did not attempt to make his presence felt in the kiva but rather stuck with his peers off to the side. Thus, even though boys were in close proximity to adult men, they stayed together at the spatial and social periphery of the adult male group. At the same time, their female age-mates were intermingling freely in home settings with groups of adult women, primarily neighbors and clan kin. When such a group congregated to make piki bread or other Hopi dishes, adolescent girls took their turns at the cooking fire along with women, and they were very much a part of the group that mixed and molded the corn puddings and shared in discussions and joking. In this respect, the Hopi resemble another tribe of southwestern United States, the Papago (Joseph et al. 1949:151–154).

These observations illustrate the point made earlier, that the exclusion of boys from adult male activities is greater than the exclusion of girls from adult female activities. Why are adolescents excluded, and why this sex difference?

A ready answer might be that adolescents have not yet learned their adult roles sufficiently to participate in adult society. While this might be true for the Hopi and Ifugao, who have fairly elaborate social systems, or for traditional states like the Trengganu Sultanate, it does not seem to hold for simple foraging societies among which a similar set of behaviors can be observed. It is not, we contend, that adolescents are not ready to participate in adult activities, since by adolescence, boys in less complex societies are likely to have acquired the skills necessary for adulthood, but rather that adults do not wish to include them. The exclusion of adolescents seems to be much more marked for boys than for girls.

Most adults in most societies spend the majority of their waking hours in productive activities. When the household is a unit of production, as it generally is in tribal and peasant communities, and household members cooperate in production, boys are likely to be working with their male kin and girls with their mothers. Within the family, then, there may be very little separation between the adolescent and his or her same-sex parent and kin. Outside the family, however, this separation can often be observed particularly for boys, as in the preceding examples. If there is a sex difference in the inclusion or exclusion of the adolescent from groups of same-sex adults, it is instructive to look at the activities of these groups.

We begin with the common observation that, almost everywhere, community decision-making is at least formally done by men—all adult men in simpler societies, leaders who inherit or are selected for their offices in the more complex ones. This is not to deny that women can control certain public institutions, the control of local markets by women among the Nigerian Yoruba (Sudarkasa 1973) being an example. Nevertheless, in almost all traditional societies, decisions concerning dispute settlement, territorial boundaries, and questions of warfare are usually made by men, even in such sexually egalitarian societies as the Hopi (Schlegel 1977) or the Philippine Bontoc (Bacdayan 1977). The occasional woman chief (Hoffer 1974) or king's councillor (Awe 1977) are exceptions that do not obviate this generalization. This implies that much of the discussion among adult men will have to do with community politics, a subject on which adolescent boys can make little contribution because they have not assumed the responsibilities of adulthood and thus have not been accepted as adults, irrespective of their skills.

Another topic of discussion among adult men in the public sphere is economic activities. It is not expected that adolescent boys will have the experience to contribute much here, either. Furthermore, without wives and children to help provide for, their personal stake in economic activities is less than that of adult men.

While inexperience and lack of personal involvement in adult activities make adolescent boys of little interest to senior males, adolescent girls are engaging alongside their mothers in the same activities that they will one day do as wives. In most places, the gulf in political power and control of property is not so great between girls and women as it is between boys and men. This is particularly true in male-dominant societies, in which the autonomy of females, whether girls or women, is restricted in comparison to that of adult men. In such societies, the girl will move from the greater subordination of childhood and adolescence to the lesser subordination of adult womanhood. Even though she will control areas of household management and child rearing, her final authority will be her husband or adult brother (cf. Schlegel 1972). Her male age-mates, however, will be making the transition from subordinates to peers, looking to the time in their adult lives when they not only claim authority over their households but also take whatever voice their social status allows them in controlling community affairs.

The adult roles that adolescents in sexually egalitarian societies anticipate differ from those of male-dominant societies (cf. Schlegel 1977 and Sanday 1981 on gender power). In some such societies, women hold power in other spheres, such as the production and distribution of goods, that balances the power of men in community decision-making. These can be called gender-balanced societies, and the Hopi are one example.

When gender is not a determining factor in the allocation of power, it is possible that the difference between boys and girls is not so marked. A muting of gender differences may be accompanied by a muting of age differences, with adolescents generally interacting more freely with adults of both sexes than they do in those societies in which gender is associated with power—symmetrically in gender-balanced societies, asymmetrically in male dominant ones. This question has not received attention from ethnographers and is open to research.

The lesser social disjuncture between girlhood and womanhood than between boyhood and manhood makes social relations of adolescent girls and women easier than those of adolescent boys and men. This suggests that adolescence may often be less stressful for girls than for boys. Blos (1979) and other psychoanalysts maintained that the adolescent transition is more difficult for girls than for boys because of girls' lesser differentiation from the mother in earlier years and consequently greater struggle for emotional autonomy at this time. We agree with the position of lesser differentiation and discuss it in Chapter 10, but we do not see this as necessarily resulting in a greater struggle for autonomy in adolescence. In other words, we see no necessity for a great or sudden differentiation from the mother; autonomy may be relative, and its realization may stretch out over many years. Blos and others rely on clinical evidence from Western society, which demands extreme individuation quite early in life for both sexes. Where the social unit in most activities is the collective rather than the individual and individualism is not expected, the struggle over individuation may be absent or very slight.

To sum up, the implications of the model are that the unlearning of child roles and character and the learning of adult modes are likely to be more difficult for boys than for girls and that women have more in common with adolescent girls than men do with adolescent boys. This may be particularly true in male dominant societies. Yet, observations of adolescents in sexually egalitarian societies suggest that, even here, girls are more fully absorbed into the "female assemblies" than boys are into the "male cohorts."

In the chapters that follow, we test this model. We will be specifically looking at separation of the sexes, that is, closer interaction with same-sex than with opposite-sex parents and siblings, and at differential association with peers. Girls, we predict, will have greater involvement with mothers and thereby with adult females in general, whereas boys will have greater involvement with peers and less involvement with fathers and adult males. Our assumption is that *Homo sapiens,* although unlike other primate species both pair-bonded and communal, shares with our kin in the animal kingdom a tendency to become sorted into groups that are analogous to female assemblies, male cohorts, and bachelor bands.

# 3

# Looking at Adolescent Socialization Across Cultures

THE model developed in the preceding chapter describes the biologically and culturally determined features that we assume to be universal in the placement of adolescents in human society. This assumption does not conflict with the observation that the structures and activities of adolescent life and adolescent behavior are variable across cultures, but it does raise the question of generic versus culturally specific culture traits. One of our objectives was to discover widespread patterns of adolescent behavior. Others were to assess the range of variability and to explain the variations. For example, adolescent boys' peer groups arise in all societies. In some, they assume primary importance as a social setting; in others, in which boys spend more of their time with adult male family members, they are less important as spheres of action and foci of interest. Why are boys more extruded from the home in one case and more incorporated into it in the other? One answer may lie in the tasks required of them. In the first instance, boys may spend much of their time out with the herds, whereas in the second they may work alongside their fathers in the family gardens. There may be other explanations, depending on the activities in which boys are engaged.

In meeting our inquiry's objectives, we necessarily dealt with two critical questions in the analysis of human development. The first question, discussed in Chapter 1, is how to sort out the determinative influence on behavior of psychogenic versus sociogenic factors, or features internal to the individual and external or situational features. Psychogenic factors are widely held to be responses to child socialization. On the one hand, then, lie those studies that trace the causality of adult behavior—and thereby adolescent behavior—to child-rearing techniques (cf. Shweder 1979); on the other are those studies that look to the present for determinants. This study tests both antecedent and situational variables as components of adolescent behavior.

The second question is whether a stage is discontinuous from or continuous with earlier stages. Obviously, without some discontinuity there would be no differentiation, but it is the degree of abruptness and magnitude of discontinuity that is in question. It is probably inevitable that any discussion of the life span as a series of stages (e.g., Erikson 1950) implies discontinuity, as it focuses upon the distinctiveness of stages. We can still ask whether the behavioral transition from childhood to adolescence is marked by continuity, ameliorating the effects of the biological changes at puberty, or by discontinuity corresponding to biological discontinuity.

Ruth Benedict (1938) brought this issue to the fore some time ago. She contrasted Samoan adolescents, or the somewhat romanticized version of them described by Mead (1928), with modern Western adolescents. The former, she said, enter and leave adolescence gradually, with plenty of opportunity to participate in or at least to observe all aspects of adult life. The latter, however, are shielded from the realities of adult life, such as sex and death. The genesis of discontinuity, according to Benedict, lies in childhood's lack of responsibility contrasted with adulthood's responsibility, submission contrasted with dominance, and markedly different sexual roles. Her major points were that discontinuity is variable across cultures and that discontinuity results in stress.

One would expect discontinuity to be greatest where adolescent initiation ceremonies mark the break between childhood and adolescence. Even here, however, the discontinuity of the abrupt change in status is ameliorated, because the ceremonies express themes that are prominent in earlier childhood socialization: social solidarity and an emphasis on sexual differentiation (Barry and Schlegel 1980b).

## A Summary of the Frequency Distributions

A list of variables used for this study is given in Appendix II. This section summarizes the frequency distributions, presenting them in the form of percentages or mean scores. Since for no variable is there information on all of the societies in the sample, the figures refer to the subsample of societies for which there is information on that variable.

### Parameters of Adolescence

Information is available on the presence or absence of an adolescent social stage for 173 societies for boys and for 175 for girls. Of these, all societies have this stage for boys; only one society lacks it altogether for girls, this being the Gros Ventre (Flannery 1953), where girls are married by about age

10. Because the Gros Ventre believe that sexual intercourse is necessary for menstruation to begin and expect wives to be virgins, marriage must occur before menarche. The child bride has the legal and social status of a woman and is expected to perform the tasks of an adult. If she is a junior wife in a polygynous household, her older co-wives are likely to be her sisters or close kin. While she has adult status in the community and takes her turn sleeping with her husband, her co-wives treat her as a little sister, which softens the abruptness of the change for so young a child. All other societies in the sample recognize an adolescent stage for both sexes.

The boundaries and descriptive characteristics of adolescence must be established. To do this, coders were asked to determine beginning and ending ages of adolescence for each society, rituals marking beginning and ending, if any, and whether adolescence was followed by an intervening youth stage before full adulthood.

A difficulty encountered in any anthropological study of the life cycle is that ages of people are rarely given in ethnographic monographs. In fact, they are often unknown by the people themselves, social role being determined more by level of maturity than by chronological age. To avoid this difficulty, this study relates social adolescence to biological adolescence rather than to any specific age. Starting age of social adolescence is measured as beginning before puberty, at puberty, or after puberty, and ending age is in early adolescence (up to about two years after puberty), mid-adolescence (about two to four years after), or late adolescence (about four to seven years after).

It is possible to make some very rough estimates of age of puberty, defined as first menstruation for girls and first ejaculation for boys. Puberty usually occurs about two years later for boys than for girls in modern industrial societies.[1] If ages of adolescence are given, but no typical age of menarche is estimated by the author, the coders were instructed to estimate 14 as age of girls' puberty unless there is evidence to the contrary. This age is derived from Eveleth and Tanner (1976:214–215), Table 15. The populations in that study closest in characteristics to the populations in the Standard Sample, peoples in Africa, Asia, and India, range from about 13 to 15 in median age of menarche.[2] We make no attempt to specify any particular chronological ages for social adolescence, nor does the study depend upon such specification. As beginning and ending ages for every society were coded by the same pair of coders, who arrived at consensus during the training period, we have every confidence that the *relative* ages in the study are correct assessments of the variation among cultures and the difference between girls and boys. By these criteria, starting age for both sexes is predominantly at or just about at puberty, 72 percent (173) for boys, 82 percent (175) for girls; the remainder start before puberty, except for one case for girls after puberty.

The movement into adolescence is often marked ritually. Data on this code, combined with that of earlier studies by Schlegel and Barry (1980a,

1980b) using the same sample, show that either a public adolescent initiation ceremony is conducted or the transition is signified in some other ritual form in 68 percent of 130 societies for which there is information on boys and in 79 percent of 126 societies with information on girls. The ceremonies are often major public events, more often for boys but occasionally for girls. Their themes express the important contribution to society the young person is expected to make in his or her future life: productivity is the most common theme among foragers, although fertility is also an important theme in girls' ceremonies, while fertility is a primary theme for both sexes in horticultural societies. (Advanced agricultural societies tend not to have public initiation ceremonies.) Thus, for about half the cases in this sample, the break between childhood and adolescence is given ritual recognition and may be the basis for communitywide ceremonies.

Ending age for boys is most commonly about two to four years after puberty, with 35 percent of 178 cases falling there and another 31 percent within two years after puberty. This estimate places the ending age for most societies at between 16 and 18, coming later for the remainder. For girls, 63 percent of 178 societies end adolescence within two years after puberty, or by about age 16. Because marriage almost always marks the end of adolescence in this sample, moving the individual into adult productive and reproductive relationships, it is safe to assume that adolescence is rather short in most societies in the sample, particularly for girls.

Modern society has nothing that corresponds to a full adolescent initiation ceremony that marks the total social transformation out of childhood. One could argue that transition rituals exist within certain domains, however. For example, the modern bar mitzvah has little effect on the way the adolescent boy is treated in society, but it does mark the end of childhood within the religious sphere of Judaism. Modern society pays more attention to the end of adolescence. For Americans, graduation from high school serves as a ritual of graduation from adolescence. Young people who do not graduate must enter the next stage without ritual recognition, although induction into military service may signify this transition for some.

In most societies, adulthood follows adolescence, but in a minority there is a youth stage before full adulthood is reached: 25 percent of 168 societies have this for boys, and 20 percent of 166 societies have it for girls. This stage exists in some traditional societies, notably those in which there is a postadolescent age-grade for young men serving in the army of the traditional state. Eisenstadt (1956:142ff.) discussed such age grading for African militaristic states like the Swazi, Zulu, and Tswana, whose young men spent a period of years soldiering and performing public works. He contrasted Sparta, which had such an age-grade for men between ages 20 and 30, with Athens, which had only a short period of service between ages 18 and 20.

Though a youth stage appears to be most common in traditional or modern states, some evidence exists for such a stage in certain tribal societies such as the Abipone of South America (Dobrizhoffer 1822), nomads with no political organization beyond the small local community. Unfortunately, the data are sparse and indicate only that young men do not marry until about age 30, at which time they become full social adults. Very little is known about the content of this stage. Given the frequency of warfare among the Abipone, full adulthood is probably delayed to facilitate the establishment of a warrior-class of unmarried men, as in the more complex traditional states.

A youth stage characterized many segments of early modern Europe as well. After a period of apprenticeship during the teenage years, young townsmen aspiring to be master craftsmen went through a period as journeymen, typically between the ages of about 18 and 26. Not yet married, they were granted neither productive nor reproductive adult status; such status came not at a specific age but rather when they were able to assume the tasks and responsibilities of full adulthood (cf. Burke 1978). In contemporary society the youth stage occurs between high school and the concomitant or sequential events of full employment and marriage. The social timetable (Elder 1975b) for modern society is to complete one's education, settle into a job, perhaps after a period of experimentation with several occupations or a stint in military service, and then marry. Research indicates that people who experience these events out of sequence may suffer adverse effects in terms of decreased lifetime earnings (Hogan 1980).

A fair bit of ink has been spilled concerning the term *adolescence*. Although the *Oxford English Dictionary* traces it to the 15th century (Bakan 1972), it may have differed in meaning then. However, the residents of 14th century Montaillou, a village in the French Pyrenees, did use the term in its modern sense. Between the ages of 12 and 14, children ceased being referred to as *puer* and became *adulescens* or *juvenis* in the records. They kept these terms until adulthood, which came at marriage for girls, not long after menarche, and after age 18 or so for boys (LeRoy Ladurie 1978:215–216).

Contrary to Bakan (1972), we do not believe that adolescence as a social condition and a social fact has been created by the term *adolescence*. Nor do social facts inevitably give rise to classificatory labels, although labels may increase the awareness of social facts and contribute to the ease of discourse about them. In other words, adolescence as a social fact can exist without a term to distinguish adolescents as a definable class of social beings. Nevertheless, it is of interest to know whether only Western society applies such a label.

Information is limited in the ethnographies, as ethnographers are more likely to report the presence of such terms than their absence. The fact that terms are reported for 14 out of 39 societies for which there is information on boys and for 17 out of 41 societies for girls does not indicate widespread terminological recognition of this stage. However, it does indicate that such recognition is not limited to modern society.

One example comes from the North American Navaho, who call a girl *ch'ikééh* and a boy *tsilkééh* between childhood and marriage. Another comes from the Trobriand Islands of Melanesia, whose adolescent life was richly described by Malinowski (1932:60). In the Trobriand Islands, the large breaks come between the periods of life characterized by different reproductive status: *wadi,* prereproductive children of both sexes; *ta'u* (male) and *vivila* (female), persons of reproductive capacity; and the post-reproductive elderly (no term given). Within these major periods, stages are designated, each with its name. The boy from puberty to marriage is known as *to'ulatile,* the girl as *nakapugula.*

In addition to labelling the adolescent stage, the Trobrianders see it as highly distinctive, a time when young people are "the flower of the village" (Malinowski 1932:64). However, the Kalapalo of Brazil, who also regard their adolescents as the epitome of beauty, have no terms for adolescence (Ellen Basso, personal communication). Further, there is no evidence that the Navajo, who do have such terms, consider this period as being in any way special. It appears that some peoples are more concerned about labelling life stages than others, for reasons having less to do with the distinctiveness of the life stages than with ideas about the need to delineate cosmic or social order. Labelling or not labelling social facts may be more reflective of the symbolic structure of the culture than the social structure of the society.

Labelling can be done visually as well as verbally. One signifier of social distinction is distinctiveness in dress, hair style, face painting, or ornamentation, all visual markers. For boys, changes in visual markers from childhood occur in 86 percent of 102 societies, while for girls they occur in 88 percent of 118 societies. Such markers may exist for one sex only. Among the Chatino Indians of Oaxaca, Mexico, girls move out of childhood when they receive a large rebozo, a kind of shawl, to replace the small rebozo of childhood. The large one enables them to carry babies about, a primary task of adolescent girls. Boys, however, do not change their appearance; their exit from childhood is signified only behaviorally, by their entering the ceremonial organization of the village where they act as pages to the adult men (Eva Zavaleta Greenberg, personal communication).

Visual markers to distinguish adolescents from adults are less common, being coded for only 32 percent of 100 societies for boys and 35 percent of 118 societies for girls. An example of distinctive adolescent appearance, differing from that of either children or adults, is the change in hairstyle of the Hopi girl. As a child, she wears the miniature version of the butterfly hairstyle, for which the hair is formed into bunches on each side of the head like butterfly wings. After a small private adolescent initiation ceremony, she puts her hair into large butterfly wings, set with the aid of wicker hoops. This is, in fact, a visual announcement that she is ready for courtship. Upon marriage, she assumes the hairstyle of adult women, in which the hair is worn in two braidlike ropes. Boys have no such visual markers. Incidentally, the

Hopi have no terms for adolescence, the adolescent being classified terminologically with the child until the girl marries and the boy undergoes his initiation into a men's society. Nevertheless, visual markers for girls and certain behaviors for both sexes are distinctive of this stage.

## Relations with the Family

In most societies of this sample, adolescents spend the majority of their waking hours with adults of the same sex—in 66 percent of 161 cases for boys and in 84 percent of 160 cases for girls—and the setting for most of their activities is the home. Relations with family members are assessed in separate segments of the code and were independently coded by different sets of coders, with the results of each supporting the other. One segment ranks agents of socialization in the family by their importance in teaching adolescents and having some control over their activities. For boys, the father is the single most important agent in 79 percent of 173 cases, while the mother is most important for girls in 85 percent of 171 cases. The other segment measures contact, intimacy, subordination, and conflict on an 11-point scale. The data reflect both the nature of the human family as an integrated unit comprising both sexes and the fact that some degree of sexual separation is widely present, even in the home. Of the societies in this sample for which there are data, girls have both more contact and greater intimacy with older female kin (excluding sisters), mothers, and grandmothers than boys have with older male kin (excluding brothers), fathers, and grandfathers. Contact and intimacy with older siblings of the same sex are similar for girls and boys.

## Relations with the Community

Adolescents are quite commonly closely integrated in adult family activities, and many participate substantially in adult community life, assuming new roles in the community. Out of 78 societies for which there is information on boys, new roles are undertaken in 64 (82 percent). These roles are economically productive, military, religious, or contributive to community welfare; no cases were recorded of new political roles. Girls are shown to have less community involvement: out of 45 societies, they take on new roles in 27 (60 percent), these being new religious roles in 14 cases. Examples of new community roles are the military activities that adolescent boys perform in a number of tribal groups. In the South and East African age-graded societies, adolescent boys are not generally warriors themselves, as the warrior grade comprises slightly older youths, but adolescent boys typically receive military training.

Adolescents of both sexes may for the first time take a meaningful part in community rituals. This is the case for the Chatino boys mentioned earlier, who enter the cargo system—the system of religious obligations—at this time. For a small number of societies, there is information on the response of the community to adolescents' new roles. Recognition can be given through such rewards as payment, feasts, or public praise. In a few cases, there is conscious selection or training for community leadership during adolescence.

In the modern world, we expect a certain portion of our adolescents to be delinquents, i.e., to exhibit behavior that violates social standards. However, what may be delinquent in European or American nations might not be so in traditional societies. Information on the question of regular, expected antisocial behavior—not including the occasional deviant—has been coded, framed in terms of what the society itself considers disruptive. Out of 54 societies for which there is information, patterned antisocial behavior of boys occurs in 24, and it occurs in 6 out of 34 societies for girls. It occurs among adolescent boys more than among younger boys in 61 percent of 31 cases and among adolescent boys more than among adult men in 59 percent of 29 cases. For boys but not for girls, adolescence tends to be the stage during which antisocial behavior most often occurs, if it occurs at all. Violence against persons and theft are more common than destruction of property. Punishment for misbehavior of any kind is fairly evenly divided between mild and severe, although it is ignored or only mildly admonished in 23 percent of 69 cases for boys and in 25 percent of 61 cases for girls.

One form of disruptive behavior is running away, and ethnographers are more likely to note its presence than its absence. For societies with information on this feature, it has been recorded for 61 percent of 36 cases for girls and for 55 percent of 31 cases for boys. Nisa, a !Kung adolescent, attempted to avoid a distasteful marriage by running into the forest and remaining there overnight in order to convince her parents of her feelings (Shostak 1983). The first author has been told of several cases of Hopi girls who used this tactic to gain relief from a tense relationship with their mothers. In these cases, they took shelter with relatives, who finally persuaded them to return.

Another form of antisocial behavior, widespread among tribesmen, is the practice of witchcraft, malevolence through magical means. In general, adolescents seem no more likely to be either victims or practitioners of witchcraft than persons of other ages.

## Relations with Peers

In the model offered in Chapter 2, the peer group is more salient for boys than for girls. This hypothesis is supported by the frequency distributions of the data. Although for both sexes most time is spent with adults of the same sex, the peer group is the single primary locus of boys' waking hours in 17 percent of 161 cases with information but in only 5 percent of 160 cases for girls. The importance of peer groups relative to the family and other social groups has been rated in 91 societies for boys and in 68 societies for girls. For boys, the figures are: more important, 27 percent; equal, 40 percent; and less important, 33 percent. For girls, the comparable figures are 7 percent, 24 percent, and 69 percent respectively. Evidence from other ratings leads us to suspect that this rating overestimates the "more important" category for boys. Nevertheless, peer groups clearly seem to be more important in boys' lives than in girls', while involvement with older kin of the same sex is greater for girls. Data on contact with peers, coded independently from importance of peer group, support this: the mean score for boys is 6.1 for 126 cases, whereas it is 5.0 for 101 cases for girls.

Peer group size also varies between the sexes. Boys' peer groups are large, numbering about 14 or more, in 52 percent of 88 cases with information and are small, about three to six, in 20 percent. Girls' groups, however, are large in 37 percent of 68 cases and small in 34 percent. Boys' peer groups more often have names than do girls' groups. For both sexes, time with peers is most commonly spent in leisure activities. Recreational activities are not confined to peer groups, however; both boys and girls are rated as "often" participating with children and with adults. Young people may get together in work groups. Several Hopi girls, for example, sometimes take the corn they have to grind over to one girl's house and have a grinding party, thus lightening the burdensome task with talk and laughter. Adolescent herd boys in African cattle-owning societies commonly herd together, away from the eyes of the village.

## Sexuality and Reproduction

For the large majority of societies, marriage choice is made during adolescence. Age of first marriage relative to puberty tends to differ between girls and boys. In 60 percent of 124 societies with information, girls are married within two years after puberty. Boys are married between two and four years after puberty in 45 percent of 132 societies, earlier than that in 33 percent. This puts the most common chronological ages of marriage roughly at 14 to 16 for girls, 16 to 20 for boys, if our estimates of age of puberty are accurate.

Unless young people are married at or before puberty, the question of adolescent sexuality arises. Ethnographers give fairly extensive accounts of premarital sexual activity. In the majority of societies in this sample, heterosexual intercourse is either tolerated or expected with a limited number of partners: in 65 percent of 155 societies with information for boys and in 60 percent of 163 societies for girls. Some controls are exerted, however; only a few societies tolerate promiscuity, and the partner is most frequently expected to be another adolescent: in 61 percent of 141 cases with information for boys and in 61 percent of 140 cases for girls.

Homosexual activity is also permitted in some societies, although these data are less complete; instances of such activity are more likely to be reported by ethnographers than the absence or prohibition of homosexuality. There is evidence in 25 societies for boys and in 17 for girls that homosexual relations are tolerated or expected.

## The Self

Adolescence is a time of new or intensified learning for both sexes in the skill areas identified: work, warfare (boys only), religion, arts and games, cognition, and social interaction. Adolescents tend to do work similar to that of adults and to dress like them but to have different leisure-time activities. Adolescence is also a time when young people are given more productive property to manage than previously in 44 percent of 102 societies with information for boys, 31 percent of 74 societies for girls. Success in adolescence is preponderantly in the area of work. The good worker gets social acclaim and is also likely to attract a satisfactory spouse later. However, physical skill is also important in determining success for boys; the activities are likely to be wrestling or competitive games. For girls, sexual attributes assume importance.

If adolescence is a time during which various skills and social roles are being learned, it is also a time during which the inculcation of character traits continues from childhood or is intensified. The traits selected for measurement were fortitude, impulsiveness, aggressiveness, obedience, sexual expression, sexual restraint, self-reliance, conformity to group, trust, competitiveness, responsibility, and achievement. Mean scores for these traits are primarily of interest in comparing girls with boys. For most, the difference is less than one point on an 11-point scale. The traits with a greater difference are aggressiveness, self-reliance, and competitiveness, with boys receiving higher mean scores in all cases. These distributions argue against radically different socialization of the sexes for most societies.

Adolescents in this sample are not free from social pressures. There is a widespread belief that adolescence in tribal or peasant communities flows smoothly, without competition for resources (which can include a desirable spouse and powerful in-laws) and without areas in which choice must be exercised. This notion is belied by the data from this study. In only a small minority of societies is there no increase over childhood in responsibility. Occupational choice must be made by at least some boys in 65 percent of 150 societies with information and by some girls in 43 percent of 141 societies. An adolescent may have to decide whether to become, for instance, a shaman, midwife, berdache (institutionalized transvestite), or master carver. Because training for a specialized role often means a long period of apprenticeship to a master, this choice can be costly in terms of time and goods. It is not made lightly. In many societies, there is pressure for excellence rather than mere competence.

Young people may also have to take the initiative in finding a spouse, even though the choice often has to be approved by others. This is the case in 58 percent of 174 societies with information for boys and in 47 percent of 169 societies for girls. Courtship in tribal societies can be as frustrating and as shadowed by fear of rejection as it is for modern Western teenagers.

Adolescence is a time during which adult character is established in the large majority of societies. Memories are long in small communities, and one carries one's adolescent reputation into adulthood.

———

The frequency distributions of the data strongly suggest that an adolescent social stage is very widespread and possibly universal for boys. Such a stage is usual for girls, although there are exceptions. Early marriage, even before menarche, does not necessarily preclude social adolescence, however; the married girl's activities may differ markedly from those of older women, and sexual relations may be delayed until some time after puberty. For any particular societies that schedule life events in a sequence different from that followed by the majority of societies, analysis has to be done on a case-by-case basis.

Compared to modern Western society, the societies in this sample tend to display a rather brief adolescence, particularly for girls. It is necessary to prolong adolescence when adult roles require lengthy training, and role training in many societies may be easier for girls than for boys. Whether in the homes of their fathers or their husbands, women remain subordinate to men in most of the societies in this sample. As women age, they assume considerable autonomy and authority within their domains, but the sphere within which they make decisions is generally more restricted than that of men. Where men hold power, adolescent boys are preparing to make the transition from child subordinates to adult peers. Girls, however, move from greater to lesser subordination within the society at large, even in those cases in which a middle-aged or elderly woman is the family matriarch. For role training, then, boys may often need a longer adolescence than girls.

The brevity of the adolescent stage for girls is related to another factor. In many places, nubile girls are political capital for the people who control their marriages, usually their fathers. Fecundity is a critical issue in these societies, for it is through his own increase—via his wife or wives—that a man assures himself of loyal supporters in his middle and later years. He expands his network of social alliances through the marriages of his children. Furthermore, in many horticultural societies and some pastoral ones, multiple wives are an economic asset: polygyny has been demonstrated to be significantly associated with high female contribution to subsistence (Schlegel and Barry 1986). For social reasons, and often economic ones as well, marriageable women are in high demand. Delaying the marriage of a daughter for many years after puberty would be letting an asset go to waste, unless there are compelling reasons to postpone marriage.

The adolescent stage itself not only is midway between childhood and adulthood but also shares some characteristics of both stages. While the adolescents in this sample are childlike in their domestic subordination and lack of political involvement in the community, they are likely to dress like adults and to perform adult productive tasks. Their absence from community decision-making does not indicate that they fail to contribute to the community, for they may take on responsibilities, particularly in religious or military activities. Although they may be sexually active, they are not reproductive.

The pattern of relationships with family, community, and peers among adolescents in this sample follows the model offered in Chapter 2. The greater contact and intimacy shown by girls with adult female kin, compared to that of boys with adult male kin, indicates greater involvement among females of all ages and greater segregation of men from boys. Conversely, involvement with peers is generally greater for boys than for girls. Although for both sexes the family is undoubtedly the most important social group and the peer group secondary in the majority of societies in the sample, a gender difference appears in the degree of involvement in these two social units.

How characteristic this gender difference is of modern society is hard to say. In the United States, for example, there may be considerable variation among ethnic groups and social classes. In the middle and upper classes, where child labor is not needed at home or in family enterprises, adolescents of both sexes are likely to spend a good deal of time with their age-mates, and the difference between boys and girls may be less marked. In working-class households or in families of Hispanic or of recent Middle Eastern or Asian extraction, girls may be expected to spend their after-school hours at home while boys may be away from home, working or at leisure with their peers.

Although adolescence worldwide might not have the *Sturm und Drang* quality attributed to it in some of the more florid 19th and 20th century literature, adolescence in this sample displays points of stress that may be widely characteristic of this stage. Life becomes a serious business at this time, for young people are under the observation of their elders as future children-in-law. Decisions made during these years can have far-reaching consequences. In small closed societies, adolescence is not just a period of training for adult life; it is the time during which the ground is prepared for adult social relations with the same people who are currently one's peers. There is no escape, no chance to begin anew somewhere else. What one will be in 10 years is strongly colored by what one is today. It is likely that adolescents are aware of this as they struggle to cope with the social pressures to conform and often to excel.

# 4

## Adolescents and
## Their Families

THE ethogram in Chapter 2 depicts our model of the social organization of adolescence. In this and the following chapters, the utility of that model is assessed and some of its implications are explored. We begin by looking at family relations.

Adolescents in modern industrial nations, anticipating the day when they will leave their families, face an important developmental task. In preparation for this move, they must begin to disengage while they are still in the midst of family activities. Within a few years they will move out, to reside for a while with roommates, a young spouse, or alone before once again living in a family circle, one that they have created. This issue does not enter the lives of the adolescents in our sample. In most of the societies, only one sex (usually girls) leaves—at marriage—and then into another family household. Even in neolocal societies, in which the married couple sets up its own household, the new home is most often within shouting, or at least walking, distance of the homes in which the young husband and wife spent their childhoods.

Such family continuity colors the relations of family members. If one's source of social support, livelihood, standing in the community, and all future aid is the family, one will avoid antagonizing relatives. Even if there are hostilities or personality incompatibilities, these feelings are suppressed to preserve a facade, at least, of family harmony. In a couple of instances it took the first author by surprise when, after being present at a cordial Hopi family gathering, she heard another side in the privacy of the field worker-informant relationship. Such suppression of animosity and preservation of family solidarity is not unusual; it characterizes family life whenever the family and not the individual is the basic unit of economic and social action.

Relations of adolescents with their families must be seen in the light of lifelong family unity. In the societies in our sample, family members need

44

one another. Adolescent and young adult children depend on the help of parents and other kin, especially when all are living together, and aging parents rely on older children for their very survival. Siblings and other relatives form the core of an individual's political and social support group and are expected to respond in time of need. Independence as we know it would be regarded as not only eccentric and egotistical but also foolhardy beyond reason.

Adolescents' relations with other family members, as recounted in the ethnographies, are generally harmonious. Subordination to elders does not seem to cause difficulties, as long as treatment is fair and the young person is being helped by the parents to achieve an honorable adulthood. Selfishness and abuse of power on the part of elders are not unknown and are resented as keenly by tribal adolescents as by any other young people. However, such cases seem to be the exception. Parental calls to duty that interfere with the adolescents' plans, and the childish thoughtlessness and foolish pranks that irritate their elders, will pass. In these families, one is in for the long haul, and present aggravations are overlooked to serve everyone's best interest, which is to maintain harmony in family relations.

Although this study's coding schedule includes questions about siblings, grandparents, and other kin, most of the information is on parents.[1] The norm is that both parents live in the home, in all of the societies of the sample except the South American Mundurucu and Callinago, among whom adult men live in the village men's house and visit their matrilocally residing wives. Only rarely is the father not the adult male who cooperates with the mother in child rearing: the Nayar of southern India and the Minangkabau of Indonesia (societies not in the sample), in which the adult brother and sister reside in the same household and the woman's husband is an evening visitor, are among the few examples worldwide.

In most societies in our sample, adolescents spend most of their waking hours with adults of the same sex—in 66 percent of 161 cases for boys and in 84 percent of 160 cases for girls—and the setting for most of their activities is the home or elsewhere with kin. In virtually all cases, the family is the primary unit of production, and adolescents work alongside family members.

Questions concerning relations with family members appear at different points in the code and were independently coded by different research assistants. One question concerns agents of socialization, ranking them by their importance in teaching adolescents and having some control over their activities. For boys, the father is the single most important agent in 79 percent of 173 cases, while the mother is most important for girls in 85 percent of 171 cases.

Other questions concern some of the features—contact, intimacy, conflict, and subordination—that contribute to the emotional tone of the relation between adolescents and other family members. These features have been rated on an 11-point scale. Mean scores are reported in Table 4.1. While

*Table 4.1.* Relations with Family: Mean Scores of Contact, Intimacy, Subordination, and Conflict

| | Boys' Mean | | | | Girls' Mean | | | |
|---|---|---|---|---|---|---|---|---|
| | Contact | Intimacy | Subordi-nation | Conflict | Contact | Intimacy | Subordi-nation | Conflict |
| Mother | 2.4 (126) | 5.3 (59) | 5.9 (92) | 2.7 (33) | 7.1 (133) | 6.4 (51) | 6.7 (111) | 2.8 (46) |
| Father | 5.3 (134) | 4.8 (56) | 7.2 (138) | 3.4 (61) | 2.5 (122) | 4.1 (47) | 7.2 (136) | 2.8 (54) |
| Older male sibling | 6.1 (46) | 6.2 (41) | 6.1 (58) | 3.7 (26) | 2.6 (40) | 5.3 (36) | 6.2 (53) | 2.6 (11) |
| Older female sibling | 2.5 (33) | 5.3 (38) | 4.5 (24) | 2.3 (8) | 6.2 (32) | 6.7 (33) | 5.2 (24) | 2.5 (12) |
| Grand-mother | 2.1 (29) | 5.9 (26) | 5.9 (35) | inadequate data (N=2) | 5.6 (40) | 6.3 (30) | 6.4 (51) | inadequate data (N=5) |
| Grand-father | 3.6 (32) | 6.0 (31) | 6.3 (47) | inadequate data (N=4) | 2.9 (33) | 5.8 (25) | 6.2 (39) | inadequate data (N=3) |

Numbers in parentheses indicate the number of societies for which there are data.

there is no rating for contemporary adolescents, data from Youniss and Smollar (1985) on American adolescents provide some basis for comparison. In eight separate studies, they sampled 1,049 boys and girls of high school age, almost all from two-parent homes and predominantly middle class. (Other class and family structures might provide somewhat different results.) We refer to their work in the following discussion.

*Contact* refers to the proportion of waking time spent together. A rating of two indicates only a small proportion; five, about half; eight, most; and ten, virtually all. For example, among the Aztecs of pre-Columbian Mexico, boys attend school while girls stay at home; thus, boys receive a rating of four for contact with father, while girls receive eight for contact with mother. Among the Balinese, however, boys work as closely with their fathers as girls do with their mothers, and both sexes are rated eight for contact with parent of the same sex. For both sexes in the sample, contact with parent of the opposite sex is rated lower than contact with same-sex parent. Mean scores indicate that boys and girls have similar levels of contact with the parent of the opposite sex; girls' contact with the mother, however, is higher than boys' contact with the father in the sample societies.

American middle-class girls and boys appear to spend nearly equal time with mothers and with fathers. Most waking hours of adolescents of both sexes are spent away from home, at school or work and with friends. In evenings or on weekends, the entire family is likely to be present in the home. There is some difference, however; Youniss and Smollar (1985) report that girls engage in more activities with their mothers and boys do more with their fathers.

*Intimacy* is evidenced by sharing secrets and expressing affection. A rating of two indicates acquaintance but no special friendship; five, a substantial degree of trust and liking; eight, strong expressions of affection and time spent together by choice. As examples, in the Trobriand Islands of Melanesia, girls are somewhat more intimate with their mothers (rating of seven) than boys are with either their mothers (six) or their fathers (five); while among the Javanese, both sexes are equally intimate with their mothers (seven), but intimacy with fathers is greater for girls (five) than for boys (two). This rating reflects an extreme distance and guardedness between Javanese fathers and sons; these fathers relax more in the company of their daughters. In the sample, girls and boys are similar in the level of intimacy with the father. For both sexes, intimacy is greater with the mother, more so for girls than for boys.

Youniss and Smollar's (1985) data do not allow us to compare intimacy levels of American adolescents with those of the sample societies, but they do provide information on the difference between boys and girls with their parents. For both sexes, intimacy with mothers is higher than it is with fathers, conforming to the worldwide pattern. Fathers exercise authority over both sexes through controlling or protective behavior, and they are turned to for advice on instrumental activities like career planning. Mothers receive confidences; and their authority, while strong, is softened by the perception that they gratify the emotional needs of their children through understanding and cooperation.

As Youniss and Smollar (1985:83) pointed out, the adolescents' depiction of parental roles is close to the instrumental-expressive dichotomy of Parsons and Bales (1955). This model, which identifies fathers with instrumental activities and mothers with expressive ones, has been much criticized, particularly for overlooking the instrumental activities of mothers. Youniss and Smollar do not report distinctions in their sample-members' families between those with and without working mothers; do working mothers, usually overextended between job and household responsibilities, withdraw emotionally from their adolescents more than mothers without jobs? Generalizing to the sample, is the greater warmth and intimacy of the mother a consequence of her usually having fewer extradomestic claims on her time and attention?

*Subordination* refers to obedience and deference. When it is prevalent, a rating of eight is given; when it is generally expected, the rating is five; and when it is not generally expected, the rating is two. Among the patrilineal Rwala Bedouin of Syria, both sexes are rated strongly subordinate to their fathers (nine), with no rating available for mother. The matrilineal Negri Sembilan of Malaysia, however, require less submission, particularly for boys: girls are rated eight for subordination to both parents, while boys are rated six for the same. Girls and boys are equally subordinate to their fathers in the sample, but boys are less submissive to their mothers than are girls.

In the American study, subordination declines as children move from childhood into adolescence and large areas of their lives are lived outside of parental awareness. Parents also relax authority as their children grow older (Youniss and Smollar 1985:72–74). Part of the diminution of authority in American households may be due to our egalitarian and democratic ideology. Part, however, may have to do with the greater length of adolescence in industrial nations. American children are adolescents until about age eighteen, by which time the young person is closer to the parents in physique, mentality, and interests than is the young adolescent of fourteen or fifteen. Two or three years' difference in age has significant effects in a stage of life when growth and change are rapid. We expect that treatment changes accordingly.

*Conflict* refers to contradictory aims or expectations and is expressed through strife, punishments, or disobedience. A rating of eight is given when quarrels or punishments are fairly frequent or severe, five indicates a moderate degree of conflict, and two signifies a mild degree. Two pastoral peoples show the range of difference. Among the Siberian Chukchee, conflict is high for both sexes, with a rating of eight for conflict of both girls and boys with father and mother. Among the African Fulani, boys and girls have little conflict with their mothers (rating of one for both sexes) but considerably more with their fathers (rating of four for girls, six for boys). For the sample, conflict scores for both sexes are low, boys having a slightly higher level of conflict with their fathers.

In the American research, conflict for both sexes tends to be higher with their mothers than with their fathers (Youniss and Smollar 1985). This may be a function of the lesser contact with their fathers and some guardedness in the father-child relationship. The greater freedom of expression with the mother also invites more disagreement and criticism by the child. Much of the mother-child conflict is rather petty, revolving around issues like cleaning one's room or talking back.

The data in Table 4.1 reflect both the nature of the human family as an integrated unit comprising both sexes and the fact that some degree of gender difference is widely present. Of the societies in this sample for which there are data, girls tend to have both more contact and greater intimacy with older female kin—mothers and grandmothers—than boys do with older male kin—fathers and grandfathers. Contact and intimacy are similar for girls and boys with older siblings of the same sex. Conflict is more often stronger between fathers and sons than between mothers and sons or between daughters and either parent. Even so, the mean level of conflict between fathers and sons is low. Subordination for both sexes to their fathers is rather high, somewhat lower to their mothers.

Of these four variables—contact, intimacy, subordination, and conflict—the one with the most complete data is contact. In order to determine the relative contact of parents with children, whether high or low as determined by waking hours spent with parents, we assessed contact with the mother versus contact with the father. It must be remembered that high and low contact do not have the same meaning for girls and boys. For girls, high contact with the mother refers to a rating of eight or above, while for boys, high contact with the father refers to a rating of six or above. As girls generally have more contact with their mothers than boys do with their fathers, a designation of high contact with the parent of the same sex means high contact relative to other societies for the same sex, not high contact relative to the opposite sex. For both sexes, high contact with the parent of the opposite sex means a rating of three or above.

With those definitions in mind, we report the significant findings, using the quantitative ratings on a scale of 0 to 10. When contact of boys with one parent is high, contact with the other is very likely to be high also ($r = .27$, $p < .003$, $N = 121$). When boys have high contact with their fathers, girls are significantly likely to have high contact with their mothers ($r = .41, p < .001$, $N = 126$), and when girls have high contact with their fathers, boys are significantly likely to have high contact with their mothers ($r = .66, p < .001$, $N = 117$). Thus, high father-son contact predicts high contact of both boys and girls with their mothers, and high father-daughter contact predicts high contact of boys with mothers. In other words, high contact of both girls and boys with their fathers indicates a high level of contact within the family generally. However, high mother-daughter contact does not predict high father-daughter contact, although there is a trend ($r = .18, p = .052, N = 119$) in that direction. High contact between mother and daughter occurs in sexually segregated as well as sexually integrated families, whereas high contact between father and son does not. When fathers and sons are less in contact, boys are spending time with peers, with other adults, or alone.

Contact has been assessed in relation to the other variables. For boys, high father-son contact is associated with high subordination, and there is a trend for high contact to be associated with high conflict (see Table 4.2). For girls, however, high father-daughter contact is associated with high father-daughter intimacy (see Table 4.2). It is clear that contact with the father has different meanings for the two sexes, tending to lead to subordination or conflict for boys and to intimacy for girls. This finding has implications for the current interest in increasing the involvement of fathers in the rearing of children. Instead of closing the gap in the differential treatment of sons and daughters, increased involvement of fathers might enlarge it, as fathers more than mothers seem to treat the two sexes differently.

There is no significant relation between intimacy and subordination or between subordination and conflict for either sex with either parent. For boys, there is an inverse relation between intimacy and conflict with the father. Applying the Mantel-Haenszel test to the entire sample (rather than dichotomizing at the median), the chi-square value is $4.32, p = .038$ ($N = 28$).

*Table 4.2* Relations with Father

|  | Contact | |
|---|---|---|
|  | *below median* | *above median* |
|  | *Boys* | |
| *Subordination* | | |
| below median | 32 | 16 |
| above median | 25 | 38 |
|  | $\chi^2 = 6.90$ | $p = .009$ |
| *Conflict* | | |
| below median | 21 | 8 |
| above median | 10 | 13 |
|  | $\chi^2 = 3.34$ | $p = .068$ (trend) |
|  | *Girls* | |
| *Intimacy* | | |
| below median | 17 | 4 |
| above median | 10 | 11 |
|  | Fisher's Exact Test $p = .052$ | |

This relationship is not significant for girls or for either sex with the mother. These findings suggest that subordination *per se* neither discourages intimacy nor exacerbates conflict, so that a more democratic household does not necessarily foster intimacy or reduce conflict. That intimacy and conflict are inversely related is hardly surprising; one would not expect a high degree of trust and affection to coexist with frequent quarrels or punishments. It is noteworthy that this inverse relation between conflict and intimacy for fathers and sons is not found for mothers and sons or for daughters at all. This may have to do with the type of conflict between mothers and children and fathers and daughters, the tribal equivalent of squabbles over keeping one's room neat or taking out the garbage. Petty bickering that no one takes seriously can be frequent between intimate persons, but a boy's conflict with his father is likely to involve more important issues, such as the son's contribution to household labor or his use of family resources.

## Family Members Other Than Parents

Very little attention has been paid to relations between adolescents and grandparents (Baranowski 1982). In the West, grandparents are not generally part of the home in which adolescents live. In traditional societies, grandparents are present in the home in stem- or extended-family households or live nearby within the community when households consist of nuclear families. However, when life expectancies are low, not all adolescents have living grandparents.

It has often been observed that grandparents can serve as a buffer between parents and children. The mean scores in Table 4.1 reflect that observation: for boys, intimacy with the grandmother is slightly higher than with the mother, and with the grandfather it is a good bit higher than with the father. For girls, intimacy with the grandmother is similar to that with the mother, and with the grandfather it is considerably higher than with the father, as for boys.

Somewhat more information is available on siblings. Relations with older male and female siblings were measured and were assessed vis-à-vis similar relations with parents. The findings indicate that relations with an older sibling of the same sex mirror relations with a parent of the same sex. When contact of the boy with the father is high, contact with the older brother is also high; when subordination or conflict with one is high, so are subordination and conflict, respectively, high with the other (Table 4.3). For girls, contact with the mother predicts contact with the older sister (Table 4.3). Data on subordination and conflict between sisters are insufficient to permit testing.

In societies in which mortality, particularly maternal mortality, is high, older siblings may have to become parental surrogates. These data suggest that there is socialization for that potential role. It has become widely recog-

**Table 4.3** Relations with Older Siblings

|  | Boys | |
| --- | --- | --- |
|  | Contact with older brother | |
|  | below median | above median |
| **Contact with father** | | |
| below median | 20 | 5 |
| above median | 5 | 15 |
|  | $\chi^2 = 11.48$ | $p = .001$ |

|  | Subordination to older brother | |
| --- | --- | --- |
|  | below median | above median |
| **Subordination to father** | | |
| below median | 18 | 3 |
| above median | 8 | 27 |
|  | Fisher's Exact Test $p < .001$ | |

|  | Conflict with older brother | |
| --- | --- | --- |
|  | below median | above median |
| **Conflict with father** | | |
| below median | 6 | 1 |
| above median | 0 | 8 |
|  | Fisher's Exact Test $p = .001$ | |

|  | Subordination to older brother | |
| --- | --- | --- |
|  | below median | above median |
| **Sibling child care: boys** | | |
| absent | 5 | 0 |
| present | 13 | 14 |
|  | Fisher's Exact Test $p = .052$ | |

|  | Girls | |
| --- | --- | --- |
|  | Contact with older sister | |
|  | below median | above median |
| **Contact with mother** | | |
| below median | 11 | 2 |
| above median | 6 | 13 |
|  | Fisher's Exact Test $p = .005$ | |

nized that much child care in tribal and traditional societies is performed by other children, following Weisner and Gallimore's (1977) influential paper surveying this practice. In the large majority of societies in this study for which there are pertinent data, adolescents interact frequently with younger children: girls in 87 percent of 95 cases and boys in 81 percent of 89 cases. Teenage child care, a source of income for modern adolescents, is a domestic duty in much of the world. Weisner (1982:323) points out the important role of sibling care in mediating parent-child tensions.

For analysis, we divided these societies into two groups, those in which adolescents are and are not significant socializers of younger children, meaning that they do or do not care for them or otherwise spend a good deal of time with them. The role of adolescents as socializers was related to the measures of family emotional tone. We reason that where adolescents are socializers, then those in the sample societies who have older siblings were socialized by them when these siblings were themselves adolescents. We expect that the relations between adolescents and siblings who socialized them will differ from relations in societies in which this is not the case.

In our efforts to discern the impact of relations of adolescents of both sexes with older siblings of both sexes, the only significant finding is the absence of strong subordination of boys to older brothers who did not care for them as children (Table 4.3). As Weisner (1982:312) pointed out, it is common for older siblings to dominate younger ones in their care. For brothers this is one way of establishing a hierarchy, in which the position of the older brother as agent for the parents can be carried forward into the adolescence of the younger brother. Whiting and Whiting (1975:95ff.) hypothesized that child care promotes responsible and nurturant behavior in children; for boys in some cases there may be an increase in dominance as well, at least toward younger brothers. There is, of course, no incompatibility between nurturance and dominance; one can be both loving and bossy. The absence of significant findings for other kinds of sibling relationships may be due to the small size of the samples. Alternatively, it may indicate that sibling relationships in adolescence are more a consequence of the setting in which they occur—the current factors promoting closeness or distance, hierarchy or equality, between adolescents and their older brothers and sisters—than of antecedent relationships, those between siblings when the adolescents were children.

## Family and Society

We looked at the co-occurrence of variables measuring family relations with variables that are measures of social organization or that are known to be associated with features of social organization. By social organization, we refer to relations that sort people into roles and categories and through which the necessary activities of life are carried on: relations of production that characterize roles within the subsistence technology and the economy; relations of reproduction embedded in kinship and marriage; and relations of power that operate within the political system, whereby decisions for the community and polity are made and enforced.

Anthropologists, practitioners of a comparative science, long ago learned that behavior, features of expressive culture, kinds of religious systems, and even the more subtle aspects of culture like values, beliefs, and styles of self-presentation do not vary randomly across cultures but fit somewhat loosely into typologies. If one knows that a society is a tropical foraging band or an East African cattle-keeping village or is matrilineal or practices general polygyny, one can make predictions about other aspects of social organization and culture.

Several ways of classifying societies have proven to be useful. One highly predictive set of variables, which encompasses many other features of social organization, is the type of subsistence technology. Another, associated with features of individual behavior, is the structure of the family. These variables tend to be intercorrelated, but not so highly as to indicate that they are tautological.

## Subsistence Technology

Subsistence technology can be characterized by a rough-hewn typology. As generally used in cross-cultural research, in which fine-grained classification would result in too few cases per type to permit testing, the classification consists of five types: foraging (sometimes subdivided into primarily hunting, primarily fishing, and primarily gathering), pastoral, horticultural (sometimes subdivided into incipient and extensive agricultural), agricultural (or intensive agricultural), and industrial. This study deals with only preindustrial societies, coded by Murdock and Morrow (1980).

Foraging societies that depend upon hunting or gathering of wild foods are generally small in scale and consist of nomadic or seminomadic bands traveling within a territory. Fishing societies are likely to be more sedentary, although they may alternate coastal fishing with inland hunting. In this case, people leave their communities to disperse during part of the year. Although most foraging societies collect food on a daily basis or every few days, some are able to acquire enough surplus to store, like the Haida and Bella Coola of the resource-rich northwest coast of North America, or to trade with outsiders, as the Plains Indians of North America traded buffalo skins and dried meat for goods of European manufacture. Thus, societies like the Oceanian Manus and Marshallese, the Haida, the Bella Coola, and the Plains Omaha, classified as foraging on the basis of primary subsistence techniques, might have features of social and political organization more in common with the more complex horticultural societies than with foraging bands such as the Australian Tiwi or the Canadian Montagnais. The great world area of foragers at the time of European expansion, between the 16th and 20th centuries, was pre-Columbian North America. Pockets of foragers have existed until recently in Australia, tropical South and Southeast Asia, the circumpolar zone, and Africa.

Horticulture, sometimes called hoe or extensive agriculture, relies commonly on root or tree crops rather than cereal grains (excepting corn in the native New World). In the absence of advanced techniques of irrigation or fertilization, it often requires extensive land, as fields are burned and cleared, used until the yield declines, and then allowed to lie fallow a number of years until new growth can be burned to restore fertility. This type of slash-and-burn horticulture is common in tropical regions of Africa, South America, and the Pacific. With a low person-to-land ratio, communities tend to be small and rather widely spaced.

Agriculture refers to intensive cultivation with advanced techniques, including the animal-drawn plow, large-scale irrigation systems, and other techniques permitting intensive cultivation of cereal grains such as corn in certain areas of the pre-Columbian New World and wheat, millet, or rice in the Old World. The person-to-land ratio is increased, allowing for the rise of urban centers where noncultivators are fed by a food-producing population.

These subsistence technologies have very different labor requirements. The involvement of the sexes, for instance, varies widely: women are heavily engaged in primary subsistence activities in gathering and horticultural societies, much less so in most hunting, pastoral, and agricultural societies, although they may contribute a good deal to the processing of raw materials (cf. Schlegel and Barry 1986). The labor demands on children differ considerably also, with relatively little contribution to the family food supply among foragers to a fair amount of contribution in the food-producing societies. Older children and adolescents are frequently used to take charge of animals in horticultural or agricultural communities in which domestic animals are raised—cattle in Africa, pigs in Oceania, sheep and goats along the Mediterranean, and the small livestock of Europe and Asia. The duck boy with his waddling flock is as familiar a figure in the Asian countryside as the little cattle herder in East Africa or the young shepherd in Sardinia. In this respect, industrial societies are somewhat similar to foraging ones like the African Hadza, where adolescents may hunt and collect to feed themselves snacks without adding to the family larder. Western adolescents who earn pin money to satisfy their optional wants are also dependent on their families for their essential needs without contributing much in return.

Although the occupations that bring parents and children together into work teams differ among societies in the sample, female domestic tasks are

usually conducted at or near the home. For this reason level of contact between adolescent girls and their mothers shows no distribution according to
subsistence system. Contact between boys and their fathers does, however.
High contact is characteristic of agricultural and fully pastoral societies,
whereas low contact is more likely in foraging and horticultural societies (see
Table 4.4).

The determining factor here is private property, for even though pastoralists claim collective ownership of watering places and grazing fields, animals are almost always individually owned. Not only are herd management
and agriculture most effectively done by two or more men working together,
but the prospect of inheriting the father's property (most pastoral and agricultural societies having father-son inheritance) also makes it advantageous
for father and son to work together, as the father teaches his son how to
manage the estate. In foraging societies, on the other hand, male subsistence
labor (hunting and fishing) is often performed individually. In horticultural
societies, while adults work in the gardens, adolescent boys might be tending

*Table 4.4* Subsistence System and Relations with Father

|  | Subsistence System | | | |
|  | Foraging | [Pastoral]<sup>a</sup> | Horticul-tural | Agricul-tural |
|---|---|---|---|---|
| *Contact: boys* | | | | |
| below median | 22 | [1] | 34 | 19 |
| above median | 10 | [4] | 20 | 24 |
| Mantel-Haenszel $\chi^2$ = 3.98 | | | $p$ = .046 | |
| *Subordination: boys* | | | | |
| below median | 18 | [3] | 20 | 13 |
| above median | 13 | [9] | 30 | 32 |
| Mantel-Haenszel $\chi^2$ = 6.42 | | | $p$ = .011 | |
| *Subordination: girls* | | | | |
| below median | 19 | [3] | 18 | 9 |
| above median | 15 | [9] | 29 | 34 |
| Mantel-Haenszel $\chi^2$ = 9.51 | | | $p$ = .002 | |
| *Intimacy: boys* | | | | |
| below median | 6 | [2] | 15 | 13 |
| above median | 8 | [0] | 9 | 3 |
| Mantel-Haenszel $\chi^2$ = 4.44 | | | $p$ = .035 | |

<sup>a</sup>Figures on pastoral systems are given to show the distribution. They were not used in comput-
ing the statistic.

cattle (Africa) or pigs (Oceania) or hunting and fishing (tropical South America), activities that take them away from the company of their fathers.

In agricultural and pastoral societies, subordination to their fathers is likely to be high for both sons and daughters (Table 4.4). There is, however, no relation between subsistence system and subordination to their mothers. Paternal authority is related to family ownership of property, land or animals, and the preparation of sons to assume eventual management of the family estate. When there is private property, children depend much more on their parents for their start in life than in tribal societies in which property is collective and each adult rightfully assumes usufruct of lineage or community land. In foraging societies, without property, each individual makes it on his own.

Societies with heritable tangible or intangible property—animals for pastoralists, use-rights to land and sometimes animals for horticulturalists, land and other wealth for agriculturalists—are less likely to promote intimacy between fathers and sons than are the foragers, who in most cases do not own heritable property (fishing societies of Oceania and the northwest coast of North America being exceptions). This distinction suggests that there are two strategies by which parents bind their children and assure themselves of lifelong loyalty. When there is property, it acts to ensure bonding through common interest. When there is not, love is an adhesive. There is, of course, no incompatibility between these strategies, for ties through property can only be stronger if they are reinforced with love. If neither love nor property binds adult children to their parents, the relationship becomes quite attenuated.

## Household Structure

The structure of the household has consequences for relations between adolescents and their parents. There is a weak trend for boys to have low contact with their fathers when residence is female-centered (matrilocal) and high contact when it is male-centered (patrilocal, avunculocal, and virilocal) (Table 4.5). Whiting and Whiting (1975:122) found a higher level of interaction with fathers among children in cultures with nuclear-family households. That is not the case in this study for contact of fathers with either boys ($r = -.03$, $N = 134$) or girls ($r = -.04$, $N = 120$). Possibly by adolescence, children in nuclear-family households are reducing paternal contact in preparation for the move away from the family when they marry. Contact of either sex with their mothers is not significantly associated with the residence pattern or the form of the household.

Thus, contact between fathers and sons is somewhat likely to be higher when men bring wives into their fathers' (patrilocal) or mothers' brothers' (avunculocal) households or to live near their male kin (virilocal). The large majority of cases with male-centered residence are patrilocal. Matrilocal res-

*Table 4.5* Household Organization and Relations with Parents

| | Residence | |
|---|---|---|
| | *Female-Centered* | *Male- Centered* |
| *Contact with father: boys* | | |
| below median | 22 | 49 |
| above median | 9 | 42 |
| | $\chi^2 = 2.13$ | $p = .145$ (weak trend) |
| *Subordination to father: boys* | | |
| below median | 18 | 28 |
| above median | 7 | 72 |
| | $\chi^2 = 14.81$ | $p < .001$ |
| *Subordination to father: girls* | | |
| below median | 15 | 25 |
| above median | 9 | 72 |
| | $\chi^2 = 10.13$ | $p = .001$ |
| *Intimacy with mother: boys* | | |
| below median | 9 | 17 |
| above median | 4 | 25 |
| | Fisher's Exact Test $p = .111$ (weak trend) | |

idence, with husband and wife living with her mother and father, is found almost exclusively where there is matrilineal descent, and in such places boys are likely to spend some time with their maternal male kin. In matrilocal households, adult men also spend time in the homes of their mothers and sisters and with their sisters' sons, away from their own sons.

In male-centered households, subordination to their fathers is likely to be high for both sexes, whereas it is likely to be low in female-centered households (Table 4.5). Patriarchy flourishes under male-centered residence, the father's authority over his children being reinforced by the presence or proximity of his close male kin. When husbands move in with wives, their paternal authority is lessened. It is considerably lower in households under the control of female heads, as among the Hopi. Furthermore, in the matrilineal societies in which most female-centered households are found, authority over children is distributed among fathers, mothers, and the mothers' matrilineal kin (usually the children's maternal uncles), the proportions varying among matrilineal societies (cf. Schlegel 1972).

We find a weak trend for intimacy between mother and son to be high in male-centered homes (Table 4.5) and low in female-centered ones. This finding reflects the often observed tendency for mothers in male-centered households to pay great attention to their sons. In part, this may be because to be the mother of sons is their major *raison d'être* in the household when the descent line is patrilineal, as is usually the case with male-centered residence. Another reason, going beyond descent, is that the mother's emotional investment in her sons in patrilocal households will pay off when they are adults, continuing to live in the household of birth. Their in-marrying wives will be subordinate to their mother, and their devotion to her will give her matriarchal power. The woman without sons in a patrilocal household is to be pitied, for in her older years she does not occupy the prominent place in the household and exert the authority over it that her more fortunate sisters do. The fact that it is only a weak trend probably reflects the discouragement of mother-son intimacy for adolescent boys in many patriarchal societies, especially where elaborate initiation ceremonies emphasize the boys' removal from the society of women and reinforce the male bonding that counteracts childhood dependency on the mother (Whiting et al. 1958).

We also assessed the relation between boys' conflict with their fathers and the form of the household. The nuclear-family household, consisting of husband and wife and their unmarried children, is the preferred and most common form in Western society. It is not the preferred form in much of the preindustrial world. More usual among peasants is the stem-family household, consisting of an older parental couple, one adult child who will eventually inherit the family estate (usually a son) plus spouse, and any unmarried children of either couple. Among tribal peoples, the extended-family household is more frequently found, in which several married couples—most commonly the parental couple plus two or more adult sons and their wives—and all unmarried children live together. We hypothesized that there would be less conflict in the larger household, as the presence of several adult males would reinforce the authority of the father and thereby suppress expressions of conflict. We found no such relationship. Thus, we cannot claim that the nuclear-family household is either more or less conflict-ridden than other forms.

Features of the productive system and of household structure contribute to the character of interaction between parents and adolescent children, as we have seen. This interaction in turn has some measurable consequences for adolescent treatment and behavior. For both girls and boys, young people choose their own marital partners when subordination to their fathers and mothers is low, but partners are chosen for them when subordination is high. When girls control their choice of spouse, their subordination is low to their fathers ( $p = .070$, $N = 98$) and their mothers ( $p = .071$, $N = 86$). There is a similar picture for boys, with low subordination to their fathers ( $p = .012$, $N = 105$) and mothers ( $p = .060$, $N = 71$). In fact, control over the choice of marriage partner is a good indicator of level of subordination.

## Marriage Transactions

In a number of societies, goods beyond small gifts are exchanged on the occasion of a child's marriage. These exchanges can take several forms, and some will be discussed further in Chapter 6 in the examination of adolescence and marriage. At this point we are interested in three general types, according to the recipient. In one type, the bride's family receives goods from the groom's family. This is bridewealth, the most common form worldwide. In another, gift exchange, there is an equal exchange of goods between the two families. In the third, the new conjugal couple receives goods. These goods originated either in the bride's family (dowry) or the groom's family, which provides the goods that the bride brings into her new household (indirect dowry). In indirect dowry, either the goods are given directly to the bride or, more commonly, goods are given to her family who then pass on goods to the new couple.

Table 4.6 shows that both girls and boys are more likely to be subordinate to their fathers when there are marriage transactions. In part, this may be due to the dependence upon parents for assembling the goods. More likely, it is the parents who enforce subordination, for if they wish to control their children's marriages—generally the case when property is exchanged— they must control the children. Only if transactions are absent are children likely to be freer from domination.

This interpretation implies that as the European form of marriage transaction, dowry, has faded as a cultural practice, the issue of parental control has become less central to family life in the West. There are additional factors, one being the rise of economic opportunities with industrialization that make young people less dependent upon inheritance or familial financing.

*Table 4.6* Direction of Marriage Exchange and Subordination to Father

|  | Recipients | | | |
|---|---|---|---|---|
|  | Bride's family | Equal exchange | Conjugal couple | Absent |
| *Subordination to father: girls* | | | | |
| below median | 25 | 6 | 3 | 15 |
| above median | 42 | 17 | 20 | 8 |
|  | $\chi^2 = 14.81$ | df = 3 | p = .002 | |
| *Subordination to father: boys* | | | | |
| below median | 28 | 6 | 5 | 15 |
| above median | 42 | 14 | 19 | 9 |
|  | $\chi^2 = 9.60$ | df = 3 | p = .022 | |

## Parent-Adolescent Conflict and Antagonism

Before leaving this discussion of the relations of adolescents with family members, we wish to dwell further on a topic that has received great attention, parent-child conflict and antagonism. Parents of Western adolescents are acutely aware of the antagonism that can be engendered by a discordance of interest between adolescents and adults. It is often assumed that this is a phenomenon of modern society, but that is not true. Duby (1980:23) related that among the French aristocracy of the early Middle Ages:

> Most heirs apparent did rebel against their fathers as soon as they out-grew adolescence, out of impatience to exercise unfettered control over the seignory, in which they were egged on by companions of their own age, equally frustrated and greedy.

Anticipation of possible rebellion surely colored feelings of fathers and adolescent sons during that time.

Although conflict and antagonism are closely related, the former behavior often being the outward expression of the latter emotion, it is important to keep them separate for purposes of analysis. As noted earlier, conflict can often be petty, the bickering or mild disobedience that indicates some discordance but not necessarily fear or dislike. Antagonism may be expressed in conflict, but it may also be expressed by withdrawal from the other or be suppressed by the need to maintain harmonious-appearing associations.

Whenever the goals and interests of parents and children are at cross-purposes, there is the possibility of more serious conflict. For example, when adults control the marriages of young people by giving or withholding economic resources, the seeds of discord are present, for those resources might be used in ways more profitable to the adults than to set up their children as householders. Among the Kyaka of New Guinea, "open conflicts occur between fathers and adolescent or young adult sons over allocation of garden land and arrangement of marriages and exchanges" (Bulmer 1965:141); and father-son antagonism leads later in life to the attribution of sickness and death to the malice of fathers' ghosts. An African pastoralist might prefer to use cattle for bridewealth to acquire a second wife for himself rather than a first one for his son. In some peasant communities, as in rural Ireland (Arensberg 1937) or Sicily (Constance Cronin, personal communication), the aging household head may delay as long as possible turning over land to sons so they can marry, for with his retirement comes his own decline in status as he enters into the category of the powerless aged. In such cases, antagonism toward the father is an expectable consequence.

Even if property is not at issue, the parental value set on family economic production and use of the adolescent's time for work in the family gardens or elsewhere may interfere with the youngster's own preference, and conflict over freedom may ensue. Closer to home, though it was in the interest of the American lower-class boy of the 19th century to get further education, it was in the father's interest to put him to work, and conflict often erupted (Rothman 1971). The first author has been given similar reports about some Hopi parents and sons from the early 20th century, when elementary and secondary education became generally available to Hopi children but their labor was often wanted at home. Children who live with their parents but do not depend on them for support can be embroiled in conflicts resulting from discrepancies between parental authority and youthful independence: the homes of 19th century English industrial workers, whose adolescent members might earn wages equal to their parents, were often strife-ridden after this fashion (Musgrove 1964:65ff.).

The impression one gets from reading many ethnographies is that conflict and antagonism between adolescents and parents in most traditional societies are not, in fact, serious problems. Adolescents do not struggle to individuate themselves from the family to the degree that Western young people do: their dependency on their families, or their spouses', will continue even after they reach adulthood, and much of their economic well-being is likely to come from their contribution to group effort rather than from independent action.

Nevertheless, conflict and antagonism can arise, so predictably as to be part of the cultural pattern. The two examples that follow are extreme types, selected to illustrate ways in which adolescent-parent antagonism can become established. The first example is of father-son antagonism among the Moose (Mossi), a herding-horticultural people living in small kingdoms of what is today Burkina Faso. The information is summarized from Skinner (1961).

> Moose fathers have very little contact with their sons, particularly the first who is most likely to be heir and successor. The oldest son is reared by his maternal relatives and does not return to his father's compound until after puberty. Although he visits his father before this, his behavior is very formal and circumspect. When he does return, he lives with other young men of the compound in special quarters for bachelors.
>
> Bachelorhood is long and difficult. Only older men usually have the social and economic resources to acquire wives, and young men make do with occasional lovers. Since the heir will inherit his father's wives as his own, excepting his mother, it is recognized that access to wives—in fact, his advancement in the community—may depend upon the death of the father. While wishing for the father's death is the ultimate treachery, Moose claim that some young men do long for it.

Open conflict between father and son in Moose society is prevented or at least softened by the limited contact between them. However, the very customs that keep father and son apart also prevent any intimacy from growing up. The institution that ensures paternal control—postmortem inheritance of women and cattle, with little opportunity to receive either during the father's lifetime—makes it difficult for the adolescent or youthful son not to look forward to his father's death.

The second example is of mother-daughter conflict, representing a transient state rather than lifelong attitudes. It comes from the Hopi. (More detailed information can be found in Schlegel 1973, 1975.) Property is not the issue here. Rather, the Hopi mother and daughter come into conflict over curtailment of the girl's freedom and escalation of her household responsibilities.

The appearance of menstruation marks the change from freedom to restriction for the Hopi girl. While her male age-mates are free to roam at will, her mother keeps her in the house. Running about the village, as she formerly did, is unseemly. She is expected to guard her chastity and her reputation and occupy her time with the laborious task of grinding corn for family meals.

At the same time that she is relatively secluded, she is expected to be choosing the boy to whom she will propose marriage, with her parents' approval. Since men marry into the homes of their wives, the burden of initiating the marriage falls on the girl's shoulders. Boys are free to refuse, and the fear of rejection casts a shadow over many girls' adolescent years. Her parents, who are urging her to marry so that there will be another worker in the house and the family line will continue, at the same time make it difficult for her to become acquainted with boys and to attract them.

These two factors, the sudden curtailment of freedom of movement and fear that she will be unsuccessful in marriage, make adolescence a trying time for the Hopi girl. Quarrels between mother and daughter, at other stages of life the most loving of kin, are common. Girls may rail at their mothers and accuse them of being "mean," i.e., unloving and uncaring in Hopi usage of English. The mother will try to sweeten the burden of household duties by telling the daughter that her corn grinding brings the blood to her cheeks and makes her pretty, and adolescent girls hold grinding parties in each other's homes, but that does not always help matters. In cases of extreme conflict, the girl might run away to a relative's house. While she gets temporary respite, she has no alternative but to return home.

In this case, mother-daughter conflict is not institutionalized, but quite the contrary. It is a response to a situational stress brought about by abrupt role change and exacerbated by parental pressures to find a husband.

Though the daughter is her mother's heir to house and status in this matrilineal, matrilocal society, as the Moose youth is to his father in their patrilineal, patrilocal one, there is none of the tension in the former that is so evident in the latter. Mothers and daughters share duties, and the transfer of household headship is gradual as the older woman ages and willingly turns over responsibility and authority to her adult daughter. The conflict in the Hopi case is not a discordance of goals, for both the mother and the daughter want the girl to learn housewifely skills and be successful in finding a husband, but rather in the way these goals are implemented. The Hopi mother does not stand in her daughter's way, as the Moose father does to his son. The antagonism that peaks in adolescence and youth for the Moose boy is an underlying feature of father-son relations, while for the Hopi family, adolescent conflict is something that simply has to be endured in the knowledge that it will pass, once the daughter has married and become an adult.

Much of the conflict between Western adolescents and parents can be understood by looking at the social institutions of modern industrial society. First, there is the nuclear-family household, which the young person will leave shortly after adolescence. Economic dependency extends into the later teen years for those who are in school full time, creating a disjuncture between adolescent dependence and the expected economic independence for many in the postadolescent youth stage. In addition, there is considerable geographical mobility. (The nuclear-family household is a centuries-old institution in preindustrial England and other parts of Europe, but as young people left home, they tended to stay within or near the community in which they were born.) This forces young people to face a rather sudden and extreme rupture from their natal families, at a time when they may fear and feel unready for such independence. It is also confusing to parents, who must encourage their adolescent children to act in mature, adult ways in preparation for leaving home at the same time that these children are still under their authority and economically dependent on them.

Second, most young people are faced with imminent responsibility for their own financial support. This independence has its advantages, in that it releases them from the parental control that can weigh heavily on young adults in societies in which parents control resources. However, the break in economic dependence also signals a rupture in the family's community of interest.

Perhaps adolescence is particularly stressful for the many modern adolescents who grow up in child-centered homes. Much attention has been paid by social historians to the cult of domesticity and the centrality of child rearing to family life since the industrial revolution. Children growing up in an indulgent and sheltered environment may be frightened by the prospect of independence, and their fear may be expressed as antagonism toward their parents. Children who have been more taken for granted will have less to lose when they leave home, and in such societies adolescence may lack the emotional intensity it has in Western nations.

————

The measures of family relations lend support to our model of the social organization of adolescence. Most waking hours are spent in the company of same-sex adults, who are likely to be family members and kin. Boys and girls have similar levels of contact with the parents of the opposite sex, but girls spend more time with their mothers than boys do with their fathers. Girls are with their mothers in the home and accompany them in their activities outside the home, whether of a productive or recreational nature. Boys, however, accompany their fathers much less and spend more time with their peers (see Chapter 5).

Fathers are generally more distant from adolescent children of both sexes than are mothers, even though boys spend more time with them than with their mothers. Both boys and girls are more subordinate to fathers than to mothers, with whom they are more intimate.

Even though mothers are the parents with whom children of both sexes are more intimate, girls are both more intimate with them and more submissive to them than are boys. Mothers have greater authority over daughters than sons, but they also tend to be closer to daughters. Even in societies that do not deliberately attempt to dilute the mother-son bond with initiation ceremonies or by other means, this bond is likely to be weaker than the mother-daughter bond. We will return to this sex difference in Chapter 10.

The relation of fathers to their children shows some differences depending on the sex of the child. As men's contact with adolescent children increases, they are more in conflict with sons and more intimate with daughters. Thus, the boy's relation to his parents, of greater conflict with his male parent and more intimacy with his female parent, reproduces itself when he grows up in his relation to his children, when increasing contact brings him more into conflict with his male child and fosters greater intimacy with his female child. Chodorow (1978) has written of the reproduction of mothering. These findings indicate that men, also, carry into parenthood the kinds of relations they had with their own parents.

We have seen that parent-child attitudes and behaviors are sensitive to the relations of production that arise with different types of subsistence techniques. Parental authority is strongest among the agricultural and pastoral peoples. On the other hand, boys' intimacy with their fathers is greater among foragers. We attribute this to the presence or absence of property: private property is most widely held among the agriculturalists; it is significant among pastoralists; it is variable among horticulturalists, where both communally held and private property exist; and it is minimal or absent among most foragers. We believe that the effect of property upon adolescents results from the facts of parental control of resources and of inheritance. When there is significant private property, anticipated inheritance becomes a ubiquitous feature of family life and child socialization, as parents consciously groom children to preserve the assets they have acquired or maintained. Furthermore, as the parents control the economic resources of the family, the child is obliged to submit to their wishes. These factors make for a more authoritarian family.

Other factors can lead to similar consequences. Acquisition of wives among the Moose makes young men dependent on their fathers. Intangible property like high offices can also be inherited. In tribal societies, the grooming of the heir is likely to occur most strongly among families of high status, among whom the anticipated inheritance of powerful political or ceremonial offices colors family interactions.

In the association between family relations and property ownership, families in modern societies may be somewhat like either traditional agricultural or foraging families. If the family owns significant property, access to it by the young person now and in the future depends upon the good will of the parents. If it does not, the young person has to rely on individual achievement through education, personal skills and talent, and luck. Based on the findings from this sample, we suggest that, in the former case, parent-adolescent interactions will tend to be more hierarchical and perhaps less intimate than in the latter. Thus, there are likely to be significant social-class differences in these relationships.

Parent-adolescent relations also respond to the structure of the household. The nuclear-family household is of particular interest to us, as it is the characteristic type in modern society. We have noted that Whiting and Whiting (1975) found a high level of interaction between fathers and children in such households, whereas we have found no difference between nuclear family households and other forms for contact between fathers and adolescents. We believe that this reflects a shift in the father-child relationship in adolescence: the decoupling from the family is accentuated in nuclear-family households, as young people prepare to make the break that will eventuate in their establishing independent households.

To summarize, we find a general pattern of parent-child relations that conforms to the model. Within this pattern there is considerable variability. We have identified at least three major factors related to this variability: subsistence techniques and the relations of production associated with them, control over property, and the structure of the household.

# 5

# Peer Groups and
# Community Participation

ADOLESCENTS operate on the fringes of adult community life. Only occasionally do they regularly interact with adults other than family and kin outside of an educational or occupational setting. When they are intensively involved with adults, it is within rather strictly prescribed limits. They are not granted admission into social groups beyond the family in which adults interact freely and adult interests are realized. In no cases in the sample do adolescents take on new political roles, being like children in their lack of power within the community. Traditional states may from time to time have their boy kings or the rare charismatic leader like Jeanne d'Arc, who was about 17 when she led the army of France. With these few exceptions, community decision-making is an adult responsibility and privilege that comes with the economic rights and social alliance-building of adulthood.

Nevertheless, in a number of places, adolescents do take on new community roles that signify an increase in social responsibility over childhood. They may begin to take part, or increase their participation, in military and religious affairs, or to perform activities for community economic production or social welfare. In such cases, adolescents usually perform these actions in groups. For that reason, we will consider community involvement along with peer group activities.

The model in Chapter 2 depicts relations with family and peers as differing between girls and boys. In most societies the family is likely to be the most important socializing institution, but the peer group as a secondary socializing agent is predicted to be more salient for boys than for girls. This prediction is borne out. For the 176 societies for which there is information for boys, peers are primary agents of socialization in 11 and secondary agents in 29. For girls, peers are primary agents in only one society and secondary ones in only 18 of 173 societies. Within this pattern, considerable variability is shown in the importance of peer groups both among and within cultures. Elder (1974), for example, related the variability in orientation toward friends and family of Oakland children during the Depression to economic factors, with a stronger orientation toward peers among the children from economically deprived families. Because the data for this present study are at the cultural rather than the individual level, this kind of intracultural variation cannot be tested. However, there is no reason to conclude that individual differences in orientation are absent from even small, homogeneous communities, although probably not to the degree that one finds in large, heterogeneous nations.

At all stages of life beyond infancy, from the rough-and-tumble play group of childhood to the poignant, ever-diminishing cluster of aged cronies, persons of similar age congregate. Such groups take on a special meaning in adolescence, when young people are temporarily released from intense identification with a family. In childhood, people depend for their very life on the natal family; in adulthood, they are responsible for the well-being of spouses and children and for pursuing the interests and position of the marital family. For the brief period of adolescence, they are neither so dependent as they were nor so responsible as they will be. It is then that peer relations can take on an intensity of attachment that they lack at other stages of the life cycle, except perhaps in old age in those places where the elderly retire from productive activities.

The transitory nature of intense peer group involvement is well known from modern society, in which it has been frequently observed that these attachments wither when young people marry or begin serious courtship. The egalitarian nature of the peer group (Gecas 1981) dissolves as occupational and social claims differentiate its members. The inevitable rupture of close ties among adolescents is a characteristic of tribesmen as well, as illustrated by the Boran, an East African cattle-keeping people. Although neither the high degree of peer group solidarity nor the competitiveness of later adult relations among the Boran is necessarily typical of traditional societies, the process described for this group (Baxter and Almagor 1978:172) is widespread:

> Sharing is urged by and on those who are equal in their juniority and limited access to those resources which differentiate men and who, in practice, have little to share but hardships and danger. . . . As men mature they become patently less equal in wealth, wives, influence, office, and power; the responsibility property brings divides as it socializes. The ideal of fraternity may remain, but it is eroded by cares and responsibilities. . . . Both a man's interests in his family herd and his individual ambitions are opposed to, and stronger than, the ideal of sharing with all age-mates.

As Sherif and Sherif (1964:251) observed, when boys move from adolescence to adulthood through marriage and employment: "The adolescent group loses its magic even in the lives of the loyal group members."

Adolescence, then, is a time when there may be something of a moratorium on family attachment, at least for boys. The peer group is likely to be the first social unit in the child's experience that acts as a group independent from adults and outside their supervision. As a socializing institution it is likely to remain secondary to the family, although in some places, particularly where there are adolescent communal houses, it can equal the family in the enforcement of behavior and inculcation of values.

An extreme form of separation from the natal family occurs within European tradition. Europe has a long history of child and adolescent fosterage, a case being the circulation of boys as pages among noble families of the Middle Ages. (The Abkhaz of the Caucasus Mountains retained the ancient practice of child fosterage into the 20th century.) In early modern Western Europe, it was common for adolescent girls and boys whose labor was not needed at home to be farm hands, apprentices, and domestic servants in the homes of others, often their neighbors. In this way, young people could contribute to their families through the remittance of cash wages, save up money to buy a farm or assemble a trousseau, or, in the case of crafts apprentices, learn a trade (cf. Gillis 1974). This practice continued well into the 19th century. Even though these young people were engaged in occupations, they were still in a domestic setting. Their employers acted *in loco parentis* and, at least in theory, treated these adolescents as they would their own children. The boarding school, then, was not an innovation in parent-child relations, but a new form of the separation from home that already had a long history in Western life.

In traditional societies, the separation is usually not so extreme, although child fosterage is not uncommon in some parts of Africa and Oceania. However, adolescents may still spend a good deal of time together and take responsibility for their own governance. The following two accounts from the Nyakyusa and the Muria of adolescent social organization, summaries of classics from the ethnographic literature, are examples of societies in which adolescents have a fair degree of independence from parental control and supervision, even though they are still dependent upon their families.

The Nyakyusa, described as they were between 1934 and 1938, are a horticultural and cattle-keeping people dwelling in the border region of what are today Tanzania and Malawi. The following account is drawn from Wilson (1963).

Up to about age 10 or 11, Nyakyusa boys live in their fathers' homes and tend their cattle. When a number of village sons have reached the right age, they are given a piece of land adjacent to the village, where they build their own huts. Along with change of residence goes an occupational change: they leave herding to the younger boys, and work in the fields with their fathers. Thus, they belong to two villages—economically to that of their fathers, and socially to that of their age-mates. While each boys' village is attached to the adult village that gave it land, boys from other villages may live there as well. Until they marry, boys and young men eat at their mothers' hearths, going from one to another in small groups. Beginning with perhaps a dozen boys, new members are added for about six or eight years, and then the village is closed. At about age 25, the senior members begin to marry and cultivate their own fields. The rationale for sending boys away is so that the parents may have privacy in their sexual activities.

Prepubertal Nyakyusa girls live with their parents (the author does not resolve the privacy question for girls), but they may visit the boys to whom they are betrothed and indulge in sex play. The initiation and marriage rituals comprise one extended ceremony. These now occur at puberty. Formerly, marriage came later, and adolescent girls lived together in a girls' house in the village, where they were visited at night by the boys.

It is not uncommon in many societies for adolescent boys to sleep away from their parents' homes. If the community contains a men's house, it is the usual sleeping place for adolescent boys, unmarried—widowed or divorced—men, and men who for various ritual reasons are sleeping apart from their wives. For example, Hopi boys after about age 10 or 11 frequently sleep in the kivas, the ceremonial buildings used as men's houses, or on warm nights, in groups on the flat rooftops of the family houses.

Less common are separate community dormitories for boys or for girls. Such dormitories for one sex or the other were rather widespread among tribespeople of Africa, southern Asia, and the Pacific; the Nyakyusa formerly had them for girls. (A survey of this custom is found in Elwin 1947: Chapter 9.) They are not limited to tribal peoples, for peasant communities in Japan, particularly in the south, often had girls' dormitories in earlier times (Norbeck 1953). Though in some cases the chastity of girls was guarded in their dormitories, often the separation from parents gave them legitimate opportunity and relative privacy for sexual adventures. Such was the case in Japan, where nocturnal visits by boys were customary.

Wherever these dormitories occurred, they were simply sleeping places, not self-contained households where goods were produced and consumed. Adolescents spent their days at home, working with their parents and eating with the family. The adolescent dormitory was the place for free evening hours, for frolic and sleep, a sort of extended slumber party as American teenagers know it, but often with the addition of sexual play.

An example of such a society is the Muria, selected because they are representative of adolescent communal organization in its most extreme form, the mixed-sex dormitory where all adolescents sleep and spend their leisure time. Described as they were between 1935 and 1942 (Elwin 1947), they are a tribe in the former princely state of Bastar, in central India. They practice plow agriculture and keep cows and pigs.

There is no particular age at which girls and boys begin sleeping in the *ghotul,* as the adolescent dormitory is called, but somewhere between six or eight seems to be the time when they first go there occasionally. The little ones act as fags to the adolescents, who teach and discipline them. All activities within the *ghotul* are regulated, from the duties the members perform for the *ghotul* or the village, to who sleeps with whom. In some *ghotuls,* semi-permanent attachments are formed, but in others adolescent boys and girls are expected to rotate among partners and are accused of selfishness and egotism if they seem reluctant to do so. At marriage the girl leaves the *ghotul* forever, but the young married man may continue to visit for some months until he can afford to give a farewell feast. Very popular married men may even be invited to retain a membership and revisit the place of happy youthful hours from time to time.

Two features of *ghotul* life are particularly striking in Elwin's account. One is the discipline that *ghotul* members exert over one another, relieving parents and other adults from enforcing conformity to culturally approved behavior. The second is the importance erotic play assumes in the activities and expressions of adolescents, making adolescence a highly eroticized time of life (we will discuss this further and bring up the question of pregnancy in Chapter 7).

These are cases of unusually strong peer group bonding. In most societies, adolescents spend most of their time in a family, usually their own. In the majority of societies, then, some accommodation must be made between attachment to family and attachment to peers.

The "parent-peer" issue, as it has come to be known, refers to the involvement of adolescents with family or peer group: where adolescents' time and energies are directed, with whom they prefer to spend time, and who is monitoring their behavior and inducing conformity. The discussion of this issue in the social and psychological literature has been cogently summarized by Coleman (1980), who noted that it is considerably more complicated than earlier investigators had assumed. In reviewing this issue several years earlier, Conger (1972:220) spoke of the "well-worn cliche that at adolescence the young person turns away from his parents and becomes the captive of his peers," a belief that "contains a considerable element of mythology." Both reviewers referred to studies carried out during the 1960s and 1970s, which indicated that weight given to influence of peers or parents may depend on the situation, that influence from both sources is often mutually reinforcing, and that parental influence is strongest when adolescents and their parents are intimate and weakest when they are not. On this last point, Bronfenbrenner (1970:102), speaking of American children, stated: "It would seem that the peer-oriented child is more a product of parental disregard than of the attractiveness of the peer-group—that he turns to his age-mates less by choice than by default. The vacuum left by the withdrawal of parents and adults from the lives of children is filled with an undesired—and possibly *undesirable*—substitute of an age-segregated peer group'' (emphasis in the original).

While strong peer-orientation may be a consequence of parental rejection or neglect among American children, this is not the case for the Muria and Nyakyusa, as just discussed. There, the values of the peer group reinforce those of parents and community. However, the implication of Bronfenbrenner's statement—that there can be an inverse relation between attachment to family and attachment to peers—receives some support from our work.

In an earlier study on adolescent initiation ceremonies, using different coders (Schlegel and Barry 1980a, 1980b), we examined the social consequences of these ceremonies, one of which is same-sex peer bonding. Separation from the family is coded for this present study along a five-point scale, from no or minimal separation, with the adolescent spending most time in or near home or with family members, to absolute separation, generally eating and sleeping away from home. The test of peer bonding and separation indicates that for boys, absence of peer bonding as a consequence of initiation is associated with absence of family separation, while presence is associated with some level of separation (Table 5.1). For girls there is no significant relationship: peer bonding is present for only six of 84 cases, and in 137 of 165 cases there is no or minimal separation.

Another relevant variable coded for this study is the importance of peer groups. This variable is measured on a three-point scale: less important than other social groups, equal in importance, and greater in importance, importance judged according to time spent and resources expended. Peer bonding

*Table 5.1* Peer Bonding as a Consequence of Adolescent Initiation: Boys

|  | *Peer Bonding* | | |
|---|---|---|---|
|  | *absent* | *present* | *% present* |
| *Family separation* | | | |
| absent (1) | 27 | 4 | 13 |
| present (2-5) | 10 | 16 | 62 |
|  | | Fisher's Exact Test $p < .001$ | |
| *Importance of peer groups* | | | |
| less | 7 | 0 | 0 |
| equal | 9 | 4 | 31 |
| more | 3 | 7 | 70 |
| Mantel-Haenszel $\chi^2 = 8.68$ | | $p = .003$ | |

as a consequence of initiation is significantly associated with the importance of peer groups for boys (Table 5.1).

Time that is spent with peers is not available for spending with family members. Table 5.2 shows the association for boys between time spent with peers and both family separation and the importance of the peer group. It also shows an inverse relation for girls between time spent with peers and contact with the mother, although in very few cases is more time spent with peers. There is a trend in this direction for sons and fathers, but it fails to reach significance.

The peer group is more prominent in the lives of its participants if young people are less involved in family life. It is more important for boys if there is separation from the family and if contact with the father is lower (below the median) (Table 5.3). As we might expect, when peer groups are rated as more important than other social groups, peers are more likely to be primary agents of socialization (Table 5.3). These results suggest that frequent or sus-

*Table 5.2* Time Spent with Peers

|  | Time spent | | |
|---|---|---|---|
|  | *more with peers* | *more with others* | *% more with others* |
| *Family separation: boys* | | | |
| absent | 11 | 88 | 89 |
| present | 16 | 41 | 72 |
|  | $\chi^2 = 6.13$ | $p = .013$ | |
| *Importance of peer group: boys* | | | |
| less | 1 | 26 | 96 |
| equal | 7 | 25 | 78 |
| more | 16 | 8 | 33 |
|  | Mantel-Haenszel $\chi^2 = 23.78$ | $p < .001$ | |
| *Contact with father: boys* | | | |
| below median | 16 | 57 | 78 |
| above median | 5 | 47 | 90 |
|  | $\chi^2 = 2.47$ | $p = .116$ (weak trend) | |
| *Contact with mother: girls* | | | |
| below median | 4 | 48 | 92 |
| above median | 0 | 75 | 100 |
|  | | Fisher's Exact Test $p = .026$ | |

*Table 5.3* Importance of Boys' Peer Group and Relations with the Family

| | Importance relative to other groups | | |
|---|---|---|---|
| | *less* | *equal* | *more* |
| *Family separation* | | | |
|   absent | 20 | 17 | 7 |
|   present | 8 | 18 | 18 |
|         Mantel-Haenszel $\chi^2 = 9.89$ | | $p = .002$ | |
| *Contact with father* | | | |
|   below median | 4 | 19 | 13 |
|   above median | 18 | 8 | 5 |
|         Mantel-Haenszel $\chi^2 = 12.39$ | | $p < .001$ | |
| *Peer group as agent of socialization* | | | |
|   primary | 0 | 1 | 10 |
|   secondary or tertiary | 8 | 17 | 9 |
|         Mantel-Haenszel $\chi^2 = 11.64$ | | $p = .001$ | |

tained contact with the father reduces the boy's participation and interest in peer activities. For girls, there are too few cases of family separation—and none where peers are primary agents of socialization—to conduct tests with these variables.

Although for boys the importance of the peer group is inversely related to contact with the father, this is not true for intimacy with the father, with which there is no significant association. Neither is there an association with father-son conflict. These results support the positions of Conger and Coleman, previously cited, that there is no simple parent-peer dichotomy. Peer groups are not the enemies of parents. In some societies, boys may flee to their peers in retreat from constrained relations with the father. In others, where the peer group is equally important, intimacy with the father may be cherished as a relief from the competitiveness of age-mates and the pressures they exert to conform to their standards. Distance between generations may appear with peer group involvement in some societies or under some conditions, but there is no general association. The reports on the Nyakyusa and the Muria, extreme cases of peer group attachment, indicate a low level of conflict with the parents.

## The Structure, Activities, and Character of Peer Groups

We begin with the assumption that social organization is the consequence of an interplay between historical traditions and the constraints and opportunities of everyday life. The structure and character of peer groups vary according to ecological, demographic, and technological features that can be identified. The size of peer groups is constrained by community size and consequently the number of adolescents who can congregate at any one time. Subsistence technology determines whether adolescent labor is required and whether adolescents work with the family or with their peers. Some foraging societies, like our own industrial cities, depend very little on the products of adolescent labor, while the participation of youngsters might be vital to family production in agrarian and pastoral societies. While peer groups *per se* meet some very important socialization needs of adolescents, it is not adolescents themselves who determine the activities of these groups. This determination is made by adults, who make the demands, provide the resources, and bestow the rewards. It is also adults who determine the amount of leisure time available to adolescents.

One of our purposes has been to investigate the structure, activities, and character of adolescent peer groups. As peer groups are not commonly described by ethnographers, the data are not so complete as one would like, and not all of the questions in the code have received enough answers to make statistical testing possible or meaningful. The analysis depends on those variables for which adequate information has been obtained.

Measures of peer groups are defined in Appendix II. Five of these are the following: (1) Importance of peer groups relative to other social groups, as measured by time and other resources expended on them. "Other social groups" includes the family. (2) The most common size of the peer groups. (3) Is this a socially recognized group, such as an age-set or a group with a name? (4) Age range of the peer group. (5) Structure of the peer group.

Peer group activities were rank-ordered according to priority: productive work, leisure, military, religious, community service, other. The sample of societies coded for the set of activities included those with a ranking on any of the items. They were divided into two categories with the use of two strategies. One strategy is a dichotomy between present and absent from mention for a specified activity, such as religious peer group activities. The assumption is that if other activities are mentioned by ethnographers and this one is not, then either it is truly absent or it exists but is inconsequential. The other strategy is a dichotomy that distinguishes a sole rank of one for a specified activity, such as productive work as the most important peer group activity. The alternative category includes societies in which the number one ranking is shared with one or more other activities, in addition to societies in which the specified activity is ranked second or third or not ranked.

Peer competition was rated on a scale of 0–10. This variable rests on the common observation that competitiveness is fostered when there are status differences and status is determined by individual achievement. Peer cooperation was rated on a scale of 0–10.

The importance of the peer group shows no significant relation to subsistence economy. Only one peer group activity does: peer groups tend not to engage in ritual as groups in foraging societies, in which ritual is more often conducted by and for an individual than the community, whereas these activities are part of peer group life in agricultural societies (Table 5.4).

The distribution of boys' peer competition is explicable by what is known of subsistence systems worldwide (Table 5.4). It is lowest where there is agriculture; only 34 percent of agricultural societies are above the median. Agricultural societies, predominantly located in Eurasia and Latin America, are highly structured. Status differences exist not only between classes but also within classes, such as the peasantry, and these differences are determined as much by hereditary position as by individual achievement, although that varies from one historical period to another. The adolescent in a peasant village may not be so concerned about his status within his peer group, for he knows that his status within the community is already established. There is less reason to compete with his peers. The adolescent in foraging societies, also, has less reason to compete with peers; since foraging societies are relatively unstructured and egalitarian, there are no material or political rewards to strive for, no markedly high statuses to achieve.

Horticultural and pastoral societies, in particular, often do reward com-

**Table 5.4** Adolescent Peer Groups and Subsistence Economy

| | Peer groups conduct religious activities | | | | | |
| | Boys | | | Girls | | |
| | present | absent | % absent | present | absent | % absent |
|---|---|---|---|---|---|---|
| Foraging | 5 | 20 | 80 | 4 | 17 | 81 |
| [Pastoralism][a] | 6 | 2 | 25 | 4 | 1 | 20 |
| Horticulture | 18 | 25 | 58 | 11 | 25 | 69 |
| Agriculture | 23 | 18 | 44 | 17 | 12 | 41 |
| | $\chi^2 = 8.30$ | df = 2 | p = .016 | $\chi^2 = 9.34$ | df = 2 | p = .009 |

| | Competition among peers (boys) | | |
| | below median | above median | % above median |
|---|---|---|---|
| Foraging | 10 | 16 | 62 |
| [Pastoralism][a] | 2 | 7 | 78 |
| Horticulture | 10 | 27 | 73 |
| Agriculture | 17 | 11 | 34 |
| | $\chi^2 = 7.57$ | df = 2 | p = .023 |

[a]Figures on pastoral systems are omitted from the tests of statistical significance, as in table 4.4.

petition. These tend to be relatively egalitarian, but there are differences in personal wealth (animals belonging to pastoralists and some horticulturalists usually are owned individually) and social rank (political and ceremonial positions in some of these give prestige and often power to their incumbents). As this finding demonstrates, the character of the adolescent peer group is shaped not only by the circumstances surrounding the group itself but also by the adult life that adolescents anticipate in the future.

The effects of the subsistence economy are mediated through social and political structures. The effects of some structural features upon adolescent groups and activities were assessed, and the results are reported in the Tables 5.5, 5.6, and 5.7. (Measures of social and political structures were coded by Murdock and Provost 1980 and Murdock and Wilson 1980.)

Boys' peer groups are likely to be more important than other social groups when community settlement is permanent, and they are less than or equal to other groups in the less sedentary communities. This finding suggests that the importance of peer groups is promoted in societies that are structured in other ways. Permanent settlements are more likely to be organized into social groups functioning for specific purposes—political, military, religious—than are less permanent ones (Table 5.5).

The size of the boys' peer group increases as community size increases up to a population of 1,000, a result of a larger population of adolescents to draw from (Table 5.6). In communities of 1,000 and over, there is a slight likelihood for smaller peer groups to be present. It is probably at this point that many communities divide into two or more neighborhoods, each with its own adolescent peer group.

Larger peer groups are also likely to be present in societies at higher levels of political integration (Table 5.6). The same mechanisms that allow for the absorption of large numbers of people into the polity seem to work toward an increase in peer group size. There is also, of course, the consideration that more complex societies tend to have larger communities. However, the size of peer group is not a simple artifact of community size, as

*Table 5.5* Importance of Boys' Peer Group Related to Settlement Pattern

| | *Importance* | | |
|---|---|---|---|
| | *less* | *same* | *more* |
| *Fixity of settlement* | | | |
| nomadic to semipermanent | 15 | 14 | 6 |
| permanent | 15 | 22 | 19 |
| Mantel-Haenszel $\chi^2 = 3.82$ | | | $p = .051$ |

*Table 5.6* Community, Society, and the Structure of Boys' Peer Groups

| | Size of peer group | | | |
|---|---|---|---|---|
| | small | medium | large | % large |
| *Community size* | | | | |
| fewer than 99 | 7 | 6 | 5 | 28 |
| 100–399 | 8 | 10 | 23 | 56 |
| 400–999 | 2 | 3 | 11 | 69 |
| 1,000 or more | 1 | 5 | 7 | 54 |
| Mantel-Haenszel $\chi^2 = 4.69$ | | | $p = .030$ | |
| *Level of political integration* | | | | |
| not above community | 14 | 6 | 18 | 47 |
| above community | 4 | 18 | 28 | 56 |
| Mantel-Haenszel $\chi^2 = 4.79$ | | | $p = .029$ | |
| Girls: Mantel-Haenszel $\chi^2 = 5.22$ | | | $p = .023$ | |

| | Age range | | |
|---|---|---|---|
| | small | medium or large | % medium or large |
| *Social stratification* | | | |
| absent | 5 | 26 | 84 |
| present but minimal | 4 | 27 | 87 |
| high | 11 | 19 | 63 |
| $\chi^2 = 3.68$ | | $p = .055$ | |

| | Social recognition | | |
|---|---|---|---|
| | absent | present | % present |
| *Fixity of settlement* | | | |
| nomadic to semipermanent | 15 | 8 | 35 |
| permanent | 15 | 26 | 63 |
| $\chi^2 = 3.77$ | | $p = .052$ | |
| *Level of political integration* | | | |
| not above community | 20 | 11 | 35 |
| above community | 10 | 23 | 70 |
| $\chi^2 = 6.20$ | | $p = .013$ | |

indicated by the fact that the size of girls' peer groups shows a significant relation with political integration but not with community size (Table 5.6).

We find a trend for the age range of members of the peer group to be related to social stratification, the smaller range being found in the stratified societies (Table 5.6). Age divisions among adolescents thus often replicate status divisions within the larger population.

Authority relationships can occur among age peers when the group has a recognized leader or a leadership hierarchy, although the presence or absence of hierarchy is not associated with any of the social measures used in this study. Speaking of the Xesibe, a cattle-keeping people of eastern Transkei, Republic of South Africa, O'Connell (1982:25) stated:

> The boys in each neighborhood organize themselves into groups based on age. These groups are internally stratified on the basis of age, fighting skill, intelligence, and personality. Good fighters and intelligent leaders are usually older in age, although a younger boy with exceptional strength and a forceful, domineering nature may become a group leader earlier than expected. Older groups of boys and youths develop more elaborate hierarchies with titles such as captain, vice-captain, treasurer, and so on. Each group collects money and sponsors periodic gatherings at which they slaughter an animal and drink beer, together with their female counterparts who are less formally organized.

Somewhat less organized, but still with a recognized leader, is the boys' peer group on Moala, Fiji. As Sahlins (1962:300) described it:

> The village gang of adolescent boys has an informal leader. Often this is the village paramount's son, or at least a boy of high rank, but he will also have to be skilled in singing, guitar-playing, and in sports. The gang leader rules by example and influence rather than by direction. The whole organization is loosely structured: there are no initiations, no offices, no titles, or the like.

There is recognized leadership of this informal sort for girls' peer groups, too, although those groups are smaller. Both boys' and girls' groups in Fiji perform communal economic tasks, the boys' groups doing more than the girls'.

Social recognition of the peer group by the community is found in the more tightly structured communities. When settlements are permanent, and at higher levels of political integration, the peer group is likely to be given a generally recognized name or to constitute an age-set or to receive other public recognition as a group (Table 5.6).

In sum, a peer group is likely to be larger, contain members with a smaller range of ages, and be recognized as a legitimate group by the community in the more complex societies. However, the internal structure of the peer group, as measured by presence or absence of leadership or by leadership hierarchy, does not correlate with the community or society variables used in this study. There are cases of egalitarian societies with hierarchical leadership of adolescent peer groups, such as the Comanche of the North American Plains, and hierarchical societies with peer groups in which leadership is fluid, such as the Lamet of Laos or the New Zealand Maori. The peer group is not the only socializing institution; as we saw in the previous chapter, the family is generally more important.

Types of peer group activities are widely dispersed over types of peer groups. In those societies with data adequate for testing, there is little association between predominant or prominent kinds of activities and the importance or structure of the peer group.

Several features of the society and community show an association with peer group activities. Boys' involvement in military maneuvers is somewhat less likely to be present in complex societies and significantly less where communities are permanent (Table 5.7). Warfare is better organized in complex and sedentary communities and requires a fair degree of skill, whereas small communities of fluid composition may need to enlist all able-bodied males in attack and defense.

Peer groups are more likely to perform collective religious acts in larger and more permanent settlements (Table 5.7). This is concordant with the test result shown in Table 5.4: in the more complex societies, rituals tend to include participation by recognized social groups as groups.

The relation of an additional variable, antisocial behavior, to peer group activities (analyzed more fully in a subsequent chapter) was assessed to determine whether types of activity might promote or suppress delinquency among boys. (There are few data on delinquency among girls.) The hypothesis was that when adolescents unite in achieving some common end, be it religious, military, or community service, there is a lesser tendency to misbehave. Conversely, leisure might promote such behavior, the assumption being that "idle hands do devil's work." That is not the case. There is no association between leisure as a major purpose of peer group socializing and antisocial behavior, but such behavior is significantly present when peer groups engage in religious or military activities (Table 5.7). This finding implies that organizing adolescent groups to perform worthy acts is not a way to prevent undesirable behavior.

We examined the nature of peer group relations by looking at cooperativeness and competitiveness within the group. Each of these variables was coded along an 11-point scale. Societies were divided into those below the median and those above (none was at the median). Competitiveness showed some relation to peer group activities: it is more likely to be above the median when peer groups engage in military training or fighting (Table 5.7). Although the inculcation of aggression is not significantly related to military activities, 67 percent of societies with such activities were rated above the median for aggressiveness. These results imply that military training, which

*Table 5.7* Peer Group Activities: Boys

| | Military activities | | |
| --- | --- | --- | --- |
| | *present* | *absent* | *% absent* |
| *Social stratification* | | | |
| present | 14 | 65 | 82 |
| absent | 12 | 26 | 68 |
| | $\chi^2 = 2.11$ | $p = .147$ (weak trend) | |
| *Fixity of settlement* | | | |
| nomadic to | | | |
|   semipermanent | 16 | 32 | 67 |
| permanent | 10 | 59 | 86 |
| Mantel-Haenszel $\chi^2 = 4.77$ | | $p = .029$ | |
| *Antisocial behavior* | | | |
| present | 9 | 14 | 63 |
| absent | 2 | 19 | 90 |
| | Fisher's Exact Test $p = .036$ | | |
| *Competitiveness* | | | |
| below median | 4 | 25 | 86 |
| above median | 17 | 27 | 61 |
| | Fisher's Exact Test $p = .033$ | | |

| | Religious activities | | |
| --- | --- | --- | --- |
| | *present* | *absent* | *% absent* |
| *Fixity of settlement* | | | |
| nomadic to | | | |
|   semipermanent | 15 | 33 | 69 |
| permanent | 37 | 32 | 46 |
| Mantel-Haenszel $\chi^2 = 4.87$ | | $p = .027$ | |
| *Community size* | | | |
| fewer than 400 | 29 | 50 | 63 |
| 400 or more | 23 | 15 | 39 |
| | $\chi^2 = 4.97$ | $p = .026$ | |
| *Antisocial behavior* | | | |
| present | 18 | 5 | 17 |
| absent | 6 | 15 | 76 |
| | $\chi^2 = 9.02$ | $p = .003$ | |

fosters individual achievement if the warrior is to succeed, stimulates competitiveness, while the competitiveness or aggressiveness of such training can stimulate or reinforce antisocial behavior. It is easy for the contained violence of mock battles to get out of hand and for boys encouraged to hone their combativeness to use these skills in achieving private ends.

Cooperativeness is likely to be above the median when peer groups are more important (both sexes), groups are large (boys), and the age range is medium or large (girls) (Table 5.8). Larger groups that are more important in the lives of their participants are more cohesive and oriented toward group tasks and goals. Cooperativeness is likely to be below the median when peer groups are less important than other social groups (Table 5.8). Competitiveness for boys is also most likely to be low when peer groups are less important (Table 5.8). This finding indicates that competitiveness and cooperation in boys' peer groups coexist and are likely to rise and fall together. This association is not seen in girls' peer groups, implying that girls are not socialized as well as boys to tolerate both competitiveness and cooperativeness within the same setting.

Whatever competitive feelings may be engendered by household interactions do not appear to carry over into the peer group. It is arguable that competition among siblings is highest in the nuclear family, in which children compete with each other for the attention of the mother and the father more than in other forms, or in extended families, in which sibling sets often compete against one another for family resources. Yet, tests showed no association with the form of the family. Presence and degree of polygyny has also been tested with competitiveness, on the assumption that polygyny, which promotes competitiveness among co-wives, may be carried over into competitiveness among their children. Even if that assumption is correct, there is no discernible carryover into the peer group. Competitiveness seems to be engendered more by the immediate situation than by feelings that arise in other settings or earlier in life.

## Peer Groups and the Community

When the peer group takes an active part in community affairs by assuming responsibility for certain rituals, community festivals, or community projects, it is at its most effective as a structure of anticipatory socialization. Adolescents may contribute their time and energy toward community service projects. It is not uncommon for adolescents to entertain their elders. In their attempts to display themselves to their best advantage in dancing or sports, adolescent girls and boys not only attract one another but also put on a show for the adults and children. Throughout small-town America, high school sports teams and cheerleading squads serve this purpose. Adolescents can also be used as agents of social control, keeping themselves and even adults

*Table 5.8* Competition and Cooperation Within Peer Groups

| | Boys | | | | | |
| | Competition[a] | | | Cooperation[b] | | |
| | below median | above median | % above median | below median | above median | % above median |
|---|---|---|---|---|---|---|
| **Importance of Peer Group** | | | | | | |
| less | 11 | 3 | 21 | 12 | 5 | 29 |
| equal | 7 | 20 | 74 | 12 | 12 | 50 |
| more | 10 | 11 | 52 | 6 | 16 | 73 |
| | $\chi^2 = 10.40$  df $= 2$  $p = .006$ | | | Mantel-Haenszel $\chi^2 = 7.18$ | | |
| | | | | | | $p = .007$ |
| **Size of Peer Group** | | | | | | |
| small | | | | 8 | 3 | 27 |
| medium | | | | 10 | 6 | 38 |
| large | | | | 13 | 21 | 62 |
| | | | | Mantel-Haenszel $\chi^2 = 4.85$ | | |
| | | | | | | $p = .028$ |
| | Girls | | | | | |
| **Importance of Peer Group** | | | | | | |
| less | | | | 18 | 6 | 25 |
| equal | | | | 5 | 6 | 55 |
| more | | | | 1 | 4 | 80 |
| | | | | Mantel-Haenszel $\chi^2 = 6.38$ | | |
| | | | | | | $p = .012$ |
| **Age range** | | | | | | |
| small | | | | 17 | 8 | 32 |
| medium or large | | | | 7 | 11 | 61 |
| | | | | | | $\chi^2 = 2.51$ |
| | | | | | | $p = .113$ (trend) |

[a]Competition: Girls' mean = 3.6, Boys' mean = 4.7

[b]Cooperation: Girls' mean = 6.2, Boys' mean = 6.2

in line through peer pressure, mockery, or punishment. Some examples of various community services will be described in the pages that follow.

One way that peer groups can take part in community life is through participation as groups in rituals. It is not unusual for adolescents to take responsibility for some portion of the community ritual cycle or certain events within it. In one Mexican village, according to Arnold (1978), adolescent girls sweep the church, assist the nuns in the catechism classes, sponsor masses for St. Theresa, and assume responsibility for singing, hiring musicians, buying fireworks, and organizing the procession in her honor. This sort of ritual involvement is widespread throughout Latin America: Chatino Indian boys of Oaxaca, Mexico, enter the village ritual system upon adolescence by acting as pages to adult men of the community.

Another way in which adolescents become active in community affairs is through the organization of festivities. This often overlaps with religious responsibility, for festivals are frequently plotted along the ritual calendar. The account that follows, for southern France, draws on Roubin (1977).

> Adolescent and youth organizations played an active role in preindustrial Provençal villages and towns. In 17th century Draguignan, there were four distinct youth groups: the *Grand Jouvent* for noble boys; the *Basoche* for the young clerks of the law courts; the *Groupe des Artisans,* a very large group subdivided according to neighborhoods; and the *Bassaquets,* or day laborers, who were similarly subdivided. An important task of these Provençal youth associations was to organize the Ball at Mardi Gras. Records from 16th century Nice, 17th century Draguignan, and 18th century Mons-du-Var all speak of these associations organizing balls according to social status. Thus, in Nice, the nobles danced at the Loggia, the merchants in front of the bishop's palace, the artisans at one town square, and the fishermen and agricultural workers at another. The leaders of these groups, the "abbots," were charged with seeing that only persons of the appropriate social station attended the respective balls. The abbots were responsible for arranging festivities on the community's patron saint's day as well. Support came from the community, in the form of a gift by the town council and also through contributions collected from house to house. This responsibility continued in Provence into at least the 1960s, under the direction of the Feast Committees elected by all young unmarried people of the community.

Adolescents in Transylvanian villages in Hungary similarly took responsibility for Christmas festivities as recently as the 1960s (Kresz 1976).

Adolescent energies in some societies are tapped for community service projects. One such case was aboriginal Palau, a Micronesian society whose description by Barnett (1949) is summarized here.

> At about age 15 or 16, boys and girls formed clubs, named age-sets separated by sex. Leaders came from among the ten most prominent fami-

lies. Young people continued to work for their families, but in addition they began to assume community service, doing assigned tasks for their village or district. They worked as clubs under the direction of village and district chiefs. The nature of these tasks is not given by Barnett, but it is likely that they had to provide labor for the construction of community buildings or for community maintenance.

In central India, specific tasks were turned over to Muria adolescents, who organized their labor through the *ghotul* described earlier. Elwin (1968:167) stated:

These boys and girls worked very hard indeed for the public good. They were immediately available for the service of State officials or for labour on the roads. They had to be ready to work at a wedding or a funeral. They had to attend to the drudgery of festivals. In most tribal villages of the Central Provinces the children were slack, dirty, undisciplined, and with no sense of public spirit. The Murias were very different.

## Peer Groups and Social Control

One of the beneficial community functions of organized peer groups can be to socialize their members by exerting pressure to behave well. Peer pressure is well understood by researchers, parents of adolescents, and adolescents themselves. While peer pressure can work at cross-purposes to the wishes of the family or the community, it can also aid in conformity to community norms and standards. Bronfenbrenner (1970) contrasted the behavior and values of Soviet and American peer groups in the 1960s along this line, finding the former to be concordant with the values of the larger society and the latter discordant. When the peer group enforces community-held norms and goals, parents can turn over some disciplining to the peer group. In this way, their burden is relieved and intergenerational conflict may be reduced.

While the concept of peer pressure is of very practical concern to the families of adolescents, it is not an especially interesting theoretical construct. One takes it for granted that any social group exerts pressures on its members to conform to the norms of the group. What is less expected is the use to which adolescent peer groups may be put to enforce the conformity of adults to accepted standards of behavior or to punish persons who are a threat to the community in some way. By giving adolescents authority to control minor infractions, adults use them for some of the social "dirty work" of the community. The examples below are of four such cases: the Mbuti Pygmies of Africa, early modern Europe, the Hopi, and contemporary Chinatown. These and comparable cases are not instances of antisocial behavior, even though certain people are discomfited or even injured or some property is destroyed by the actions of adolescents as enforcers of the norms.

Mbuti adolescent boys and youths are actors in the *molimo* ceremony, the great celebration of the spirit of the forest for the entire band. While much of the ritual occurs at night and involves singing led by older men, boys contribute their share. As Turnbull (1962:82–84) described it:

> But in the mornings the youths came into their own completely. Before the first glimmer of light filtered through into the camp, those of us who had managed to get to sleep were waked by a violent and raucous trumpeting from just outside the camp. . . . From the far end of the camp, near the path leading to Cephu's clearing, a wild cavalcade of youths swept into view, shouting and yelling, clustered so thickly that it was impossible to see the trumpet they were carrying. . . . [The procession] blasted and shrilled and growled and bellowed, and it rampaged around the camp, overturning any of the crude chairs that had been left outside, scattering the remains of fires in all directions, and beating on the roofs of huts to wake everyone up. . . . If anyone had given offense the previous day, usually by being too argumentative, the youths in the morning rampage paid particular attention to the offender's hut. Cephu's camp of course came in for the most attention, and although Cephu complained loudly each time, at the time, he never brought it up later as an issue for discussion or dispute. One morning, after two brothers, Masalito and Aberi, had been fighting, the "animal of the forest" [the trumpet-playing group], making more noise than ever, circled all around Masalito's hut and finally pounced on it, beating on the roof and tearing off leaves and sticks. Some of the youths climbed up a tree that overhung the hut and broke off a heavy branch, which fell on the hut, blocking the entrance, but doing no real damage. The couple inside screamed their protests; then there was a sudden silence. Masalito had done the most dreadful thing of all. He had told the youths to take "that animal" away and throw it back in the water and stop all the noise. This spoiled the whole illusion, which is only a pretence in itself, that the women think that *molimo* is an animal and do not know that it is a trumpet surrounded by a lot of noisy youths. The silence was followed by cries from all over the camp—cries of shame shouted by both men and women. The "animal" was galvanized into even greater action, and Masalito's hut was in danger of being completely destroyed. Then Njobo came sleepily out into the clearing and told the youths to go away. They had probably had their fill by then anyway, and they left, making a few last defiant noises, some in the direction of Njobo. As soon as they were gone the women came out of their huts, looked around to see how much damage had been done, then went to wash themselves and get breakfast. Children scampered around the irate Masalito as he cleared up the wreckage

outside his hut, and as they danced up and down I heard one of them, bolder than the others, give a tiny hoot in imitation of the trumpet. Masalito tried to grab the child but they all ran away, laughing, to torment someone else.

For the peaceable Mbuti, arguing and fighting are violations of socially acceptable behavior. It is these violators who become the victims of the adolescent enforcers.

A different sort of infraction was the concern of adolescent boys and youths in country villages throughout much of preindustrial Europe. Marriage was necessary for a youth to move into adult status, and a village youth had to have the wherewithal, a farm or a small business, to support a wife if he were to marry; thus, marriage and property were interlocked. Other things being equal, the most desirable brides, usually the ones with the largest dowries, went to the most prosperous grooms. Yet, unlike the practice in many societies, marriages were not formally arranged by adults, and young people had veto power over any manipulations their elders might attempt. Furthermore, not all young men were likely to assemble the necessary property. If they were second sons of poor families, they neither were heirs to what little the family estate contained nor had access to other resources. In such cases, marriage was problematic. This may account for the popularity of European fairy tales in which some poor but brave lad wins the hand of the princess, often with magical help. For many boys, magic offered the best hope.

Marriage and sexuality, therefore, became the focus of young people's enforcement of the norms. Not only did the communities consider it unseemly for older people (usually men) to marry the young (usually girls); such an event also threatened the young by reducing their pool of potential brides (and grooms) and by giving older and wealthier men (and women) an unfair advantage. Groups of adolescent boys and youths responded to such infractions, and also to the adulteries and sexual misdemeanors of their elders, by the *charivari,* as it was called in France, or *rough music,* as it was known in England. (This ritual was given other names in other lands.)

Village youth groups in early modern Europe consisted of all village adolescent boys and youths from about age 14 until marriage, or until about age 30 if still unmarried. Leaders were the bachelors in their mid-twenties. Girls sometimes formed auxiliary groups, but the boys' groups were the most active. Numerous accounts exist of these groups in the English-, French-, and German-speaking areas. In some parts they served as a local militia, in others they were mobilized for church or civic festivities; but everywhere, a primary function was control over marriage and sexuality through shaming of offenders. As Gillis (1974:30) stated:

Youth has at its disposal an ancient stock of frightening effigies, rough music (profane songs), and mocking pantomime with which to deal with its enemies. Ready with tin pans and horns under the lecher's window, and quick to join the charivari of the second wedding of an old man and a young bride, the *Bruderschaften* [Germany] and the Abbeys of Misrule [France] were self-interested enforcers of the moral and social equilibrium of village life.

In a typical rural charivari, a recently remarried widower might find himself awakened by the clamor of the crowd, an effigy of his dead wife thrust up to his window and a likeness of himself, placed backward on an ass, drawn through the streets for his neighbors to see. Paying of a "contribution" to the Lord of Misrule might quiet his youthful tormentors, but by that time the voice of village conscience had made their point.

While the Hopi had no such institution as the charivari, they quite enjoyed adolescent boys' shaming of villagers who were committing adultery. If a man were discovered by the roaming boys to be visiting a woman at night when her husband was away, the village might wake up the next morning to find a trail of ashes between his house and hers. The message was plain, and the victims were helpless to protest or to avenge themselves.

The final example comes from contemporary Boston rather than a preindustrial society. Kendis and Kendis (1976:14 and 16) described the community service of Chinatown's street boy gangs:

> The street boy group performs a function for the larger Chinese society as well as for the boys; it serves as an interface between the American and Chinese societies in situations of confrontation. When confronted by whites the boys identify themselves as Chinese. Chinatown becomes their community, and it is their job to protect it and its members from attacks by anyone from the outside. The boys see threat and encroachment in a number of situations. If they feel the prostitutes and pimps are beginning to cause problems in the community or are in any way acting as though they "owned" Chinatown, the boys run them out of town. If someone *dao* [fails to pay] checks from one of the Chinese restaurants, it is their job to catch him and beat him into submission, thereby getting him to pay his bill and discouraging him from a repeat offense. If members of non-Chinese communities come into Chinatown in order to ridicule the Chinese, the boys make it their duty (as well as their pleasure) to intercept them and beat them as a warning that neither they nor their territory are to be violated. Finally, if one of the street boys should be beaten up by outsiders, the boys bring out their knives, chains, and lead pipes and prepare for a "jam." . . .
>
> The activities of the boys directed against the members of the outside community visiting Chinatown serve as a form of community expres-

sion—an expression of hostility. This can be clearly seen in the reactions of community members to the boys' activities. When the boys are policing Chinatown and beating *dao* checks, the old men join in, kicking the offender once he is down and defenseless. Others express their approval to the boys, and the restaurant owners may treat them to dinner. In addition, the activities of the boys are public and the community is aware of them. As long as they remain functional and not counterproductive the community permits the continuation of these activities. To the extent that their activities represent the community's sentiments regarding American society, the boys are tolerated.

Adolescent boys are used by this community as the first line of attack against threatening outsiders. Their policing activities are rewarded by the approbation of their elders and, in a more direct way, with treats.

In these cases adolescents are given license to do what under other circumstances would be intolerable as rebellious or even criminal behavior. As policing, however, it is approved by the community and even rewarded. It is clear that final control rests with adults, that adolescents do not simply rampage away at will. It is unlikely that Mbuti village men would permit the destruction of innocent people's huts, that European peasant boys would be allowed to carry on their rowdy displays before the houses of village notables, or that Chinatown elders would tolerate a fatal beating, which would bring in the police. Adolescents must know and keep their place. In these closed communities, power is given to them by adults, and it can be taken from them if they misuse it through excesses or by directly attacking the most powerful. Like our own Halloween tricks, adolescent pranks can go too far. As early as the 16th century in some parts of France, youth clubs of the village became, in the larger towns, class-based associations of all ages, and their attendant rambunctiousness was turned against the authorities in expressions of class conflict. Increasingly, they were banned from the towns, although they continued to flourish in their original form in the villages well into the 19th century (Gillis 1974:32–35).

Whether as enforcers of norms and morals, as organizers of local events, as workers for public welfare, or as entertainers, adolescents can provide valued community services. They generally do so in groups of same-sex peers, under the auspices of adults in the community who make available the resources and provide tangible or intangible rewards. However, as much as community service may be appreciated or even needed, it is no prophylactic against delinquency. We will discuss this further in Chapter 8.

It is striking that so much of the data in this chapter come from boys' peer groups rather than girls'. That in part results from reporting bias, as boys' activities are discussed more frequently than are girls' in ethnographic accounts. Possibly this bias is due to the fact that the majority of ethnographers in times past have been men, who would either be more interested in boys' activities or have more access to them.

The cause does not lie entirely in reporting bias, however; for even when there is ample information on girls, there is generally less variation across cultures than there is for boys. There are not enough cases of separation from the family for girls to permit testing; and in the large majority of societies, the girls' peer group is less important than other social groups, such as the family. Girls' peer groups in general are smaller and play a lesser role in their lives than do boys', whereas, as we have seen in the preceding chapter, contact of girls with their mothers is greater than contact of boys with either their mothers or their fathers. Taking the test results of this and the preceding chapter, we see a difference in the adolescent experience of girls and boys. Girls spend more time with same-sex adults than do boys, and in particular, they have greater contact and intimacy with their mothers than boys do with either parent. On the other hand, girls tend to have smaller peer groups that are of less importance to them than peer groups are to boys. Our major finding regarding the parent-peer question, then, does not bear on whether parents and peers are opposed to one another, for we have seen that in general they are not. Rather, there is a difference in emphasis between attachment to one or the other depending upon gender, which has nothing to do with the general quality of relationship between adolescents and their parents, as far as can be judged by cultural norms and widely observed behaviors. For both sexes, the strongest attachment is likely to be to the family, which is to be expected in human society in which people cluster in small mixed-sex groupings related through kinship or co-residence.

This gender difference has several implications. One is that the passage into adolescence is easier for girls, because there is not so much of a break from childhood. The transition is less smooth for boys, who experience more of a decoupling from the family. Girls grow into adult status within the community of females of all ages, their socialization for adulthood being gradual. Boys spend more time with age-mates, with whom they form horizontal rather than vertical age-related bonds.

The difference in social setting has its consequences for the nature of group relationships. As we have seen, for girls, cooperation and competition are not associated, whereas for boys, competition and cooperation occur within the same setting. In the roughly egalitarian peer group, one competes with the same people with whom one cooperates in meeting the goals of the group. Not only are boys' peer groups more likely than girls' to be of primary or secondary importance in their lives, but they are also more likely to be activity-oriented rather than merely a setting for leisure time. Thus the social setting for boys differs in several ways from the social setting for girls, which often includes girls and women of differing ages. Girls are frequently directed in their activities by adult women rather than directing them themselves. By structuring the setting of socialization in this way, competitiveness is reduced. We have found no evidence that girls are innately less competitive than boys: on an 11-point scale for competitiveness, the highest rating that any society received was nine, and girls were rated at this level for two societies (with 20 cases of this rating for boys.)[1] As girls are certainly capable of behaving just as competitively as boys, we must look to the social settings that promote or inhibit competition to explain differences in behavior.

# 6

# Mating, Marriage, and the Duration of Adolescence

SOME of the character of adolescent life, including the length of adolescence itself, is determined by marriage considerations. While adolescence predates marriage chronologically, the anticipation of marriage is in the minds of adolescents and those responsible for them. In this chapter we look at reproductive concerns of the society as a major factor in the kinds of lives adolescents lead.

Unlike other species, in which individuals select their mates, humans reproduce in a social setting that limits and often determines their reproductive fates. Human reproduction, played out in terms of kinship and household arrangements, is social as much as biological, since reproductive relations are embedded in long-term social attachments between the mated pair and among their kin.

The view of kinship as biologically based has fallen out of favor in some circles. Schneider (1984), probably the most explicit opponent of this view, even denied the universality of a common definition of *kinship*. Whatever the arguments about definition of kinship and the principles of recruitment to the kindred and the descent group, there is no society known to us in which biological parent-child and sibling ties and extensions thereof are not recognized and are not accompanied by prescriptions for appropriate behaviors toward these categories of persons.

There is a direct association between mating and selective advantage for the individual in species in which individuals control their own mating strategies. Among humans, however, individuals less commonly control their own mate selection. Modern societies are somewhat aberrant in this respect; among preindustrial peoples, marriage is often under the control of kin, particularly the parents of one or both partners, and then the criteria for mate selection are as much to further their own interests as to benefit the young people getting married.

In societies without private property, "economic capital" is nonexistent or very limited and "social capital," the alliances forged through kinship and social linkages such as marriage, is the means to enhance one's position and enlarge one's support base. Even in complex traditional societies with private property, marriage seals other kinds of alliances between families. Dynastic marriages are not just found among the aristocrats of traditional states, but are commonplace where ties of a political or economic nature are created or cemented through the marriages of children. Marriage is too critical a social and political issue to be left to the fancies of the young themselves. In only 18 percent of 141 societies do boys make their own selection; girls select their mates in 13 percent of 131 societies. In the remaining societies, kin, primarily parents, are involved in the choice. It is therefore the social arrangements of parents that most frequently determine the reproductive relations of young people.

The assumption underlying this link between marriage and mating is that most biological reproduction occurs within marriage. There are two possible counter-arguments to this: first, the fact that many societies permit premarital sexual relations for girls and, second, that in a fairly large number of societies, widespread adultery and such customs as wife sharing or privileged sexual unions with certain permitted relatives of the spouse can lead to pregnancies that are socially but not biologically contained within the marriage.

We will return to the question of sexual permissiveness for adolescent girls in the following chapter. To anticipate, it is rather uncommon for unmarried girls in preindustrial societies to produce children. Either sexual intercourse is prohibited, or, where it is not, infertility in young adolescent girls reduces the likelihood of conception. When adolescents in permissive societies do get pregnant, in most cases either marriage legitimizes the child or the fetus is aborted.

There is considerable variability in the tolerance of sexual partners other than the spouse. Gaulin and Schlegel (1980), using the same sample that we did, found that about half of the societies for which there is information are rated as having high paternal confidence, meaning that the woman's husband can be confident that any given child is his own. In the remainder of cases, in which there is wife sharing or a moderate to high degree of extramarital sexual activity, paternal confidence is lower. However, the authors point out that even in societies with low paternal confidence, most births are likely to be the result of marital intercourse, simply because it is the husband who, over time, has greatest access to the wife. There are the rare exceptions: the Nayar of southern India (Gough 1961), for example, where the recognized father of a woman's child is her current lover and not her official husband; or the Australian Tiwi (Hart and Pilling 1960), where extreme age difference between spouses and the frequent albeit illicit access to young wives by the young bachelors increases the likelihood of adulterous pregnancy. These cases are noteworthy because they are so atypical.

Thus, we assert that marriage is the principal way in which biologically reproductive partners are allocated. In the majority of societies in this sample, adults control this allocation, at least when the persons to be married are young. (It is not uncommon for subsequent marriages of older people to be decided by the prospective spouses themselves.) To be an actor in reproductive strategies in many societies, one may have to wait until one is a parent and gains control over the reproduction of one's children, as one's own reproductive career was designed by others.

## The Importance of Marriage in Preindustrial Societies

Peoples of contemporary Western nations put little emphasis on marriage compared to those of most known societies, where few remain single or childless by choice. Why is marriage such a central issue in preindustrial societies, and how does this affect adolescents?

Marriage means different things in different places. The romantic love and sexual exclusiveness of the European and American marriage pattern would be difficult for the Hima, an African pastoral society, to understand (Elam 1973). There, the wife who does not give her sexual favors to her husband's friends is considered churlish and unneighborly, and her husband upbraids her for her lack of hospitality. The ideal of partnership between spouses that we carry into marriage is foreign to peoples who live in large, extended-family households, in which the household members one works and relaxes with are primarily of one's own sex, and marital privacy and attachment are limited.

Despite the diversity of marital arrangements, however, almost everywhere marriage entails a relation between spouses that includes living together and cooperating in reproduction in the broad sense, from the child's conception to its adulthood. Exceptions, such as the Nayar noted above, among whom adult sisters and brothers live together and women are visited by their consorts at night, are rare; the overwhelming evidence is toward the formation of a mated pair, whatever the kinship or residence patterns may be, who take primary responsibility for feeding and socializing their offspring. The pair may be part of an extended-family household, in which case productive tasks are allocated among household members and many goods are pooled, and child care tasks are to some degree shared. Nevertheless, alongside the unity of the group is a sense of unity of the conjugal family, comprising spouses and their children, which competes with and can override attachment to a larger group.

Examples of the unity of the conjugal family can be taken from many kinds of societies with a variety of household arrangements. In the polyandrous households of Tibet (Peter 1963), where several brothers share a common wife, the wife and her children (by whichever brother) accompany the oldest brother if the fraternal group separates. Among the Hopi, when the size of the matrilocal extended family outgrows its space, older daughters split off with their husbands and children into new households. A striking example of conjugal unity overriding clan affiliation among these very matrilineal Hopi is given by Titiev (1944:92–93) in his discussion of the factional split of the village of Oraibi in 1906. While various factors entered into factional alignment for men, in several cases men joined with their wives and in general women joined with their husbands instead of their brothers as lineage politics would dictate.

Why should the mated-pair bond and the bond between parents and children be so widespread in spite of the great variability in the meaning of marriage and in household structure? The duolocal pattern of the Nayar is enough to show that other kinds of arrangements could be made, that is, with siblings forming the cooperative pair. In fact, there would be some advantages to the primary (but nonsexual) bond being between sisters and brothers, for that would perpetuate into adulthood the close ties of childhood and eliminate such difficulties as sexual jealousy between the cooperating pair and abrasive relations with in-laws. There must have been strong selective pressures toward the mated-pair bond for it to have arisen, and strong pressures of a similar or different kind for it to persist in spite of the broad diversity in family settings.

A problem with universals or near universals is that they cannot be tested comparatively but only addressed logically. Fortunately, it is possible to test pair bonding across species, as Ember and Ember (1979) did. Basing their finding on a sample of 40 species, they rejected explanations of pair bonding that rely on division of labor by sex, male sexual competition, and duration of infant dependency, finding that pair bonding occurs in species in which the female's feeding requirements would interfere with her care of the young. Cooperation of two individuals ensures better survival for the offspring, whether in birds, some other mammals, or ourselves.

While Ember and Ember disposed of several kinds of cooperative arrangements such as that between two females, two males, or among a group of promiscuously mated individuals, they did not address the male-female sibling pair. In spite of the advantages noted above, sister-brother pair bonding would be likely to occur only when large extended-family households with a stable resource base ensure that enough male kin are contributing at any one time to the care of sisters' children, and no children are without maternal uncles in the home. When families are smaller and more mobile, there is no guarantee that there would be a brother available at all times for a reproductive sister to rely on, even when the definition of sibling is broader than it is in the European kinship system and includes many persons whom we would consider to be cousins. Marriage circulates men among fertile women, distributing them more effectively than would brother-sister pair bonding. The privilege for men of producing children is accompanied by the duty to cooperate in their care. Marriage ensures that all children have a socially acknowledged male who is responsible for them.

Is marriage just for the benefit of children, or do marriage and parenthood serve the interests of adults as well? As Ware (1978:2) baldly stated: "Parents have children because they benefit thereby." Since techniques of contraception and abortion are widely known, and infanticide may be practiced as a last resort, we have to assume that the number of children typically found in families is a consequence of choice. The psychic benefits of parenthood are gained with one or two children, who could be born at any time during the woman's reproductive lifespan of 20 years or more. Additional children can place a severe economic burden on families in industrialized societies, which reduce their family size accordingly. Optimal family size may be very different in other circumstances.

Children can be an economic asset as soon as they are able to relieve adults of light but time-consuming tasks such as hauling water, caring for infants, washing laundry and dishes, feeding chickens, collecting sticks or dried dung for firewood, or scaring birds away from ripening grain. They can begin these tasks as young as four or five. While they are not very productive in their early years, their productivity increases with their increasing skills and strength, and they may be net contributors rather than consumers by the time they reach adolescence. In her study of economic activities of children among the Nigerian Hausa, Schildkrout (1978) listed some of the ways in which children earn money, including the selling of cooked foods their mothers prepare. Both boys and girls might be market sellers as early as seven or eight.

It is not only the anticipated labor of young children that makes them welcome as contributors to the family economy. Even more is the anticipated labor of adolescents and young adults, as long as there are labor opportunities for them and the fruits of their labor, cash or produce, are controlled by adults. Thus, in horticultural, pastoral, or agrarian economies in which there is room for territorial expansion, as in much of Africa, the limiting factor in wealth is scarcity of labor rather than scarcity of land. Though additional labor does not increase the surplus per laborer, it does increase the absolute surplus of whoever controls the goods produced. Children, and the wives to bear them, become a valued resource under such conditions.

Of equal or greater weight is the issue of future security. Almost everywhere, support in old age is taken over by children. Though other kin may provide assistance, the aged person without grown children is unlikely to get very solicitous care or receive much respect from juniors. Thus, children have economic value even if their labor does not contribute much to the household economy. This fact can explain the value of fertility to foragers, among whom adolescents and children do not generally contribute much toward household subsistence (see Schlegel and Barry 1980b for a discussion of the theme of fertility in the adolescent initiation ceremonies of girls in foraging societies). When this value is overlooked, as Meillassoux (1981:19–22) apparently did in his discussion of reproductive relations among foragers, one can derive a picture of the foraging band that mistakenly dismisses the bonds between parents and children and thereby provides no basis for the importance of marriage to men in band societies.

Even in the extended-family household, in which the elderly childless man or woman in most cases receives sufficient food and clothing to stay alive, old age lacks the compensations of loving children and grandchildren, whose labor allows the elderly person to enjoy leisure. As Ware (1978:21) put it: "Each lonely old woman gathering sticks is an object lesson in the need for security in old age, and such crones are not rare in societies with high mortality." It is widely appreciated that when the mortality of young and middle-aged people is high, parents expect to lose some children and take this into account in adjusting family size.

Children can be an economic asset even if they are far from home, as long as wage labor is available and parents control their wages. The remittances sent back by overseas children at present play an important role in the domestic economies of many poor countries. A family's best long-term strategy may be to produce many children in the hope that some, at least, will leave and send remittances home. Considering the low cost of child rearing in areas with outmigrating labor like Cape Verde or the rural Philippines, such a strategy makes considerable economic sense. Given the economic value of children in nonindustrial societies, and the high mortality rate that creates the need for replenishment, we can see why the reproductive value of women should be so high in preindustrial societies.

Reproduction is problematic for men. Women, of course, can reproduce within or outside of marriage and enjoy the present and future benefit of children regardless of the presence of a spouse, as long as they have some way of supporting themselves. Thus, women gain socially from reproduction, at the same time that they bear heavier physical costs. Men, for whom physical reproduction bears very little cost, do not gain socially from it unless they attach themselves to women who are or become mothers. For men, marriage is a commitment to a woman to help support her and her children in return for the social gains of parenthood. Other benefits of marriage for both sexes, not to be overlooked, are the expectation of domestic services and sexual relations as a right rather than a privilege, to be taken for granted rather than to be negotiated. In economies in which services have not become commodities, activities such as feeding, construction and upkeep of clothing and shelter, and care in time of illness arise out of personal relationships, and claims on such services are critical to well-being and even survival.

The benefits of reproduction are not problematic for a woman, but the support of herself and her children is. Barry and Schlegel (1982) found that the mean contribution of women to subsistence in the Standard Cross-Cultural Sample of preindustrial societies is 35.5 percent. Much of the women's labor goes into reproductive and domestic activities and into the processing rather than the procurement of raw materials. In almost every society (the Hadza, an African foraging group, being one possible exception), women rely heavily on men for assistance. This is most likely to come from their husbands, who claim fatherhood of their children. One view of marriage, then, is an exchange between the sexes: men provide support for children in exchange for claims on them, and women acknowledge these claims of men who help provide for them.

Such a free-exchange model, however, would apply completely only in societies in which individuals make their own marriage decisions, and, as we have seen, such is not the case for the majority of societies in this sample. Reproductive women are a valued asset to their kin, and the disposition of women in marriage becomes a political act in the establishment of claims on loyalty and the maintenance of networks. When children are of value to men, men assert fatherhood and seek marriage. It is only when other sources of economic advance, support, and political alliance-building outweigh children as a source of these benefits that paternity claims may not be so strongly pressed and abandonment is a realistic fear for women.

One way of attempting to increase the total fecundity of individual women is to get them married as soon as they give evidence of becoming fertile, at or very shortly after puberty. (Ironically, very early marriage and sexual relations may actually reduce the total fecundity of women, as stillbirths and miscarriages, not uncommon with early pregnancies, particularly when health care is poor, can damage their reproductive organs [cf. Nag 1962:87–88].) Of 178 societies for which there is information on girls, in 112, or 63 percent, adolescence ends within two years after puberty, almost always through marriage. (For boys the corresponding percentage is 31.) Among the Chatino, Indian peasants of Oaxaca, Mexico, girls may marry as early as 11, with 13 not being uncommon. However, sexual relations do not begin until after the bride's menarche; if she marries before then, she shares a bed with her mother-in-law until her first menstruation. In spite of such an early age of marriage, she is considered socially to be a woman (James Greenberg, personal communication). These figures support the assertion of a widespread interest in fertility in preindustrial societies. The question to be addressed concerns the remaining 37 percent. We cannot assume *a priori* that these societies are less interested in fertility than the majority; rather, we must look to other factors to explain the delay in marriage and the consequent lengthening of adolescence.

## Age of Marriage and Economic Considerations

An important step in understanding the reasons for age of marriage has been made by Whiting et al. (1986), who examined what they call *maiden-*

*hood strategies* for a subsample of the Standard Cross-Cultural Sample. The term *maidenhood strategies* refers to the length of time between a girl's menarche and her marriage and to the type of sexual activities permitted, if any. Length of maidenhood varies from longer than five years to none, when marriage takes place at or before menarche.

The concordance between the Whiting coding and that for length of adolescence in this study is expectably very high. Our definitions differ somewhat from Whiting's. Coders were asked to determine at what point social adolescence ends: early (up to about two years after puberty), middle (between about two and four years after puberty), late (more than about four years after puberty). Barring other information, early adolescence for girls is early to mid-teens, middle is to mid- to- late teens, late is late teens to about twenty. For boys, early is mid-teens, middle is later teens, and late is late teens to early twenties. As we have noted earlier, we take age 14 to be the age for puberty for girls, 16 for boys, if there is no information on this. Although in a very few societies like the !Kung, African foragers, girls may often marry before puberty, we know of no societies in which boys do.

When the duration of maidenhood was plotted according to level of social complexity, foragers were shown by Whiting et al. (1986) to have absent or short maidenhoods, middle-range societies such as horticulturalists and subsistence pastoralists to cluster around one to three years, and complex societies such as traditional agrarian states to have either absent or long (five-year) maidenhoods. These researchers believe that this distribution has to do with control over fertility, as women married early have a longer reproductive span than women married late. Given a period of at least two years of adolescent subfertility after menarche, only societies that delay marriage for more than three years do not make full use of the woman's fertility. Therefore, Whiting et al. adduced other factors to account for the choice between absent and short maidenhood. Parents, they believe, resort to the earliest marriages when population is sparse and marriages must be arranged for children before they reach puberty. These authors explained long maidenhood in the complex societies in their sample by a diminution of concern over paternity: these are bilateral societies where descent is traced through both parents, and Whiting and his co-authors assumed that paternity concerns are weaker in bilateral than in patrilineal societies, in which one belongs to one's father's descent line.[1]

The focus of their study was on fertility, which, we assert, is a central concern in preindustrial societies. However, the degree of concern may vary according to the economic or political value of children, and marriage may be delayed when large numbers of children are not advantageous or capital rather than labor is the key to economic success.

Additional factors may advance or delay marriage. One of these is control over labor, an economic advantage. We looked for a relation between length of adolescence and residence patterns to assess this factor; and although the difference in the distribution does not reach significance, an early end of adolescence for girls is most often found for this sample among matrilocal societies, in which daughters bring in husbands (68 percent). Next come societies in which wives reside in their husbands' households (62 percent). Early end is found least among neolocal and ambilocal (57 percent) societies, in which both sons and daughters leave (neolocal) or either the son or the daughter leaves to join the spouse at her or his home (ambilocal). We suggest that matrilocally residing families tend to encourage very early marriage for their daughters, as this is the means by which male labor is brought into the household. Neolocal households, on the other hand, might wish to delay marriage, as they lose the labor of daughters without any replacement by daughters-in-law. There is, however, no association between end of adolescence and female contribution to subsistence: women's labor is equally valuable to their parents and their husbands.

Although labor considerations may be of great importance to these families, which constitute units of production in preindustrial societies, we cannot overlook the emotional bonds that could discourage parents from sending children out into new households. In neolocal households, the parental couple is left alone after its children leave. The loss of female companionship may be particularly difficult for the mother, whose social circle is likely to be somewhat more circumscribed than her husband's. Even for the patrilocal stem family, in which an in-marrying daughter-in-law replaces a daughter, one reads of the "psychic cost" of a daughter's marriage. Speaking of Boeotia, Friedl (1963:122) wrote that the mother "loses the companionship of a friend, confidante, and working partner" and that mothers "commonly speak longingly of how much they miss their absent daughters."

Labor patterns differ according to differences in subsistence technology, and we tested the covariance of these with the point at which adolescence ends. Like Whiting et al. (1986), we found that the concentration of early marriages for girls is higher for foragers than for people with other technologies, although this distribution does not reach significance. Unlike them, however, we posit an economic rather than a demographic reason.

One of the features of marriage in foraging societies is the frequency with which bride service accompanies marriage (Schlegel and Eloul 1988). In such cases, a man works for his father-in-law or mother-in-law for a period of time to earn the right to his wife, whatever the residence pattern may be. In horticultural or pastoral societies, property is usually under the control of men and bride service is generally thought of as a limited period of labor for the bride's father; a Biblical account is the herding that earned Jacob his wives Leah and Rachel, told in the Book of Genesis. In foraging societies, bride service is more commonly defined as the long-term provisioning of the wife's mother with meat and possibly other goods, as among the !Kung and the Tiwi. Both parents are to some degree dependent upon the labor of their son-in-law. Women are scarce in these small communities, there being evidence of considerable competition among men over women in foraging societies. Each nubile girl is a prize, and men, far from resisting the demands marriage puts on them, are eager to lay claim to a wife. (For further discussion, see Schlegel and Eloul 1988). Here, as in the matrilocal societies previously noted, the promotion of early marriage is to the economic advantage of parents of daughters. That girls in foraging societies do not necessarily welcome such early marriages is made plain in the recollections of Nisa, a !Kung adolescent (Shostak 1983); this determined and strong-willed young person exhausted every means at her disposal—complaints, running away, refusal to join her husband—to rid herself of the unwanted burden of marriage, finally giving in to pressure from her parents and others.

Another economic factor in determining age of marriage has to do with transfer of property at marriage. Schlegel and Eloul (1987) coded marriage transactions for this sample, the types being bridewealth, token bridewealth, bride service, gift exchange, women exchange, dowry, and indirect dowry, along with the absence of transactions.[2] Using that code, we find that the end of adolescence is preponderately early for all societies with one exception, the dowry-giving societies, in which adolescence ends later (cf. Goody and Tambiah 1973:10). The difference between dowry societies and others is significant at the .002 level (Table 6.1).

In only two dowry-giving societies, the ancient Romans and the Haitian peasants (who do not give much dowry because they have very little property), does adolescence end early. Those in which girls' adolescence ends after a median duration, about two to four years after puberty, are the Chinese, Korean, Punjabi, Uttar Pradesh, and Basque. Those in which it ends later, about four to seven years after puberty, are the Irish, Burmese, Japanese, and Russian. These last two categories were collapsed for testing.

In spite of the tendency for dowry societies to delay the end of adolescence, the ancient Romans often had child betrothal with marriage following the girls' menarche. This deviant case forced us to examine the dowry societies in the sample.

The puzzle is resolved when we consider the social segments from which information was derived for coding. The customs coded for Romans were

***Table 6.1*** End of Adolescence and Form of Marriage Transactions: Girls

|  | Marriage Transactions | |
| --- | --- | --- |
|  | *dowry* | *other* |
| *End of adolescence* | | |
| early | 2 | 110 |
| middle and late | 9 | 57 |
|  | Fisher's Exact Test $p = .002$ | |

mainly those of the aristocracy, whereas peasant villages are the source of information for the remaining societies. Age of marriage in dowry-giving societies would seem to vary according to status and wealth, with higher-status and richer families marrying daughters off early and lower-status families marrying them off later.

Other evidence supports this hypothesis. In India, it is prescribed for the higher castes that girls be married early, even sometimes before puberty, although in that case cohabitation should be delayed. A very large portion of the population does not follow this high-caste rule and marries its girls well after puberty (Dumont 1970:110–111); thus, very early marriage is a custom of the elite or of those who emulate them. Considering the financial burden of providing a dowry—this being the main cause of debt among Indian peasants (Dumont 1970:110)—it is hardly surprising that poorer families should not be eager to hasten the marriages of daughters.

The evidence from preindustrial Europe, where dowries were given, points in the same direction. Without specifying ages, Trumbach (1978:16) related that in medieval Genoa, "Aristocrats married early, artisans married late." Early modern Europe was highly unusual in having quite late marriage for both sexes; but even there, the aristocracy generally married somewhat earlier than artisans and much earlier than the peasantry. In the 16th century, daughters of the upper landed classes married at about age 20 (Laslett 1965), and noble brides of the following century were also about that age (Stone 1977), while among small-property owners and laborers, women were marrying between ages 24 and 27 (Stone 1977).

The explanation for this discrepancy requires a consideration both of the economic value of women as laborers and reproducers of laborers and of the dowry itself. In the most complex societies, those in which dowries are customary, women of the food-producing sector have a lower economic value than they do in many simpler societies. Women's contribution to subsistence is high in societies in which gathering or tropical horticulture are major subsistence activities; but when there is plow agriculture, women make a lesser contribution to subsistence, although their processing and domestic activities expand (Ember 1983). In addition, in complex societies land and raw materials are not free, and there has to be a balance between the number of mouths the farm or shop can feed and the number of hands required to maintain it. Under such conditions, fertility cannot be unrestricted among peasants or artisans of limited means, and neither the labor power nor the reproductive capacity of women is high relative to women in many simpler societies. (For a more detailed discussion of marriage transactions, female contribution to subsistence, and other relevant variables, see Schlegel and Eloul 1988.)

Thus, we propose, first, that there is less pressure on peasant than on horticultural or pastoral families with marriageable daughters to give them as brides. Second, it is to the advantage of dowry-giving families with limited means to delay the marriages of daughters. This puts off the time when family property must be assembled to accompany her into her new home, and it also allows for a longer period in which she will contribute her domestic labor to the household, in compensation for the cost of rearing her.

While these factors must be considered in the marriages of girls of peasant or artisan families, they do not apply to the elite. Female domestic labor is replaced or augmented by the labor of servants or slaves, and there is no economic advantage in keeping the girls at home. While the elite family may be no more eager to part with its property in the dowry settlement than the poorer family, it is in a better financial position to do so. Furthermore, substantial dowries are used to "buy" the best possible son-in-law (and this is often the spirit in which these negotiations of property and status are held). A family can improve its social connections by using wealth to marry a daughter to a man of a higher social position, a well-known custom in India and one that was practiced by upwardly mobile families in Europe since at least the 16th century. While the family loses some of its property, its social gains are considerable. Mercantile families can bring a poor but clever son-in-law into the family business with the dowry (or anticipated inheritance), his loyalty assured by his economic dependence on his wife's family. This practice has been documented for mercantile families of Latin America (Socolow 1978).

Dowry, therefore, allows land-owning peasants and elites to use the marriages of their daughters in order to gain alliances with men who provide them with economic or social advantages. Dowry as a custom was found among all propertied classes in Europe, where land ownership even by peasants has been widespread for centuries, and among the property-owning sectors of Asia. In prerevolutionary China, where the elite and the more prosperous peasants gave dowries, people of lesser wealth, who were renters of land or poor artisans, engaged in other types of marriage transactions, such as indirect dowry. Such is still the case in India (see Schlegel and Eloul 1988).

With marriageable daughters as a sort of social capital, there is no advantage for elite families to delay putting this to use. Furthermore, with no economic constraints on fecundity, elite women have high reproductive value when high infant mortality threatens the perpetuation of the family line and the integrity of the family estate.

To this point, the discussion has been about girls' marriages, but not only the marriages of daughters are of concern to parents. Kin (primarily parental) control over the marriages of girls is only slightly greater than over those of boys in the sample. Low kin control is defined as marriage choice being made by the individual alone or with only advice from kin. This freedom is allowed to boys in 57 percent of the 138 societies with information, to girls in 50 percent of 129. Kin exert control when they have veto power over the marriage choice or they make the decision. Families are more likely to

**Table 6.2** Control Over Marriage and Form of Marriage Transactions

|  | *Marriage Transactions* | |
|---|---|---|
|  | *dowry and indirect dowry* | *other* |
| *Control over girl's marriage* | | |
| individual primarily | 6 | 59 |
| kin primarily | 18 | 46 |
|  | $\chi^2 = 6.41$ | $p = .011$ |
| *Control over boy's marriage* | | |
| individual primarily | 6 | 73 |
| kin primarily | 19 | 40 |
|  | $\chi^2 = 12.18$ | $p < .001$ |

control the marriages of offspring of both sexes when property goes with the girl into her conjugal household, especially in the form of dowry or indirect dowry (Table 6.2).[3]

Concordance between girls and boys is high for the end of adolescence as well (Table 6.3). In most societies the sexes are treated somewhat alike in the length of time between puberty and adulthood, although boys are generally older at marriage than are girls. Because for both sexes adolescence usually ends with marriage, this finding indicates that young people usually marry spouses fairly close to them in age, brides being generally no more than four years younger than their grooms.

The greatest discrepancy exists in those societies in which adolescence ends early for girls but late for boys. Discounting seven cases of boys' adolescence not ending with marriage, we are left with 16 cases with a large age difference between the sexes. Nine of these, all but one in Africa, give bridewealth, supporting Mair's (1977:56) observation that bridewealth can delay the marriage of boys, whose families must assemble the goods, at the

**Table 6.3** End of Adolescence: Concordance Between Girls and Boys

|  | *Girls* | | |
|---|---|---|---|
|  | *early* | *middle* | *late* |
| *Boys* | | | |
| early | 50 | 5 | 0 |
| middle | 38 | 21 | 2 |
| late | 23 | 18 | 20 |
|  | Mantel-Haenszel $\chi^2 = 49.09$ | $p < .001$ | |

same time it speeds the marriage of girls, whose families are eager to receive bridal payments. Nevertheless, in the majority (55 percent) of the 56 bridewealth-giving societies for which duration is coded for boys, end of adolescence for boys is not late (16 cases early, 15 cases middle adolescence).

Foragers have the lowest percentage of boys ending adolescence late and the highest percentage of those ending adolescence early, with societies with other subsistence techniques generally extending adolescence for a longer time. The difference in distribution does not reach the level of statistical significance, but it suggests that marriage may be delayed in some of the more complex societies when there are questions of property distribution, or in a few cases when schooling or other training lengthens the period needed for boys to learn adult skills. This is not usually the case for girls, as girls marry early (up to two years after puberty) in 106 of 178 societies for which duration of adolescence is coded for girls.

We have seen that there is a higher percentage of early-marrying girls in matrilocal societies and late-marrying girls in neolocal and ambilocal societies, although the distribution does not reach significance (as the majority of societies for all residence patterns have early marriage). This pattern is similar for boys, and it does reach statistical significance (Table 6.4). However, almost as many boys have an early as a late end to adolescence in neolocal and ambilocal societies. We suggest that adolescence is prolonged in those neolocal societies in which it is difficult for boys to assemble the wherewithal to establish a household (cf. Stone 1977:51–52) or to achieve by other means the readiness for adult status that enables them to take a wife. Understandably, parents would be reluctant to give their daughter to a very young husband if the couple had to support itself, and they might insist that he prove himself capable of carrying the responsibility of male household headship before he could marry her.

In the majority of societies in this sample, young people of both sexes have been married within about four years after puberty, girls by their midteens and boys by their late teens or very early twenties. They are likely to

*Table 6.4* End of Adolescence and Residence Pattern: Boys

|  | Residence pattern | | |
|---|---|---|---|
|  | *female centered* | *neolocal and ambilocal* | *male centered* |
| *End of adolescence* |  |  |  |
| early | 13 | 8 | 33 |
| middle | 20 | 3 | 39 |
| late | 4 | 10 | 47 |
|  | $\chi^2 = 15.47$ | df = 4 | $p = .004$ |

marry someone close in age. In spite of the high concordance between girls and boys, however, adolescence ends for boys in most societies at a chronologically later age than it does for girls, and boys' adolescence is longer than girls' in many societies.

The length of adolescence, we argue, is determined in most societies by the age of marriage, which in turn is the consequence of decisions made by persons controlling the marriages of very young people, who are rarely in an economic or political position to make such determinations themselves. The result may be either early or later marriage for either sex: there is no association between parental control over marriage and length of adolescence for girls or boys. When exchanges of property take place or when a family stands to gain or lose a significant portion of its labor force, parents and kin take a keen interest in the marriages of children and use them to their own advantages. This is not to imply that adults are deaf to the wishes of children, and in the great majority of cases children can refuse a marriage that is distasteful to them. However, parents can be much less subtle than they are in modern societies about directing their children's interest toward appropriate partners; they are usually free to advise about or veto proposed spouses, and they can use their control over property to advance or delay children's marriages.

Our emphasis has been on the economic aspects, broadly construed, of age of marriage, not because we minimize the importance of concerns about fertility, but because we take it for granted that fertility is always a consideration in preindustrial societies, even in those in which child spacing is a necessary consequence of women's labor patterns (cf. Schlegel and Barry 1986) or excess children are abandoned (Boswell 1989). But marriages serve social and economic as well as reproductive ends, and these factors must be taken into account. Important points to consider are labor patterns in conjunction with household structure, the reproductive value of females and the interest in accelerating or delaying childbearing, whether or not long periods of education or apprenticeship are required for economic success, and whether or not large amounts of goods must be accumulated to make an individual marriageable or to provide for marriage transactions. The length of adolescence is not arbitrary but results from a complex of factors in the cultural manipulation of biological givens.

# 7

# Adolescent Sexuality

THE compelling pressures of burgeoning sexuality in adolescence are channelled into heterosexual relations, homosexual acts, and masturbation. Some data are available on all three forms of sexual activity.[1] By far the most information is on heterosexual intercourse and the least on masturbation, although the latter is probably much more common than the former except in the very rare cases when other sexual outlets are available on demand. Homosexual acts are not widely reported, but more data can be retrieved than one would expect, given the longstanding reticence about discussing the subject.

In the sections that follow, we discuss permissiveness and restrictiveness toward heterosexuality and homosexuality. We attempt to identify social and cultural features leading to one or the other attitude and to test for concomitants and consequences. In particular, we are interested in the ways in which sexual behaviors are associated with other kinds of adolescent behaviors.

## Permissiveness and Restrictiveness
## Toward Heterosexual Intercourse

As we have seen in Chapter 3, more societies are permissive than restrictive toward adolescent sexuality. The variability ranges from the prohibition of any sort of flirtatious behavior, or even contact, to a kind of amused tolerance of the sexual exploits of young people. The Middle Eastern village girl who should speak to no man outside her family after puberty, and even with kin assumes a modest demeanor, is a far cry from the saucy girls and boys of Polynesia, bathed, scented, and decked with flowers, strutting about or trooping to neighboring villages for festivities that end in amorous embraces.

The Muria described in Chapter 5, and similar societies with unsupervised adolescent dormitories like the Ifugao and Bontoc tribes of the Mountain Provinces, Philippines, reach the peak of permissiveness. The following summary of Muria *ghotul* life is taken from Elwin (1968), an abridgement of Elwin (1947).

During the afternoon, girls sweep and clean the yard. The adolescents are responsible to the village for keeping the building and its compound clean and will be fined if it is left untended. At sunset, boys come to start the fire, the only light for the evening's activities.

After the evening meal taken at home, the boys straggle into the *ghotul* carrying their sleeping mats. The smaller boys bring firewood, and they may be called on to massage the legs of the older boys if they are tired. Meanwhile, the girls are assembling somewhere outside, and they enter as a group. A troop of girls from another hamlet may be visiting. Some girls sit with the boys, others sit together and talk, and fatigued boys and girls nap in quiet corners.

For an hour or two the mood is very informal. People gather in groups to talk; someone will tell a story or pose riddles; plans for a dancing expedition to another *ghotul* may be made or duties at a village wedding allocated; or there may be dancing. Sometimes boys sing taunting songs to the girls, who reply in kind.

By about 10 o'clock, the girls collect around the girl leader, who allots to each her sleeping partner. Every girl then goes up to a boy, often but not necessarily this partner, to comb his long hair and massage his back and arms. This, of course, brings them into close contact with one another, and the boys often call out sexy remarks about themselves or others.

When the massages are finished, it is bedtime. Girls visiting from another *ghotul* are now expected to leave. (If any visiting girl is discovered by her own *ghotul* boys to have remained the night, they get very angry and she is punished with a heavy fine.) The younger children go to sleep in a row. The adolescents pair off, two on a mat. Extra boys share a mat. Elwin notes that there are more often extra boys than girls. This is possibly because menstruating girls do not go to the *ghotul*. Those who intend to have intercourse may retire to a small hut in the compound. Soon all is quiet. Everyone arises before dawn, for they should be at home and working when their parents arise.

While girls are expected to have intercourse at least some of the time, forcing the girl is extremely offensive and can result in a heavy fine. In some *ghotul*s, couples are paired off and expected to remain faithful to one another, although it is unlikely that one's "*ghotul* husband" or "*ghotul* wife" will be one's eventual spouse. In others, there is a rule against sleeping together too often, which the boy and girl leaders enforce. Even in this sexually charged atmosphere, there are strong rules of propriety and sanctions against speech or actions in bad taste. Elwin speaks of a boy who tried to peep under the skirts of the girls when they were dancing. They stopped, grabbed him and bound his hands, tying them to the roof. He remained in this uncomfortable and undignified posture for 15 minutes and had to apologize to each girl before he was released.

In such a society, the adolescent years must seem idyllic to those who have passed beyond them, particularly to young adults who have to bear the burdens of adult responsibility and yet have not attained the satisfactions and honored position of middle age. The Muria, certainly, look back with fond nostalgia on those days. Nevertheless, they appreciate the privacy of the home and the generally greater freedom of sexual expression with a spouse.

There are several snakes in this adolescent paradise. One, of course, is pregnancy. The Muria have various beliefs about conception, that it is likely immediately after the girl's menses or that it is unlikely if one changes partners frequently, and they take steps to avoid it. The young people in the *ghotul* practice *coitus interruptus* when they fear the possibility of a pregnancy, and abortions are performed. Probably most often, though, the couple are married, or she is married to her betrothed, who is expected to accept the child as his own.

Jealousy is another problem. Younger boys are jealous of older ones, and the "drab-looking older girls" of 18 or so (!) may be jealous of the "young and beautiful" ones in their early teens (Elwin 1968:216). *Ghotul* members resent it when others are assigned to sleep with their preferred partners and are known to have temper tantrums.

The effects of such extreme permissiveness on one's sex life in later years are in dispute. Elwin speaks of the apparent marital happiness and fidelity and the low divorce rate among the Muria. On the other hand, Barton contrasts the low divorce rate among the Kalinga, who do not have adolescent dormitories, with the high frequency of adultery and divorce among the neighboring Ifugao and Bontoc, who do. He believes that this "period of promiscuity" (Barton 1969:54) establishes habits that are hard to break and lead to discontent and boredom with one partner.

The findings from our study support Barton, although not necessarily for the reasons he gave. As Table 7.1 shows, adultery is likely to be frequent among men when adolescent boys have sexual freedom, and it is likely to be frequent among women when adolescent girls have sexual freedom. Thus, there is consistency in behavior between adolescence and adulthood. This is also true for the double standard, or the attitude toward adultery: for both sexes, adolescent permissiveness is related to the absence of a double standard. We note especially the association between restrictiveness toward boys and the presence of a double standard. Restricting the sexual freedom of women, adolescent girls, and adolescent boys is part of a general pattern of control over subordinate persons, most likely to be found where sexual freedom is one of the privileges accorded to dominant adult men only.

Whatever the cause of marital infidelity among the Bontoc, Ifugao, and

*Table 7.1* Adolescent Sexual Freedom Related to Adultery[a]

| | Adolescent Sexual Freedom[b] | | | |
| | Boys | | Girls | |
| | N | Mean | N | Mean |
|---|---|---|---|---|
| *Double standard*[c] | | | | |
| absent | 34 | 6.5 | 32 | 5.8 |
| present | 60 | 5.1 | 63 | 4.5 |
| | $F = 9.20$ | $p = .003$ | $F = 6.37$ | $p = .013$ |
| *Frequency: men*[d] | | | | |
| high | 31 | 6.1 | | |
| low | 15 | 4.2 | | |
| | $F = 8.19$ | $p = .006$ | | |
| *Frequency: women*[d] | | | | |
| high | | | 26 | 5.9 |
| low | | | 23 | 4.1 |
| | | | $F = 6.74$ | $p = .013$ |

[a]Source for data on adultery: Broude and Greene 1980.

[b]Adolescent sexual freedom is measured on an 11-point scale, a higher mean indicating greater freedom.

[c]Absent means allowed equally or punished equally; present means allowed to husband, or wife punished more.

[d]High means almost universal or moderate; low means occasional or uncommon.

others, Elwin's report suggests that it does not necessarily lie in permissiveness toward adolescent sex. As one Nigerian Ijo informant, quoted by Hollos and Leis (1986:404), averred, one can never tell: "A young woman with much sex experience before marriage may never commit adultery after marriage, whereas one who has not could go to other men after marriage."

Finally, Elwin brought up the question of whether the continual contact does not reduce desire, and he suggested that the massages and other intimacies are a stimulus to the boys for impulses that otherwise might flag. His own account, however, contains evidence that boys are always eager but girls are not always willing, even though the Muria maintain that women are insatiable and take the lead in seduction. Elwin took note of Havelock Ellis's (1906) belief that sexual feelings are dulled between those who have been brought up together. However, his reports of passionate attachments that lead to elopement, cause extreme jealousy, or result in long periods of despondence when the beloved *ghotul* partner gets married to somebody else belie his concern. Recent research on sexuality indicates that the inhibition of sexual impulses toward another is strong if the intimate contact occurs when at least one of the pair is a young child (cf. Parker 1976); however, the continual contact of Muria adolescents does not begin until the children are into middle or late childhood.

Some societies may allow a great deal of freedom to girls and yet expect them to maintain their virginity. The East African Kikuyu in earlier times had a youths' dormitory, to which adolescent girls came for entertainment and what American teenagers have called "heavy petting," that is, all but penetration. This custom, termed *ngweko,* involved lying together with intertwined legs while fondling and going through the motions of copulation. The girl kept her leather pubic apron in place all the while. It seems quite certain that the young men would come to orgasm. Whether the girls did or not is not stated. These girls had had clitorectomies; but only the tip was removed, so perhaps there was enough erectile tissue for girls also to be stimulated to climax. This sexual activity was encouraged. It would have been shameful for the girl to get pregnant, however, and so the precaution of the apron was taken.

It is not uncommon for people to feel ambivalent about the sexuality of their adolescents, and this is often reflected in the ethnographic reports, in which one can read about parents admonishing and scolding girls but not going to any great lengths to keep them away from boys. When adolescents have freedom of association and can get away from adult supervision, some instances of sexual contact are almost assured. Among rural Haitians, for example, a tolerant attitude toward premarital relations is combined with a strong disapproval of pregnancy and threat of punishment for shaming the family (Herskovits 1971). To avoid this, girls use magical contraceptives and the more effective abortions. On the contrary, the Hopi supervised their daughters to some degree and considered out-of-wedlock pregnancy unfortunate, but neither the family nor the girl was strongly sanctioned and the child suffered from no stigma.

Broude (1981) provided a detailed summary of cross-cultural studies of the management of sexuality, including premarital sex norms for females. (Little attention has been paid to males.) As most girls in most traditional societies leave social adolescence at marriage, the females in question are by and large adolescent girls.

Two kinds of studies have been done. One tests the influence of features of social structure on premarital sex norms to determine the kinds of societies that are permissive and restrictive. The other considers psychological factors such as anxiety over sex in promoting or inhibiting premarital heterosexual relations. None, to our knowledge, compares permissive with restrictive societies for other regularities of behavior.

The summary by Broude (1981) greatly simplifies our task in presenting relevant material. Studies by Murdock (1964), Goethals (1971), and

Eckhardt (1971), and a later one by Paige (1983) all examined the influence of social structural features. In brief, premarital sexual permissiveness for females has been found to be associated with the simpler subsistence technologies, absence of stratification, smaller communities, matrilineal descent, matrilocal residence, absence of belief in high gods, absence of bridewealth, high female economic contribution, little or no property exchange at marriage, and ascribed rather than achieved status. In addition, Barry et al. (1980b) reported an association with an evaluation of girls as equal to or higher than that of boys. All of these variables are characteristic of lower social complexity and, as Broude pointed out, are highly intercorrelated.

The influence of psychological factors has been assessed by Ayres (1967) and Broude (1975), who considered restrictiveness to be the result of sex anxiety. They found associations with their measures of sex anxiety—for Ayres, long pregnancy taboos; for Broude, severe socialization for sexual propriety and inaccessibility of the caretaker, which, she posited, lead to distrust. Both assumed that premarital restrictiveness results from an aversion of adolescents to sex. It seems more likely, however, that it is adults who impose their standards of sexual behavior on adolescents. In other words, restricting adolescent sexuality is done by adults for reasons of their own. We should note, as Broude (1975) pointed out, that premarital sex norms show no significant association with adult sex anxiety, measured by a scale constructed by Minturn et al. (1969), thus casting doubt on sex anxiety as a factor in premarital sexual permissiveness or restrictiveness.[2]

Earlier work by the first author and the research of others described in Chapter 6 led us to consider two other factors in the determination of premarital sex norms: the age at which adolescence ends and the absence, presence, and type of marriage transactions as described in Chapter 6.[3] The latter are highly correlated with social complexity: indirect dowry and especially dowry are found in the most complex societies, while bride service, women exchange, and absence of transactions are more often found in the least complex (cf. Schlegel and Eloul 1988). Following Whiting et al. (1986), we hypothesize that parents are not so concerned about premarital pregnancy, and therefore girls' sexual activities, if marriage follows soon after menarche. Common observation shows that early postmenarchial sexual intercourse rarely results in pregnancy, a phenomenon known as adolescent sterility or subfecundity. We also hypothesize that permissiveness and restrictiveness are related to the type of marriage transaction, on the grounds that families are more concerned about a girl's virginity when some forms of property exchange are part of the marriage arrangement. When parents wish to control her choice of marriage partner, a daughter's pregnancy might force them into an unwanted alliance if the seducer makes paternity claims on the child. (This hypothesis has been developed in Schlegel 1991.)

The association between the end of adolescence and sexual permissiveness and restrictiveness was tested. Ending age was divided into early and later, or up to two years after adolescence begins and later than that. Permissiveness means that sexual intercourse is tolerated or expected, and restrictiveness means that it is prohibited. The result is significant (Table 7.2). However, even when adolescence ends later, more societies in the sample are permissive than restrictive. Thus, premarital sex norms are not simply a function of female biology.

The relation of marriage transactions to premarital sex norms was assessed and found to be significant (see Tables 7.3 and 7.4). Marriage is also more likely to be late in dowry-giving societies; in all other cases, there is no association between the age of marriage and the type of marriage transaction (see Chapter 6). Societies are more often permissive than they are restrictive except those having dowry, indirect dowry, and gift exchange.[4] Permissiveness characterizes most societies in which exchange is absent, women are exchanged, or bride service is performed, that is, when either nothing is given or something other than property changes hands. When property is exchanged, people are less permissive. However, contrary to the assumption that with bridewealth men "buy" a virgin, bridewealth-giving societies are more frequently permissive than restrictive. A typical example of a permissive bridewealth-giving society is the Ijo of Nigeria, among whom "many men claim to want to marry women who have already proven to be fertile" (Hollos and Leis 1986:402).

Societies with gift exchange, indirect dowry, and especially dowry deviate from the more general pattern. The case of dowry is of historical as well as ethnographic interest because dowry has been the preferred form of marriage transaction in most of Eurasia and was a European tradition until fairly recently. The rationale for restrictiveness when dowry is given has been discussed by Schlegel (1991).

By seducing and impregnating a girl, a man could press his claim to take her as wife along with her property. Her parents would be reluctant to refuse, since the well-being of their grandchildren depended upon their inheritance from both of their parents; and another man would be unlikely to marry the mother if it meant that he had not only to support her chil-

Table 7.2 End of Adolescence and Premarital Sex Norms: Girls

| | End of adolescence | |
| --- | --- | --- |
| | *early* | *later* |
| *Sexual intercourse* | | |
| prohibited | 24 | 27 |
| permitted | 76 | 35 |
| | $\chi^2 = 5.90$ | $p = .015$ |

*Table 7.3* Distribution of Marriage Transactions and Premarital Sex Norms: Girls

| | | | | | | Marriage Transactions | | | |
|---|---|---|---|---|---|---|---|---|---|
| | Bride wealth | Token bride wealth | Bride service | Gift exchange | Women exchange | Dowry | Indirect dowry | Absent |
| *Sexual intercourse* | | | | | | | | |
| prohibited | 15 | 3 | 3 | 8 | 1 | 9 | 9 | 4 |
| permitted | 32 | 4 | 22 | 8 | 6 | 2 | 5 | 32 |

Source: Schlegel and Eloul (1987).

**Table 7.4** A Test of Marriage Transactions and Premarital Sex Norms: Girls

| | Marriage Transactions | | | | | |
|---|---|---|---|---|---|---|
| | Bride wealth[a] | Bride service | Gift exchange | Dowry plus indirect dowry | Absent | Total |
| **Sexual intercourse** | | | | | | |
| prohibited | 18 | 3 | 8 | 18 | 4 | 51 |
| permitted | 36 | 22 | 8 | 7 | 32 | 105 |
| | $\chi^2 = 33.14$ | | $df = 4$ | p < .001 | | |

Source: Schlegel and Eloul (1987). Women exchange is omitted because of the small number of cases.

[a]Includes token bridewealth.

115

dren but also to make them his heirs. The widow with children would be a different matter, since these children would have received property through their father and would make no claims on their stepfather beyond support, for which in any event their labor would provide compensation.

To illustrate that upward mobility through marriage with an heiress is not foreign to dowry-giving societies, consider a common theme of European fairy tales, already offered in Chapter 5 as an indicator of men's anxiety about marriage. A poor but honest young man goes through trials to win the hand of the princess, who inherits her father's kingdom. Or he wins her heart, and through the good offices of a fairy godmother or other spirit helper, they evade her wrathful father and eventually are reconciled with him. This more or less legitimate means to upward mobility is not so different from the illegitimate one, by which he wins the heiress through seduction.

Families guard their daughters' chastity in dowry-giving societies in order to protect their property against would-be social climbers and to ensure that they can use their daughters' dowries to attract the most desirable sons-in-law (cf. Chapter 6). The Mediterranean world, the home of the "honor-shame" complex that links family honor to the chastity of its female members, has been a center of dowry-giving since the ancient civilizations of Egypt, Greece, and Rome. Other historical centers are northern Europe, China, and India. Indirect dowry, as in the custom of the *mahr* almost universal among Muslim peoples, has often been confused with bridewealth; in fact, it was so coded in the *Ethnographic Atlas* (Murdock 1967). (The confusion results from considering only the transfer of goods from the groom's family to the bride's while ignoring the equally important transfer of goods from the bride's family to the new conjugal couple.) Perhaps it is the well-known emphasis on virginity in Muslim societies that has given rise to the erroneous impression that bridewealth-giving societies are overwhelmingly concerned with premarital virginity.

The two exceptions to restrictiveness among dowry-giving societies in this sample deserve comment. The Haitians turn a blind eye to a daughter's sexual activity but punish her severely if she should become pregnant. Haitian peasants have so little property that, while they do give some goods to a marrying daughter and therefore are classified as dowry-giving, they are unlike the prosperous land-owning peasantry, bourgeoisie, and elite that constitute the bulk of the dowry-giving category. The Burmese allow sexual intercourse before marriage, but only between those who have become publicly betrothed and are thereby considered to be as bound to each other as are married partners elsewhere. These cases have been more fully described in Schlegel and Eloul (1988).

One factor that may account for an emphasis on virginity in many societies that give neither dowry nor indirect dowry is inheritance of titles, which are a form of inherited property. A case in point is Samoa. Although untitled girls have considerable sexual freedom, titled girls, particularly the *taupou,* the village "princess," are expected to go to marriage as virgins. As titles pass through both parents in Samoa, it is important that daughters not produce bastard children—the maternity of bastards is undeniable, unlike their paternity—or form unsuitable attachments (cf. discussion in Schlegel 1991).

Another feature of the Samoan elite that promotes virginity is the exchange of valuable gifts between the marrying families. Although no one comes out ahead economically in such an exchange, it serves to ensure that marriage occurs only between people of comparable wealth or social power, in that they can call up wealth from kin and dependents. Here also, an ambitious boy might try to impregnate an elite girl in order to force her family to recognize him as a son-in-law, even though his social status would not normally make him an eligible spouse for her. In many gift-exchanging societies, virginity is not an issue for ordinary people, for whom status concerns are not major factors and few gifts if any are exchanged. The Omaha, a Plains Indian tribe, are similar to the Samoans in this respect: high-status families exchange valuable gifts and expect virginity, while ordinary people do neither. Similar arguments apply to variations by class in maintaining daughters' virginity in Europe and Asia at different historical periods.

Families do not simply rely on sex norms to ensure the chastity of their daughters. As we have seen in Chapter 4, the patterning of subordination of daughters to parents is consonant with the form of marriage transaction, low subordination being linked to the absence of transactions. We have interpreted this association as an indication that subordination of adolescents to parents is partially a function of property relations. When these property relations focus around marriage, parental control of girls is strict, a major objective being to ensure the daughter's virginity for reasons already discussed. Parental control is looser when property relations are absent and virginity for girls is not at issue.

It seems likely that both age of marriage and type of marriage transaction together have an effect on sexual permissiveness. The relations with premarital sex norms are indicated in Table 7.5, which shows that the percentages follow the predicted direction even though they are not statistically significant.

We conducted further tests controlling for the end of adolescence to determine whether property is or is not a factor in premarital sex norms. When adolescence ends early, that is, when girls marry early, societies that give no property are more often permissive (91 percent) than those that do give property (63 percent). The difference is significant ($p = .002$ by Fisher's Exact Test). However, when adolescence ends later, the difference between socie-

*Table 7.5* Property Contribution, End of Adolescence, and Premarital Sex Norms: Girls

| | | Premarital sex norms | | |
|---|---|---|---|---|
| | *End of adolescence* | *restrictive* | *permissive* | *% permissive* |
| *Contributor* | | | | |
| groom's kin | early | 9 | 26 | 74 |
| only[a] | later | 9 | 10 | 53 |
| bride's kin[b] | early | 11 | 8 | 42 |
| | later | 14 | 7 | 33 |
| none: no | early | 4 | 42 | 91 |
| property[c] | later | 4 | 18 | 82 |

[a]Bridewealth and token bridewealth.

[b]Dowry, indirect dowry, and gift exchange.

[c]Women exchange, brideservice, and absence of transactions.

ties that do give property (43 percent permissive) and those that do not (82 percent permissive) is also significant ( $p = .003$ by Fisher's Exact Test).

It seems likely that whenever families attempt to marry their daughters to men of equal or higher status, that is, when status considerations are an important feature of the marriage, they restrict the girls' premarital sexual activity. This is most likely in property-owning societies, those that give dowry and those in which the elite exchange gifts; it is also the case for some peoples giving indirect dowry. To allow sexual freedom would make it too easy for a social-climbing suitor, seeking to better his social position or at least that of his children, to seduce and impregnate the girl and then press paternity claims. These concerns will be strongest in societies in which girls marry later, when there is greater danger of pregnancy.

Although both age of marriage and property exchange have an effect on sexual permissiveness, there are other factors, outside of the scope of this study, that should also be considered for a fuller understanding in specific cases. Along with dowry, there is the girl's future inheritance at the time of the parents' death, another source of goods that she will, in time, bring to the marriage. Emulation of those of higher status, particularly when a rise in status through marriage by daughters is possible, is another factor. So is the assumption of a new morality after religious conversion. The value placed on chastity as linked to spiritual purity, promoting celibacy and aversion (at some historical periods) to the remarriage of widows, is a feature of religions that arose in the ancient dowry-giving areas of the world: the Mediterranean and Anatolia (Christianity) and India (Hinduism and Buddhism).

## Concomitants of Permissiveness and Restrictiveness

We have seen that subordination to parents is associated with types of marriage transaction, and these factors in turn are associated with premarital sex norms. It seems likely that subordination to parents is related to permissiveness and restrictiveness toward premarital sexual relations. We found this to be the case: girls are more likely to be highly subordinate to their mothers in societies that prohibit sexual relations (Table 7.6).

Because control over one's body is fundamental to personal autonomy, the control of others over one's sexuality is likely to be highly associated with control in other areas. (In some mammalian social units that are hierarchically structured, high-ranking animals react aggressively to sexual activity among subordinates and reserve that privilege for themselves [cf. Bischof 1975a:51].) For this sample, premarital sex norms are significantly associated with control over the choice of spouse. When kin rather than the individual are primarily responsible for selecting the spouse, sex norms are more likely to be restrictive (Table 7.7). On the other hand, sexual relations may become part of the courtship pattern for adolescents who choose their own spouses.

Subordination does not seem to affect other aspects of the relations between girls and their mothers, as there is no significant association between premarital sex norms and contact, intimacy, or conflict between mothers and daughters. Apparently, autonomy is not so much desired in these communally based societies that its absence sours the relations between parents and children.

Boys' relations with family members seem little affected by permissiveness or restrictiveness. Subordination to the father and contact, intimacy, and conflict with him show no association with premarital sex norms for boys. Nor does separation from the family affect whether or not adolescent boys have sexual freedom. There is, however, an association between sex norms for boys and control over selection of spouse, as there is for girls (Table 7.7). For parents who control their children's marriages, it simplifies

*Table 7.6* Girls' Subordination to the Mother and Premarital Sex Norms

|  | Subordination | |
|---|---|---|
|  | *low* | *high* |
| *Sexual intercourse* | | |
| prohibited | 15 | 19 |
| permitted | 47 | 22 |
|  | $\chi^2 = 4.52$ | $p = .034$ |

*Table 7.7* Premarital Sex Norms and Control over Marriage

|  | Control over marriage | |
|---|---|---|
|  | *individual primarily* | *kin primarily* |
| *Sexual intercourse* | | |
| Girls | | |
| prohibited | 11 | 29 |
| permitted | 49 | 30 |
|  | $\chi^2 = 11.32$ | $p = .001$ |
| Boys | | |
| prohibited | 7 | 17 |
| permitted | 64 | 31 |
|  | $\chi^2 = 10.09$ | $p = .001$ |

matters if young people are not permitted to form sexual attachments that may be at odds with their wishes.

We hypothesized that sexual restrictiveness might lead to aggression, on the assumption that sexual frustration makes itself felt in antisocial ways. That is the basis for Stone's (1977:52–53) interpretation of youth of the 18th and 19th centuries, when marriage was delayed for many:

> In view of the low recorded level of illegitimacy, it is reasonable to assume that for many young men this delay involved considerable sexual denial at a time of optimum male sexual drive, despite the usual nonprocreative outlets. If one follows Freudian theory, this could lead to neuroses of the kind that so regularly shattered the calm of Oxford and Cambridge colleges at this period; it could help to explain the high level of group aggression, which lay behind the extraordinary expansionist violence of western nation states at this time.

There is no evidence from this study to indicate that sexual frustration, inferred from the prohibition of heterosexual intercourse, leads to aggressive behavior. Premarital sex norms are not significantly associated with aggression among peers, a high level of aggressiveness as a character trait, or antisocial behavior toward the community. We propose that the young men to whom Stone referred were expressing the effects more of social than of sexual frustration, as their immediate prospects for marriage were dim and their unmarried state kept them from attaining full social adulthood.

We further hypothesized that competitiveness among boys as a character trait would be exacerbated in societies that are sexually permissive to adolescents, on the grounds that boys would compete with one another for the available girls. That hypothesis was not supported by our data. It is possible that in some societies sexual success with girls is a reward for achievement in

*Table 7.8* Premarital Sex Norms Comparing Girls and Boys

| | Sexual intercourse, boys | |
|---|---|---|
| | *prohibited* | *permitted* |
| *Sexual intercourse, girls* | | |
| prohibited | 29 | 14 |
| permitted | 2 | 108 |
| | $\chi^2 = 78.39$ | $p < .001$ |

other areas. In such cases, there may be an association; however, it does not show up as a widespread pattern.

The data from our study allow us to assess the prevalence of a sexual double standard for adolescents. Overwhelmingly, societies that are restrictive for one sex are restrictive for the other (Table 7.8; see also Frayser 1985:203).

We do not have the relevant data on the youth stage, but we suspect that the double standard is most likely to exist if marriage is long delayed and both sexes pass through a youth stage. Attempts to suppress the sexuality of young men who have moved somewhat beyond parental control are probably seen as futile, whereas young women can be kept in line through fear of pregnancy or withdrawal of support. In such cases, the young men will visit prostitutes, as do Muslim youths of Thailand (Anderson and Anderson 1987), if they are available, or attempt to seduce girls of a lower social class in class-stratified societies.

When heterosexual relations are permitted, the partner is most often limited to another adolescent: in 72 percent of 120 societies for boys and in 77 percent of 111 societies for girls. Sexual activity seems to be primarily an amusement. While the occasional passionate attachment can develop, for most people sexuality lacks the emotional meaning it has in the more restrictive societies.

## Courtship

Courtship implies at least the stimulation if not the satisfaction of sexual desire, even when desire hides beneath a veil of romanticism. When there is sexual freedom or clandestine sexual adventures are permitted even though the sexes maintain distance in public, courtship may be merely an intensification of the usual attentions that boys and girls pay one another. A more formal kind of courting occurs along with strict segregation between the sexes. Hoebel (1978:28) related the anxiety-laden courtship of the North American Cheyenne boy:

After adolescence [Hoebel means *puberty*], boys and girls do not associate with each other, so there is no direct opportunity to develop camara-
derie. Once a boy has seen a girl whom he hopes to make his sweetheart,
he approaches her furtively. He knows the path from her family lodge to
the stream where she gets water or the grove where she gathers wood.
Hopefully, he stands along the path. As she passes, he gives her robe a
little tug. Perhaps he feels this is too bold. If so, he whistles or calls to
her. She may stonily ignore him, much to his mortification. Or she may
make the stars shine by stopping to talk about this and that, but never of
love. If all goes well, they may later begin to meet and talk outside her
lodge. In time, they may exchange rings (either the old-time horn ones or
those of metal obtained from traders) that young people wear. They are
then engaged. Except for the exchange of rings, a suitor rarely gives presents directly to a girl. When the time comes, these go to her male relatives.

Tootling on a medicine flute is supposed to be a means of casting a
love spell over a reluctant maiden. Certain medicine men can concoct a
spruce gum to help a hapless swain to win his goal. If the girl chews the
gum, her thoughts cannot leave the boy who gives it to her.

Hopi courtship also has its anxious moments, but for the girl rather than
for the boy (cf. Schlegel 1973).

Getting a husband is not easy for the Hopi girl. In this matrilocal society
in which houses are owned by women, it is up to the girl to invite her prospective husband into her home, thus putting the burden of initiating
courtship on the girl. She does so by presenting the boy of her choice
with a special cornmeal cake. He is obliged to receive it, but he does not
have to act on its invitation. The girl waits for a few days to see if he will
respond, for no self-respecting boy would appear so eager that he would
rush to accept unless they had already discussed marriage. If he does not
let her know in a few days, the girl becomes anxious. After a week or so,
she realizes that he is refusing her proposal, and she will, according to
her temperament and the attraction she feels toward the boy, either cast
her hopes elsewhere or become despondent. Adolescent girls, the Hopi
believe, are susceptible to depression, particularly at rejection by a
hoped-for bridegroom.

The Hopi are not unique in making the initiation of courtship the responsibility of the girl. The Garo of Assam, also matrilocal, do this too. This
description is drawn from Nakane's (1967) account.

A Christian Garo girl writes a letter of proposal to the boy of her choice,
who initially replies in the negative, even if he has hinted to the girl that
he is willing. (Boys often receive such letters from several girls.) After a
time, his *amour propre* permits him to accept. The custom among the

pagan Garo is for the girl's father to propose the marriage to the boy and his family, which is always refused at first. If it is not a serious refusal, the prospective bridegroom at some later point is kidnapped by boys of the girl's lineage and brought to her house, where self-respect obliges him to run away. Once again, he is kidnapped. After one or a few times, he will stay if he truly wants the girl. If not, he will keep running away until she and her family finally give up.

Although research into courtship customs is beyond the scope of our study, it is probable that the burden of courtship falls upon the partner who will have the greater domestic power, at least initially, in the marriage. We propose that when households are matrilocal and the in-marrying husband stands in a rather lowly position, the initiative will be taken by girls or their parents. Sharing of initiative seems likely for more egalitarian neolocal households. When the husband is the head, we suggest, it is up to him to invite his prospective wife to join him. Any of these forms of courtship may be conducted chastely or be accompanied by sexual intercourse.

## Lovers and Peers

We pointed out in Chapter 5 that peer group attachments fade somewhat as men marry and take on adult responsibilities. This change may be due in part to the greater attention paid to household economic status and activities and, frequently, to the corroding effect that inequality among adult men has upon the *esprit de corps* of the peer group. There is an emotional factor to be considered as well, affection toward a wife competing with attachment to peers.

The love of a man for his wife and the hold that her sexuality has on him are widely recognized as dangerous to the solidarity of various kinds of male-bonded groups. In patrilocal extended families, whose core is the cluster of father and sons and brothers, attachment to these men is supposed to override attachment to the wife, and it is considered unseemly for husbands to show any public signs of affection to their wives. Wife sharing can be interpreted as an attempt to enhance bonds among men.

Love and war are also at odds. In some parts of New Guinea where warfare is endemic, men normally sleep in the men's house in order to be ready to rush to the defense of the village if attacked. Men's loyalty to their peers is expected to supersede that to their wives. Men are teased if they spend too much time in their wives' huts when they visit them for meals or in the evening for sex, and the secret male lore contains many themes and beliefs that devalue women and reinforce male-male ties (cf. Schlegel 1990).

Accordingly, we looked at whether peer group attachments are weaker when adolescent girls and boys are permitted to have sexual relations with one another. We found no significant association between the importance of the peer group and sexual permissiveness, perhaps because many permissive societies discourage the formation of close ties between couples by encouraging or enjoining boys and girls to spread their favors widely. We have already observed this among Muria adolescents, among whom, in the majority of the *ghotuls*, girls and boys are expected to rotate partners. As already noted, this does not entirely prevent the formation of strong attachments, but such attachments are not encouraged.

Another example is the traditional Kikuyu, discussed earlier. As in other age-graded societies of East Africa, male peer bonding is—and is expected to be—strong. Efforts are made to reduce close attachments to girls. The summary below is drawn from Worthman (1986) and Whiting et al. (1986).

> Circumcision marks a change in status for both sexes. Girls are circumcised, i.e., the very tip of the clitoris, the "male" part, is removed, just before menarche, and they pass into the adolescent stage. Boys are not circumcised until about age 18, when the "female" part, the prepuce, is removed. They move into bachelor huts for a period of several years and their responsibility to the community changes as they assume a warrior role (we would call this a youth stage). Young men and adolescent girls have sexual relations without penetration, as described earlier. They are expected to change partners, and it would be selfish and unsociable to restrict one's attentions to a special friend.

Lovers, not parents, are the enemies of the peer group.

## Adolescent Homosexual Behavior

Homosexuality has emerged as a subject of anthropological investigation in the past few years, following paths broken by literary and historical scholars. Reports, often only passing mentions, of homosexual activity occur in the ethnographic literature, particularly in the accounts of peoples of parts of Melanesia, but only recently has much of this material been assembled and made readily accessible. Much of the credit goes to Herdt, who wrote an ethnography (1981) of the Sambia (a fictitious name), a Melanesian people practicing ritual homosexuality. He also edited a collection of papers (Herdt 1984) on ritualized homosexuality in Melanesia.

One of the pervasive themes in the parts of Melanesia in which ritualized homosexual behavior occurs is the growth-giving quality of semen. In order to grow, boys must be rubbed with semen, one of the practices of the Kimam, or inseminated by older boys or adult men, through either fellatio or anal intercourse. Adolescent boys in such societies are either the inseminated partners of older men or, as among the Sambia and the Kimam, the inseminators of younger boys.

The following description of the Kimam is drawn from Serpenti (1977). The practices had been defunct for some time before Serpenti lived among the Kimam, so there are some lacunae in his account.

The lives of adolescent boys and youths center around the men's house, where a series of rituals is held and where they sleep from first initiation until marriage. Boys go through their first initiation at about 10, before puberty, when they enter the first grade and become *munaka*s. Each *munaka* has as a mentor a member of the second grade, a *tjutjine,* a boy from about 14 to perhaps 17. The *munaka*s go through various hardships during the initiation, and their arms and legs are periodically rubbed with semen. The initiatory process consists of several major feasts and a number of rituals over a period of about three years. At this time new boys enter the cycle, the *munaka*s become *tjutjine*s, and the *tjutjine*s graduate into the highest grade of older teenagers, the *mabureede,* those apparently about 17 and older. These youths remain in that grade until they marry, seemingly one to several years later.

The *mabureede* are permitted to have discreet sex with unmarried girls, with the exception of their fiancées. For the younger boys, homosexual activity is expected. Each *tjutjine* is fellated by the *munaka* for whom he is the mentor.

The Sambia, also, practice fellatio between preadolescent boys and adolescents. Unlike Serpenti, whose account is rather matter of fact, Herdt (1981), who had the advantage of witnessing initiations and talking with participants, discussed the meaning of these practices to the boys who conduct them. We summarize his account:

Although the younger boys often have to be pressured into performing, once they get accustomed to it they do not object, and some enjoy it. Most adolescents, who are the fellated, enjoy it very much, often engaging in it with any appropriate initiate. After they marry, to girls not yet mature, they continue to be fellated by the smaller boys at the same time that their little wives are also fellating them, since young girls as well as boys need semen in order to grow. Once the wives reach menarche, or at least by the first birth, men give up fellatio and restrict their activity to vaginal intercourse—to do otherwise would be considered odd, and only a few cases were reported to Herdt about men who continue in homosexual practices. Most men claim to prefer coitus.

Not surprisingly, this and similar information on ritual homosexual activities caused a sensation when it first appeared. It indicated that early homosexual behavior, even when approved and enthusiastically practiced and enjoyed, did not necessarily imprint the sexual proclivities of the mature years. Even though the Sambia consider women dangerous and polluting—much of the initiatory ritual is to remove female contamination and create masculinity through the "milk" of males, the semen—they are not sexually inhibited toward them; nor do most Sambia men prefer sex with other men, although a few do and there is certainly experience in it and the opportunity for it. Except for a brief period between the wife's menarche and the birth of the first child, most men do not even behave bisexually and appear to see little attraction in doing so.

Herdt was primarily concerned to make explicit the symbolic system that incorporates homosexual activities. In a penetrating analysis of institutionalized homosexuality, which included a discussion of Herdt's book, Creed (1982) pointed out that symbolic analyses of the subject have overlooked the power dimension. He proposed that these systems, whereby older males dominate younger ones sexually as well as socially, are extreme cases of sex and age hierarchy: men over women, and seniors over juniors. (This criticism is more applicable to those societies in which adult men are fellated than those, like the Sambia, who restrict fellatio to adolescent boys.) It appears highly plausible that when male gender dominance over women is expressed as sexual dominance and through metaphors of sexual penetration, it is but a short step to the expression of men's dominance over other men through homosexual acts, the dominant partner always taking the inseminator role. It is certainly the case that the sexual lives of adolescent and prepubertal boys in these societies with ritual homosexual activity are highly controlled. Homosexual acts between adult men and adolescent boys have been noted in militaristic states such as the African Azande and among ancient Greek and Germanic peoples (Dumézil 1967). A study of sexual and social dominance over boys, when man-boy or youth-boy sexual relations are institutionalized, would be timely.

The most common kinds of homosexual relations reported for adolescents in the sample are of a casual, transient nature. In virtually all cases, if homosexual relations are tolerated or permitted for one sex they are for the other as well (Table 7.9). There are 13 societies with information on boys but not on girls. In general, as more information on all subjects is available for boys than for girls, we believe that the concordance would approach 100 percent if full information were available on girls. The two exceptions of which we are aware are the Papago, Indians of the American Southwest, who tolerate these relations for boys but do not recognize them as occurring among girls, and the Chiricahua of the same general region, who tolerate them for girls but prohibit them to boys, except for berdaches (transvestites, discussed later).

In most instances, homosexual relations appear to be a substitute for heterosexual intercourse when intercourse is prohibited or access to girls is problematic. The Nyakyusa, who do permit adolescents to have heterosexual relations, are an example of the latter. Wilson (1963:87–88) stated:

Homosexual practices are said to be very common in the boys' villages—they begin among boys of ten to fourteen herding cows, and continue

*Table 7.9* Homosexual Behavior Comparing Boys and Girls

|  | Girls | |
|  | --- | --- |
|  | *prohibited* | *permitted* |
| *Boys* | | |
| prohibited | 8 | 1 |
| permitted | 0 | 15 |
|  | Fisher's Exact Test $p < .001$ | |

Note: *Prohibited* means coded as prohibited. *Permitted* means tolerated or expected. Societies where homosexuality is coded as unrecognized are omitted.

among young men until marriage, but they are said never to continue after that, and are regarded simply as a substitute for heterosexual pleasure. . . . If a boy's own father, or a village father, finds a son with another youth he will beat him, but provided both parties were willing, there is no court case, and the older men treat the practice tolerantly as a manifestation of adolescence.

These relations among the Nyakyusa generally take the form of interfemoral intercourse, also the common form of sexual activity with adolescent girls.

As permissiveness toward homosexuality shows no significant association with either permissiveness or restrictiveness in heterosexual relations, it cannot be said to be an indication of general sexual permissiveness or restrictiveness. Nor is such an attitude significantly associated with any of the features that might be thought to promote it, such as those that enhance strong male bonding like separation from the family, the importance of peer groups, the separation of male and female peer groups, or participation in military activities. (This last does not imply that a people are particularly bellicose; as we have seen in Chapter 5, it is most commonly in the simpler societies that adolescent boys go to battle.) Permissiveness toward homosexuality also shows no association with any of the measures of the father-son relationship: contact, subordination, intimacy, or conflict. In most cases, it appears to be a more or less tolerated substitute for heterosexual intercourse, a concession to the sexual desires of adolescents until they are socially ready for mature sex. It is what Gregersen (1982) labeled "youthful experimentation."

To address the question of whether there is an association between adolescent and adult homosexual activity, we assessed the relation between attitudes toward homosexual behavior among adolescent boys (using our data) and the attitudes toward adult male homosexuality and its frequency (using data from Broude and Greene 1980). As Table 7.10 shows, there are no cases in which homosexuality is permitted to adolescents but punished among

*Table 7.10* Attitudes toward Male Homosexual Behavior in Adolescence and Adulthood

|  | *Adolescence* | |
| --- | --- | --- |
|  | *prohibited* | *permitted* |
| *Adulthood* | | |
| tolerated | 1 | 9 |
| punished | 4 | 0 |
|  | Fisher's Exact Test $p$ = .005 | |

Source: Broude and Greene 1980.

adults. In the societies that prohibit homosexual behavior by adolescents, only one (Trobrianders) tolerates it among adult men. Frequency of adult homosexuality shows no association whatsoever with attitudes toward homosexual behavior in adolescent boys. While the number of cases is very small, these findings suggest that tolerance toward adolescent homosexual activity goes with tolerance of adult male homosexuality. However, the majority of the societies that tolerate adult homosexuality actually disapprove of it, indicating that they regard adolescent homosexuality as a harmless outlet for boys' sexual urges but as inappropriate to adult life.

Contrasting with this casual kind of homosexuality is the institutionalized role of the recognized homosexual assumed by the occasional man in certain societies. Although the North American Indian berdache or transvestite was by no means always a homosexual, he (or rarely she) often was, and this role transition frequently began in adolescence. That is the case for the Chiricahua noted above. A similar sort of institutionalized homosexual role was available to Tahitian men: the *mahu,* a male homosexual transvestite recognized by these Polynesian people, seems also to have made his role change in adolescence (Levy 1973).

We have asserted that lovers, not parents, are the enemies of the peer group. That assumption may have to be qualified when the sexual partners are of the same sex. In a cross-cultural study of adolescent initiation ceremonies (Schlegel and Barry 1980b), we discussed the promotion of solidarity among those who go through the ceremony together. Although the age range within an initiation cohort is variable across cultures, in most cases the range is rather small and the set of initiates consists of age peers. Boys are initiated in groups in more than half of the societies with information, whereas girls are single initiates in 87 percent of the cases (Schlegel and Barry 1980a). Initiation ceremonies are one, although by no means the only, way of inducing solidarity and gender consciousness in adolescent boys. In those societies that put boys through a ceremony, adults are more likely to accept their adolescent homosexual behavior and less likely to prohibit it than in those that do not (Table 7.11). (For girls, the relation between attitude toward girls'

*Table 7.11* Adolescent Initiation Ceremonies and Boys' Homosexual Behavior

|  | Homosexual Behavior | | |
| --- | --- | --- | --- |
|  | prohibited | tolerated | accepted |
| *Ceremony* | | | |
| absent | 11 | 12 | 5 |
| present | 2 | 1 | 7 |
| Mantel-Haenszel $\chi^2 = 5.57$ | | $p = .018$ | |

homosexual behavior and girls' ceremonies is in the same direction but short of significance: $p = .139$). We are not suggesting that male solidarity promotes homosexuality—we do not have the data to make that claim—but rather that there is more acceptance of adolescent homosexuality when male solidarity is valued and encouraged.

## Sexual Abuse of Adolescents

Adolescent sexuality has been painted here as generally lighthearted, leading in some cases to despondence over unrequited passion or frustrated love but rarely having more serious consequences. There is a darker side, however, of adolescent (or even younger) girls as the sexual objects of older men, against their will. It is difficult to find information on this subject, because it is part of the hidden side of social life. Usually there is only anecdotal information. Instances of abuse are reported from societies in which women are sexually subordinate, that is, men control women's sexual activities and "benevolent" control can be perverted into brutality. Homosexual abuse is also not unknown.

One must be cautious in making assumptions about the disturbing effects of sexual experience on very young girls, a suggestion to the contrary coming from early accounts of marriage among Australian Aboriginal peoples of Arnhem Land. Infant girls were betrothed to young men who "grew up" their young wives, providing them with food and paying a good deal of affectionate attention to them. Sometime before menarche, after their breasts had begun to develop, the girls joined their husbands, with whom they were thoroughly familiar. It was believed that this long and affectionate acquaintance gave rise to a deep attachment, particularly on the part of the girl (cf. Burbank 1987). Under such conditions, even prepubertal sexual relations with an adult man were probably not traumatic or even unpleasant.

Adolescent girls, like adult women, might be raped. It is not easy to get information, but there are some scattered accounts. According to Henry (1964), rape by an adult man is the usual introduction to sex for young girls of the Kaingang of tropical Brazil. In spite of this, these girls grow up to be sexually assertive women who take on a number of lovers. No mention is made of their attitude toward men in general or those who raped them. We are not told whether this rape is violent, whether girls are prepared for it, or what the relation is between the rapist and the girl, so it is wise to be cautious in judging the trauma of the experience.

A culturally accepted practice that can cause severe physical and emotional distress and long-lasting bitterness is gang rape, the punishment in a number of tribal societies for females who have violated a cultural proscription. The Mehinaku of central Brazil, for example, thus treat a woman or girl who has accidentally seen the men's sacred flutes (Gregor 1985). Gang-rape for another purpose is resorted to by the Kimam, mentioned earlier, and the victim is frequently an adolescent girl. Serpenti's (1977) account is summarized here.

> The Kimam believe that semen has the power to give life and is needed by the sick to be cured and by young boys in order to grow. Women, and very often young girls, are selected as the vessels for the collection of the semen that will later be rubbed on the bodies of those deemed to require it. When the time comes, as many as 10 to 15 men take away the girl, who is not supposed to resist, and have intercourse with her. Everyone else pretends to be ignorant of what is happening. The early mission reports indicate that girls were often absent from school for a number of days due to illness following this treatment.

We simply have no idea of how much rape of adolescent girls occurs where virginity is highly valued, as in Latin America or the Muslim nations, particularly rape by relatives like uncles or older cousins who have more contact with girls than unrelated boys and men do. Incidents are reported, but there is no way, to our knowledge, of estimating frequency. In such cases, the family usually hushes it up, to protect both the allegedly virginal status of the girl and the reputations of the man and the family.

A final bleak addition to the sexual abuse to which adolescents may be subjected is the use of young people as prostitutes. Child and adolescent prostitution has not been a subject of much ethnographic investigation until recently, and accounts of it in the older literature tend to be incidental. Korbin (1987) summarized and gave references to much of the current research on child sexual abuse, including prostitution in such traditional states as Thailand, Turkey, and prerevolutionary China. This abuse is not foreign to Europe and the United States, either: adolescent prostitutes of both sexes are on view to anyone who walks the streets of our large cities. With no marketable skills to offer, these unfortunate young runaways or "throwaways" have only their bodies to sell.

---

All the evidence leads to the conclusion that permissiveness toward heterosexual intercourse by adolescent girls in preindustrial societies is heavily influenced by two factors. The first is the age of marriage. When marriage follows closely upon menarche, girls are often allowed to enjoy their sexuality to the fullest extent. The second is the presence and type of property transferral. If no property accompanies marriage, there are likely to be few sexual restrictions. Restrictions are found to be more often associated with property exchanges and become predominant when status is an important consideration in the marriage. Both of these factors are related to premarital pregnancy. Parents are less worried about daughters' pregnancy when experience has shown that no or few girls get pregnant. Parents are very concerned, however, if a daughter's pregnancy could result in a paternity and marriage claim by an undesirable son-in-law. Although we did not ask about abortion, some of the ethnographies do give accounts of girls resorting to it, as among the Haitians and the Muria. Considering the danger of abortion under primitive medical conditions, it can only be considered a backup to other precautions, of which abstinence is the most certain.[5]

Our evidence indicates that the double standard is rare at the adolescent stage. This is a curious finding, because the double standard is so widespread for adults, most societies being more tolerant of male than of female adultery. We ask: if boys were permitted to have sex but girls were not, whom would the boys seek out for sexual partners? When prostitutes are available, boys can be directed to them. In societies divided by rank or class, elite boys, not having access to girls of their own status, may turn to lower-status girls. This may be somewhat condoned, as it was in Samoa, where the child of a low-ranking girl by an elite boy could be an asset to its family as a claim on the father's favor. Alternatively, it may be deeply resented by lower-status parents trying to protect the reputations (and possible upward mobility) of their own daughters, as in much of Europe and America. If neither prostitutes nor other females were available to adolescent boys, sexual permissiveness for boys but not for girls would encourage boys to seek out the wives of adult men. Men are hardly likely to allow a double standard for adolescents if their wives would be the objects of seduction.

There is no evidence from our study that permissiveness or restrictiveness *per se* have much effect on personality features. Neither competitiveness nor aggressiveness show any relation to the frustration or satisfaction of sexual desires. Girls tend to be more subordinate to their mothers in restrictive societies, which we interpret as an indication of parental watchfulness over the daughter's virginity. Subordination does not, however, seem to affect the level of intimacy or conflict between mother and daughter.

While adolescents in permissive societies can legitimately satisfy their sexual desires, they are not necessarily freer of conflicts or anxieties over sex than are adolescents in restrictive ones. Partners are in theory available, but getting one, or the right one, may not be easy. We have seen the distress of disappointed Muria adolescents, and how Nyakyusa boys resort to homosexual acts for lack of access to girls in their permissive setting. Sexual intimacy can only increase the attachment to a special friend and thus make jealousy, despondence over a breakup, or the pain of unrequited love even harder to bear. In permissive societies there can be a conflict between attachment to the lover and bonds to peers, and adolescents who love each other may face the censure of their peers and the disapproval of their elders.

The ethnographic information makes it clear that there are several varieties of homosexual experience, with different causes and consequences. The form most commonly reported is the very casual sort, which is seen as a substitute for heterosexual intercourse. There is no evidence that this bespeaks, or leads to, a preference for homosexuality or even to the performance of homosexual acts in adulthood. Nor does the institutionalized homosexuality of some New Guinea societies seem to result in a preference for such relations, although we need information on more societies on this question. Permissiveness toward homosexuality does allow the individual with a homosexual preference to express that preference, which he or she cannot do, or can do only clandestinely, when homosexuality is prohibited.

It would seem, thus, that homosexual acts among our own adolescents should be regarded with tolerance. It is particularly unwise to label a young person a homosexual for youthful experimentation or for turning to members of the same sex because he or she is too shy and socially awkward to approach one of the opposite sex. There is no evidence here to suggest that people are "by nature" bisexual; it appears that even when homosexuality is not restricted, most people prefer heterosexuality. The tolerance that modern society is finally beginning to show toward homosexual persons should also be extended to those adolescents who are not by preference homosexual but who occasionally engage in a homosexual act.[6]

Other findings about adolescent sexuality across cultures are also relevant to contemporary Western society. Given the absence of property exchanges at marriage, along with alternatives to abstinence for preventing pregnancy, it is understandable that Europeans and Americans have become tolerant toward premarital sexuality (cf. Schlegel 1991). It is unlikely that an earlier morality could be reinstituted, even if that were deemed desirable. A sensible course of action in a world in which young adolescent mothers and their children are highly disadvantaged and sexually transmitted diseases are a serious threat to health and even life would be to educate our young people to be responsible about their sexual freedom and to induce them to take precautions against pregnancy and disease. The success of the Kikuyu in preventing pregnancy, using the girls' pubic apron as a sort of external diaphragm, indicates that socialization for responsibility can work.

# Ȣ

---

# Violating Cultural Norms

---

A major topic of research on adolescence has been social and psychological deviance, particularly in the form of delinquency. In this chapter we address some types of violation of behavioral norms and examine some of the antecedent and current conditions in the lives of adolescents that seem conducive to such deviance. We emphasize three areas for which there is good information: antisocial behavior; sexual license, or deviance from the cultural ideal of sexual behavior; and running away as a means of escape from stressful situations.[1]

Deviant behavior is, by definition, behavior that departs from what is generally accepted as appropriate. It may be tolerated, mildly punished, or severely sanctioned. Cross-cultural research forces us to be very specific in defining what is and is not appropriate; inducing a trance may be deviant in contemporary America but quite normal in many other societies; in other places, responding to a grave insult with fisticuffs indicates a pathological lack of self control. Therefore, deviance must be defined cross-culturally as violation of a particular society's standard of appropriate behavior, not from some arbitrary standard based implicitly on our own expectations and values.

A problem for researchers is how to interpret a high degree of deviance. On the one hand, it could represent disregard of norms; on the other, it could indicate changing norms, such as the increasing openness about sex among American and European adolescents. What was considered deviant 40 or 50 years ago is accepted by many today as normative.

For our purpose, antisocial behavior is defined by community standards. We are concerned with *expected* antisocial behavior, not the occasional deviant who is probably found everywhere. Expectations vary from culture to culture. If a sizeable proportion of adolescents are observed to commit antisocial acts and if people acknowledge that a number of adolescents behave in this way (always hoping their children will not), we coded the presence of expected or regular antisocial behavior. This is the case for the

United States, in which theft and violence, while deplored, are expected and observed to be committed by a significant number of adolescents. We would code expected antisocial behavior as present in this nation.

Antisocial behavior is not always so disruptive as it is among modern urban peoples, who seem to be at the high end of the continuum. For example, among the Basques, for whom the difficult age (*la edad defícil*) is between 14 and 18 for boys, Caro Baroja (1944:137) described it thus:

> Esta edad es la más desdichada de todas. Es cuando el chico quiere paracer hombre, y para romper su natural timidez se finge el borracho, aunque no haya bebido más que agua cristalina; quiere hacer chistes y cae en patoso; es grosero con las chicas, porque no sabe ser galante, y tiene instintos dañinos, residuos de la infancia, contra plantas y animales. (This age is the most miserable of all. It is when the boy wishes to appear manly and to cover his natural timidity he feigns drunkenness, even though he has drunk nothing more than plain water. He wants to be funny but falls flat. Not knowing how to be gallant, he is boorish to the girls. He is childishly destructive of plants and callous toward animals. [Trans. A.S.])

The boy may be irritating to his elders, but his antisocial behavior would not be considered delinquent under American or European law.

Most ethnographies concentrate on the social norms, and deviance is poorly documented. Nevertheless, we were able to make judgments about expected deviance in a substantial number of societies. We could identify characteristics of societies in which particular types of deviance are present or absent and compare features of societies that have one but not another form of deviance.

Deviance is often thought to be less frequent or less intense in tribal societies that are more homogeneous and socially cohesive than are modern industrial states. There may be some truth to that; the scarcity of information on serious deviance in the ethnographies of many such societies may reflect reality. Nevertheless, without better direct evidence, such an assumption is unwarranted and tends to romanticize the little community. In the small-scale society in which the first author did fieldwork, the Hopi, it was recognized in earlier times that adolescent boys sometimes behaved badly, mainly by destroying property. This was in a society renowned for its emphasis on social harmony and its suppression of violent acts and angry words.

## Antisocial Behavior

Antisocial behavior includes such diverse activities as hostile speech, fighting or crimes against persons, theft, sexual misbehavior (as socially defined), destruction of property, and drunkenness or misuse of other drugs (as socially defined). There is direct information about expectations of antisocial behavior by adolescent boys in 54 societies, present in 24 and absent in 30 (Table 8.1). There is less information about girls, for whom such an expectation is coded present in six societies, absent in 28. Reliable differences between these categories of societies are difficult to demonstrate for girls because of the small number of cases coded present, although the sample for boys is adequate to permit testing.

In all but one of the 30 societies in which this expectation is coded absent for boys, it is coded absent for girls as well. In one society (Tiwi) it is coded present for girls and absent for boys. In four societies (Abkhaz, Burmese, Trobrianders, and Cubeo) it is coded present for both sexes. In one society (Hadza) it is coded present for girls but information on boys is lacking. In the remaining 20 societies listed in Table 8.1, in which the expectation is present for boys, there is no information on girls.

There may be several reasons for the scarcity of information on girls: inattention to girls' antisocial behavior by the ethnographer, failure to report observations of such behavior, or true absence of this expectation, the ethnographer neglecting to mention that such behavior is not expected. As we shall discuss further, we believe that the last of these reasons provides a plausible explanation for many of the "no information" cases.

Among the 24 societies in which boys' antisocial behavior is expected, it takes the form of theft in nine, physical violence in seven, verbal abuse in four, sexual activity in three, drug use in two, destruction of property in one, and "other" (a residual category) in six. These different forms add up to more than 24 because in several cases two or more forms were identified for the same society. Among the six societies in which girls' antisocial behavior is expected, sexual activity is the form in three, theft in one, physical violence in one, and "other" in two. In addition to the cases coded present, there is evidence of theft, violence, or sexual deviance in some societies that either do not expect deviance or on which information on expectation is lacking.

## The Social Setting

In the large majority of societies, same-sex adult kin are the principal companions of adolescents of both sexes. The first two variables of Table 8.2 refer to adult companions. In most cases, the adult men (first variable) are fathers, and the adult men who are principal companions outside the home (second variable) are kinsmen. The findings indicate that deviance from this pattern is associated with deviance from social norms. This is also true for the following variable: in most societies, productive work is the principal skill area in which adolescents are trained.

We thus infer that the majority of societies select socializing agents and locations that are conducive to adolescent conformity (discussed further in Chapter 9). We also infer that the negative association between regular anti-

***Table 8.1*** Antisocial Behavior Expected in Adolescent Boys[a]

| *Present (N = 24)* | *Absent (N = 29)* | *Not coded (N = 10)[b]* |
|---|---|---|
| Bambara | !Kung Bushmen | Nyakyusa (S-B) |
| Fur | Ashanti | Turks (V) |
| Masai (T) | Songhai | Basseri (S-G) |
| Amhara | Hausa (S-G)[b] | Balinese (S-B) |
| Rwala Bedouin | Azande (V) (S-B)[b] | Fijians (V) |
| | | |
| Basques (V) | Teda | Kaska (V) |
| Lapps (T) | Egyptians | Wadadika (V) (S-B, G) |
| Abkhaz (T) | Uttar Pradesh | Callinago (T) |
| Burmese | Lakher | Yanomamo (T) |
| Alorese (T) (V) | Lamet | Mundurucu (S-G) |
| | | |
| Kapauku (T) | Vietnamese | |
| Trobrianders (S-B, G) | Rhade | |
| Siuai | Andamanese | |
| Ingalik (T) (S-B) | Tanala | |
| Gros Ventre (T) | Negri Sembilan | |
| | | |
| Hidatsa (V) | Javanese | |
| Omaha (V) | Tiwi (S-B, G) | |
| Creek (V) | Kimam | |
| Huichol (V) | Tikopia | |
| Aztec (T) (S-B, G) | Pentecost | |
| | | |
| Quiche (T) (S-B) | Samoans (S-B) | |
| Goajiro | Yapese | |
| Cubeo (V) (S-B, G) | Palauans | |
| Nambicuara | Ifugao | |
| | Yukaghir | |
| | | |
| | Slave | |
| | Comanche | |
| | Zuni | |
| | Warrau | |
| | Lengua | |

[a]Where one of the three following types of antisocial behavior is reported for boys, the type is indicated: violence (V), theft (T), and sexual deviance (S-B). It is also indicated where girls show sexual deviance (S-G).

[b]In these societies, antisocial behavior is not expected or there is no information. However, when such behavior is mentioned, it is of the type indicated.

*Table 8.2* The Social Setting of Adolescent Boys and Their Expected Antisocial Behavior

|  | N | r | p |
|---|---|---|---|
| *Relations with adults* |  |  |  |
| Adult men are principal companions | 50 | −.36 | .024 |
| Adult men are principal companions outside the home | 42 | −.43 | .014 |
| Productive work is principal skill area | 48 | −.59 | <.001 |
| *Relations with peers* |  |  |  |
| Principal peer activity is leisure | 44 | −.37 | .033 |
| Peer competition is high | 37 | .36 | .029 |
| Peer group has a name | 25 | .51 | .020 |

social behavior and the variables related to adult companionship signifies that boys are less likely to misbehave when they are included in adult society. (As productive work by adolescents in this sample is in most societies done in or near the home, that variable indirectly measures activities with the family and socialization by older family members.) The first variable related to peers supports this conclusion, for antisocial behavior is more likely to be expected when peer groups have names, that is, when they are institutionalized.

We also see that misbehavior is less likely when leisure is the principal activity of the peer group. This variable reflects the same social dynamic as the productive work variable, that is, most activities in which the adolescent is engaged are in the company of adults.

In our discussion of peer activities in Chapter 5, we noted that antisocial behavior is more likely when adolescent boys are organized into groups that engage in religious or military activities. This association challenges the popular belief that getting adolescents to do something worthwhile, as determined by adults, is a sure way to keep them occupied in good works and out of mischief. The reverse seems more likely (cf. Table 5.7). We interpret misbehavior as a consequence of time spent with adolescents away from adult companionship, rather than the direct result of peer activities. It is the setting more than the form of the activities that appears to influence how they behave.

The nature of adolescent interaction has consequences for social deviance. Competitiveness is high when antisocial behavior is expected. We should note that status competition is less likely in mixed-age groupings like the family: there the lower status of adolescents compared to adults is given, and adolescents have no incentive to compete with adults for status because to do so would be pointless. In the more egalitarian peer groups, status competition can arise, even to the point at which fighting breaks out or boys steal to acquire more goods than their age mates.

We find no association between boys' antisocial behavior and intimacy with either the father or the mother. Thus, there is no evidence that antisocial behavior in these societies is a protest against parental distance or lack of warmth. There is also no evidence that boys' antisocial behavior is associated with heightened conflict with either parent.

To summarize, in this sample, antisocial behavior is less likely when adolescent boys are more in the company of adults, more likely when peer groups have organized activities and peer relations are unusually competitive.

As we pointed out in Chapter 4, adolescents in most preindustrial societies spend much of their time with their families and with same-sex adults. Expected antisocial behavior is most often found in communities whose social settings deviate from the norm. For this reason, we feel confident that adolescent antisocial behavior is not likely to be a regular feature of most of the societies in this sample for which there is no information; that is, it is limited rather than widespread.

We can ask why some societies are organized in ways that appear to promote adolescent misbehavior. A certain amount of deviance may be carried by a society, no matter how much it is deplored, because the conditions that lead to it are not recognized or to correct them would be too costly or would disrupt other arrangements. For example, it may be advantageous to the domestic economy to have adolescent boys working apart from adults and out of their supervision. For various reasons, boys may be thrown in the company of other boys much of the time, resulting in aggressive or otherwise antisocial acts.

Such is the case for the African Masai, whose adolescent boys herd cattle. Boys are suspected sometimes of stealing cattle to add to their own herds. For the Abkhaz of the Soviet Union, whose boys also spend much time together, theft is such a central feature of economic and political life that boys are trained to steal. However, sometimes this thievery is turned against community members and even other peers, and then it is punished. Temptation and opportunity join to make theft possible and attractive. Gros Ventre boys, roaming in packs, are also expected to steal, robbing women of meat placed on drying racks. This is tolerated by these Indians of the North American Plains even though it is not approved.

Among the Aztecs of pre-Columbian Mexico, prepubescent and adolescent boys spend much of their time in school (see Chapter 9). The great chronicler of the Aztec people shortly after the conquest, Fray Bernardino de Sahagún, recorded the following observation (translated from the Aztec into English, with annotations from Sahagún's Spanish translation, by Dibble and Anderson 1961:12, 13, and 87):

The bad boy [is] always inhuman, incorrigible, disloyal, corrupt, perverse. He flees constantly; [he is] a thief; he lies; he does evil, is perverse.

The bad youth goes about becoming crazed; [he is] dissolute, mad; he goes about mocking, telling tales, being rude, repeating insults.

The lewd youth is a madman. He goes about drinking crude wine—a drunkard, foolish, dejected; a drunk, a sot. He goes about eating mushrooms. . . . [He is] vain, proud, debauched; a pleasure seeker, a libertine—revolting, filthy, vicious, a keeper of mistresses; a talker. He lives in concubinage; he is given to pleasure.

From this unflattering picture, we can see that some Aztec boys are liars, thieves, runaways, tale bearers, consumers of alcohol and hallucinogenic mushrooms, and libertines, all misdemeanors for which they are severely punished. Girls are very closely guarded by at least the noble and "respectable" families, so it must be to wayward daughters of the lower classes that the following description applies:

The bad maiden [is] one who yields herself to others—a prostitute, a seller of herself, dishonored, gaudy. She goes about shamelessly, presumptuously, conspicuously washed and combed, pompously.

From the evidence in Table 8.2 and the illustrative cases, we draw the conclusion that some degree of antisocial behavior is predictable in our society and in any that draws youngsters from the company of adults into the company of other adolescents for many of their waking hours.

## Antisocial Behavior and Features of Adolescence

The findings reported in Table 8.3 show that many demands are made upon adolescents whose antisocial behavior is a regular occurrence. Adolescence is recognized as a sharp break from childhood. Adolescence itself is characterized by new roles in the family and community, which contribute to the break from childhood. Adolescents own productive property, thus receiving strong pressure to behave responsibly. New roles in family and community exert similar pressures. The result can be a conflict between compliance and assertion.

It is in adolescence that adult character is established, putting pressure on boys to behave maturely. Furthermore, boys have considerable opportunity to choose a spouse, thus adding the need for them to make a critical decision about their future along with the potential for anxiety and frustration that accompany real or feared rejection. This decision and others affecting their future must be made within a rather short period of time, as adolescence ends early.

Finally, adolescent antisocial behavior is found in conjunction with de-

*Table 8.3* Characteristics of Adolescent Boys and Their Expected Antisocial Behavior

|                                                  | N   | r   | p       |
| ------------------------------------------------ | --- | --- | ------- |
| *Adolescence as a new stage*                     |     |     |         |
| Sharp break from childhood                       | 54  | .37 | .007    |
| *Characteristics of adolescence*                 |     |     |         |
| New roles in the family                          | 25  | .65 | .001    |
| New roles in the community                       | 34  | .50 | .006    |
| Ownership of productive property                 | 37  | .44 | .008    |
| High degree of opportunity to own property       | 30  | .52 | .005    |
| *Anticipation of adulthood*                      |     |     |         |
| Adult character established in adolescence       | 52  | .49 | < .001  |
| High degree of opportunity to choose spouse      | 52  | .38 | .006    |
| Early ending of adolescence                      | 54  | .26 | .060    |
| Antisocial behavior by adult men                 | 27  | .55 | .005    |

viant adult behavior. Deviant adults do not provide role models for conformity. A case of this type is the Alorese, a tribal people of the eastern Indonesian islands. DuBois (1944:62) related:

> The responsibility of boys for misdeeds, especially theft, is illustrated in a number of incidents in the autobiographies. Perhaps even more far-reaching in its implications is the inclination of people to blame any mishap, destruction, or theft on children. On several occasions when I complained of the theft or destruction of my property, I was answered with a shrug and the comment that boys must have done it and that therefore there was little chance of discovering the guilty one. Actually, in those instances that could be followed up adults were the real culprits.

When infractions are minor, it may be perceived as better all around to blame children and adolescents, known to be imperfectly socialized, than to identify the actual adult perpetrator, with unpleasant consequences far exceeding the magnitude of the offense. Adult lies and concealment of their own misdeeds lead to cynicism and do not help adolescents learn to control their antisocial impulses.

## Antecedents of Adolescent Antisocial Behavior

Expected antisocial behavior is likely when the socialization of infants and children tends to be more harsh than is commonly found (Table 8.4). Mother and infant do not share the same bed, the infant's movements are

*Table 8.4* Antecedents of Adolescence and Boys' Expected Antisocial Behavior

|  | N | r | p |
|---|---|---|---|
| *Infancy and early childhood* | | | |
| Mother and infant sleep apart | 27 | .50 | .005 |
| Bodily restrictiveness in later infancy | 36 | .35 | .036 |
| Child is trained by example[a] | 41 | .42 | .007 |
| Child is trained by gifts[a] | 46 | .39 | .009 |
| *Later childhood* | | | |
| Child is trained by example[a] | 41 | .47 | .003 |
| Child is trained by gifts[a] | 48 | .38 | .009 |
| Child is trained by lecturing[a] | 40 | .42 | .009 |
| Fortitude is inculcated | 44 | .35 | .021 |

[a]This indicates not only the mode of training but also the intensity with which it is administered, that is, frequent showing by example, giving of gifts, or lecturing.

restricted, and fortitude is inculcated in the older child. This sort of socialization is neither permissive nor indulgent.

The measures for socialization in infancy and early childhood were independently coded for this sample (Barry and Paxson 1980; Barry et al. 1980a). Several direct techniques for child socialization were coded; they include training by example, training by public opinion, training by lecturing, teasing, scolding, warning, corporal punishment, rewarding with ceremonies, and rewarding with gifts. Two of these variables show a strong association with the presence of regular antisocial behavior: a high reliance on training by example and by gifts. A high reliance on training by lecturing is also significant in later childhood.

When children are frequently lectured or shown how to do things, they are not allowed to discover the world for themselves. Rather, they are constantly under pressure by adults to perform well. This does not make for a permissive environment. These findings support the others in this table related to permissiveness. Training children through the use of gifts rewards the good behavior but does not punish the bad.

In addition to the intensity of training, it is likely that these modes are not very effective in stopping antisocial behavior in childhood, thus setting the stage for antisocial behavior in adolescence. In a study of "problem" boys age two to 15, the large majority between five and 12, Patterson (1982) examined various methods of punishment. He found that lecturing (rule-giving) alone, without a backup punishment, is largely ineffective when dealing with antisocial children. Example and gifts may be equally ineffective in stopping misbehavior. If antisocial behaviors are not checked in childhood, they can persist into adolescence. In some of the societies with expected anti-social behavior, those boys who misbehave may be the products of child so-cialization that failed.

## Varieties of Expected Antisocial Behavior

The two most frequently reported forms of antisocial behavior are theft and physical violence (Table 8.1). They correspond to the distinction be-tween theft and personal crimes included in a cross-cultural study of crime by adults, coded for a different sample (Bacon et al. 1963). These are also the forms that we consider the most troublesome in modern society. Analyses in our study indicate under which conditions these types of behavior are most likely to be found among adolescents.

Adolescent violence in this sample is rarely life-threatening. Among the Amhara of Ethiopia, for example, physical aggression is the result of verbal aggression that gets out of hand. The Amhara consider the appropriate use of insult and mockery to be a form of verbal art, and adolescent boys are learning to become adept at this as they disparage and taunt one another. Although fights do not generally occur among adult men, mockery and in-sult among boys can lead to shoving and wrestling.

When weapons are involved, adolescent violence is dangerous. Among the Huichol, Indians of northern Mexico, the adolescent boy is allowed to join the older men at feasts, where a considerable amount of alcohol is con-sumed. As Zingg (1938:127) described:

> He drinks too much at feasts, is too apt to insult his elders, sometimes going so far as to engage in fights and knife-play. Oftener than others, the youth sobers up with his feet in the stocks in the dark room of the *Casa Real.*

As indicated in Table 8.1, physical violence is a form of antisocial be-havior in seven societies in which antisocial behavior is expected. In addition, it is present in one society in which antisocial behavior is not expected and in four societies for which there is no information on the regularity of antisocial behavior. These 12 societies are compared with the remaining 50 societies for which regular antisocial behavior is coded either present or absent or for which theft or sexual deviance are reported present. The results are reported in Table 8.5.

Child socialization in these societies is neither indulgent nor permissive. There is low contact with the mother in infancy, and in later childhood there is strong training for self-restraint. This non-indulgent socialization may be an attempt to train children to conform, when the danger of violent behavior in adolescence is perceived. That total conformity is not achieved is indicated by antisocial behavior and lack of sexual restraint on the part of adult men.

Boys' peer activities are characterized by high competition and low co-

*Table 8.5* Violence as the Form of Boys' Antisocial Behavior

|  | N | r | p |
|---|---|---|---|
| *Antecedent socialization* | | | |
| Contact with mother in infancy | 44 | −.55 | <.001 |
| Self-restraint inculcated in early childhood | 51 | .29 | .040 |
| *Characteristics of adolescence* | | | |
| Peer competition is high | 42 | .47 | .002 |
| Peer cooperation is high | 40 | −.41 | .010 |
| Conformity is inculcated | 44 | −.33 | .032 |
| Trust is inculcated | 20 | −.59 | .011 |
| Competitiveness is inculcated | 39 | .36 | .028 |
| *Anticipation of adulthood* | | | |
| Choice of vocation | 31 | .55 | .003 |
| Adult men commit antisocial behavior | 31 | .44 | .015 |
| Adult men indulge in sexual license | 35 | .40 | .021 |
| Frequent deviance by adult men | 25 | .56 | .006 |

operation. Neither trust nor conformity is inculcated, although competitiveness is. Boys have before them the example of men who indulge in sexual license, engage in antisocial behavior, and rate high on frequency of deviance.

Societies in which some adolescent boys are expected to steal show a different constellation of features. Theft is the primary form of antisocial behavior in nine of the societies in which antisocial behavior is expected. Additionally, it is found in two societies without information on the regularity of antisocial behavior. These 11 cases are compared with the 51 remaining societies in which antisocial behavior is coded either present or absent or in which violence or sexual deviance is reported present. The results are reported in Table 8.6.

There is no evidence that infancy and childhood in these societies are particularly harsh. Beginning in childhood, importance is attached to material reward by means of training children through gift-giving. Aggressiveness is an inculcated character trait (to be discussed further in Chapter 9).

Adolescent boys are likely to own productive property, such as animals, but unlikely to receive much training in productive work. Thus, a desire for material reward is instilled, but there is little emphasis put on working for it. One obvious way of gaining desired objects without work is through theft. Leisure is not a principal peer group activity, suggesting that boys are spending more time together on activities other than just relaxing. Since

*Table 8.6* Theft as the Form of Boys' Antisocial Behavior

| | N | r | p |
|---|---|---|---|
| *Antecedent socialization* | | | |
| Training by example in early childhood | 48 | .35 | .016 |
| Training by example in later childhood | 48 | .31 | .032 |
| Training by gifts in later childhood | 51 | .28 | .046 |
| Aggressiveness is inculcated in later childhood | 52 | .32 | .021 |
| *Characteristics of adolescence* | | | |
| Opportunity for property | 34 | .36 | .037 |
| Productive work is principal skill area | 56 | −.36 | .013 |
| Principal peer activity is leisure | 50 | −.36 | .010 |
| *Anticipation of adulthood* | | | |
| Differentiation from adults in work is expected | 54 | .38 | .017 |

adolescents' work differs from that of adults, boys are not likely to be working alongside men.

Theft by adolescents is usually directed against the community rather than the family. In small communities where everyone is known and people are always about, much theft would have to be planned. It is therefore less likely than violence to be a spontaneous act.

Patterns of theft and violence are quite distinctive. Violence is always hostile, the infliction of harm on others; theft may be a disapproved way of gratifying wishes for ownership rather than necessarily a response to anger. The underlying impulses are different. A case-by-case analysis would show variation within these patterns; for example, the Gros Ventre "meat raid," committed by the peer group, appears to be of a different order from the clandestine individual theft of a cow by a Masai or a reindeer by a Lapp.

Patterson (1988) distinguished between violence and theft as different tracks in the misbehavior of American children. Working with ten-year-old boys in the Oregon Child Aggression project, Patterson and others found that many of the stealers, in contrast to the other antisocial children, follow "a sneaky aggression path that does not include fighting" (Patterson 1988:127). In an earlier study, Patterson (1982:262) found that the stealer tends not to have close ties with family members, who "did not want to be responsible for training him" and "are not attached to the role of parent." In our sample, boys who steal tend to be infrequently in the company of adults and family members. We are not suggesting that parents are indifferent to sons in places where boys steal, but there does appear to be a generally low level of contact and continuing socialization by adults in these cases. Intracultural variability in a large, complex society like the United States, with a multiplicity of socialization styles, has its counterpart in cross-cultural variability.[2]

Taken together, the findings on violence and theft do not suggest that expected antisocial behavior necessarily represents hostility toward parents or even toward the adult world generally. These forms are not associated with either a low level of intimacy or a high level of conflict with either parent in adolescence. Rather, they result from situations that stimulate impulsive behavior and the failure of early socialization in teaching how to control it.

Violence in almost all cases is directed either toward peers or toward persons outside the community; either adolescents do not wish to behave violently toward adults or children in the community, or such behavior is not allowed. When violence is directed toward peers, it may be deplored but tolerated: "boys will be boys." Since boys' fights rarely lead to death or permanent injury, adults may not think it important to prevent them. In our view, fights can best be interpreted as an extension of the competitive behavior fostered by social settings that emphasize relations with peers rather than adults, coupled with imperfect socialization for self-restraint. This impulsiveness, also seen in adult men's sexual license, is an ironic outcome for such rigid child socialization.

While thieving is most often from community members rather than peers or family—in fact, theft is sometimes committed by groups of adolescent boys—it need not be interpreted as hostility toward the community. There may be secret admiration of boys who steal successfully, as in the case of the Gros Ventre mentioned above: boys who steal meat will one day transfer their daring to the theft of horses from other bands. In such cases, adult ambivalence toward theft makes it clear to boys that stealing is tolerated if they can get away with it. Theft appears to be more of a device for getting the material possessions one has been trained to desire, without seeing the necessity to earn them, than an expression of alienation or hostility.

A further consideration is that in misbehaving, adolescent boys may be imitating the antisocial behavior of their elders. Of the 24 societies in which there is expected antisocial behavior by adolescent boys, in 17 cases boys are believed to misbehave more than men. Even in these 17 cases, antisocial behavior by men is often reported. To the determinative features of delinquency we have identified, we have to add socialization *for* antisocial behavior in some cases, those in which boys imitate men.

## Sexual Deviance

Only a few societies give clear evidence of sexual deviance in adolescence, 12 for boys and 8 for girls (Table 8.1). They are compared with the remaining 50 societies for boys and 32 societies for girls for which expected antisocial behavior of the same sex is coded either present or absent or for which violence or theft is coded present for the same sex.

Sexual deviance means that adolescents are violating the accepted standard of sexual behavior. We have already seen in Chapter 7 that the majority of societies permit sexual intercourse with other adolescents. Deviant behavior includes more than occasional sexual intercourse when this is prohibited, rape, homosexual behavior when this is prohibited, and sexual relations with forbidden partners such as married people.

Sanctions on sexual deviance may vary from mild, as when Nyakyusa elders ignore or mildly punish the homosexual play of boys (see Chapter 7), to shaming, beating, or even incarceration. Sexual offenses are just one of a list of misdemeanors for which adolescents may be imprisoned, at the request of their parents, in the Quiche Indian village of Chichicastenango, Guatemala. If boys have relations with prostitutes, the parents may lodge a complaint, and sexual affairs with Ladinas (non-Indian Guatemalan women) may be punished by whipping.

It is not adults, but rather other adolescents, who punish the sexual offenses of Trobriand Island young people. The following account of this Melanesian society is drawn from Malinowski (1932).

> Boys from one village will alert their secret girlfriends in another village that they are coming on a *ulatile,* an amorous expedition. As previously arranged, the girls go surreptitiously out to meet their lovers in the bush or at some pre-arranged meeting place. If the boys of the visited village detect this, they will try to chase the visitors away and fights might ensue. In former times, such fights could lead to war between the communities, as in those days the boys went armed.
>
> Girls have their expeditions as well, but these are public and, in theory, decorous. On some pretext, such as the desire to see a new yam house, the girls dress in their finery and go to visit a neighboring village. They sit openly in the village grove, where the entire community comes to sit facing them except for their rivals, the girls of the host village, who are sulking. After a time, each boy gets up and presents a small gift to the girl of his choice. The young people retire to some spot in the jungle, where they sing and chew betel nut—but no one remarks if a couple withdraws to a more private place. On returning home, the girls try to sneak into the village, for if their local boyfriends catch them, they may be abused or beaten, no matter how loudly they protest their innocence.

Social practices associated with sexual deviance are shown in Table 8.7. Only one antecedent condition emerges as significant for boys, training by involving children in ceremonies. For girls, training by rewarding with gifts is significant. These may not be effective ways of teaching self-control, as we have suggested earlier. The remaining antecedent conditions for girls are those that push toward social maturity: the inculcation of responsibility, industry, and most strongly, achievement. The most common form of sexual

*Table 8.7* Sexual Deviance as a Form of Antisocial Behavior

| | Boys | | | Girls | | |
|---|---|---|---|---|---|---|
| | N | r | p | N | r | p |
| *Antecedent socialization* | | | | | | |
| Training by gifts in early childhood | 49 | −.04 | — | 31 | .41 | .025 |
| Training by gifts in later childhood | 51 | −.11 | — | 31 | .37 | .040 |
| Training by ceremonies in later childhood | 55 | .30 | .028 | 32 | .17 | — |
| Responsibility inculcated in early childhood | 52 | .11 | — | 34 | .35 | .044 |
| Responsibility inculcated in later childhood | 56 | −.01 | — | 35 | .41 | .016 |
| Industry inculcated in later childhood | 60 | .09 | — | 37 | .35 | .037 |
| Achievement inculcated in later childhood | 55 | .05 | — | 32 | .56 | .002 |
| *Characteristics of adolescence* | | | | | | |
| Opportunity for current work | 55 | .34 | .013 | 36 | .33 | .051 |
| Choice of current work | 47 | .10 | — | 29 | .55 | .004 |
| General permissiveness | 51 | −.08 | — | 31 | −.51 | .005 |
| Opportunity for drug use | 43 | .36 | .020 | 24 | .27 | — |
| Achievement is inculcated | 30 | .42 | .025 | 15 | .29 | — |
| Contact with father | 51 | −.13 | — | 26 | .41 | .042 |
| *Anticipating adulthood* | | | | | | |
| Sexual license by adults | 35 | .60 | <.001 | 23 | .49 | .022 |

deviance for girls is disapproved sexual intercourse. Girls who have been encouraged to behave maturely, like women, may feel ready to assume adult privileges like sexual relations.

Opportunity for work means that there are many tasks that adolescents can do, while choice of work means that they can decide whether or not to do them. Girls' sexual deviance is strongly associated with choice of work, that is, girls have opportunities to do various productive activities and they can choose among them. This implies a measure of independence. However, a low level of general permissiveness is associated with sexual deviance. For boys, the opportunity to indulge themselves with drugs is related to physical indulgence in sexual behavior.

Contact with the father has opposite effects on girls and boys. A high degree of contact is positively related to girls' sexual deviance, negatively related to boys', although the latter is short of statistical significance. It is possible that when girls are in frequent contact with their fathers, they are less under the control of mothers and other female kin who are more likely to monitor their sexual behavior. Both sexes are likely to be sexually deviant when there is sexual license by adults.

## Adolescent and Adult Antisocial Behavior

Although the number of societies in which antisocial behavior is expected of adolescents is rather small, in quite a few at least one form of antisocial behavior appears to occur more among adolescents than among adults. For boys, there is more antisocial behavior in 32 societies, equal or less in 58. For girls, the figures are 19 and 64 respectively. This finding suggests that adolescence is commonly a period of less rather than of more misbehavior. Table 8.8, based on a composite subsample combining several measures of antisocial behavior, indicates the socialization features associated with greater occurrence of antisocial behavior in adolescence. Some of these are associated with expected antisocial behavior, such as features of antecedent socialization. We will comment on the new correlations.

More deviant behavior is found for boys than for men when adolescents are visually differentiated from adults. This is a measure of the distinctiveness of the adolescent stage, similar to another such measure, a sharp break from childhood (Table 8.3). The exclusion of younger children from recreational activities also emphasizes the distinctiveness of the adolescent stage.

Another feature is the inculcation of obedience in boys during adolescence, a continuation of socialization for this trait in childhood. It is likely that mothers are exerting pressure to comply, since boys have conflict with the mother but only in a few cases with the father. Greater antisocial behavior for boys than for men is here shown to be associated with low intimacy with the father. The pattern appears to be one in which fathers do not participate as strongly in the socialization of boys as do other adults, in many cases probably the mother. (In most of these societies, adolescents live in homes that contain both parents.) The implication of these results is that when the burden of socialization of adolescent boys falls most heavily on mothers, they are more likely to exert pressure for obedience and less likely to get it. In these societies, misbehaving boys are likely to receive corporal punishment, possibly because deviant behavior generally is not as tolerated as it is in societies in which adults often deviate from what is expected.

Only three features of adolescent life are significantly associated with a greater likelihood of misbehavior of girls than of women. First, this likelihood is found when girls have less contact with peers, suggesting that for girls, unlike boys, peers socialize for conformity to community standards. Second, there is conflict with the father, possibly as a result of the misbehavior, but there is no indication that this behavior leads to conflict with the mother. Third, a higher degree of girls' misbehavior is likely to occur when

***Table 8.8*** Deviance More Likely for Adolescents than for Same-Sex Adults[a]

| | Boys | | | Girls | | |
|---|---|---|---|---|---|---|
| | N | r | p | N | r | p |
| *Antecedent socialization* | | | | | | |
| Training by ceremonies in early childhood[b] | 66 | .27 | .032 | 63 | .17 | — |
| Training by ceremonies in later childhood[b] | 74 | .29 | .013 | 67 | .15 | — |
| Training by gifts in early childhood[b] | 71 | .35 | .003 | 68 | −.13 | — |
| Training by gifts in later childhood[b] | 74 | .36 | .002 | 72 | −.15 | — |
| Obedience inculcated in early childhood | 83 | .26 | .017 | 81 | .16 | — |
| Obedience inculcated in later childhood | 84 | .27 | .014 | 81 | .18 | — |
| *Characteristics of adolescence* | | | | | | |
| Differentiation from adults by visual markers | 55 | .44 | .003 | 62 | .01 | — |
| Corporal punishment | 37 | .44 | .022 | 36 | .30 | — |
| Low intimacy with father | 34 | .49 | .005 | 32 | −.05 | — |
| High conflict with mother | 19 | .56 | .018 | 29 | .17 | — |
| High conflict with father | 38 | .32 | .053 | 32 | .40 | .025 |
| Contact with peers | 69 | .04 | — | 54 | −.30 | .031 |
| Younger children excluded from recreational activities | 44 | .32 | .034 | 37 | .17 | — |
| High evaluation of adolescents of this sex | 58 | .17 | — | 57 | .28 | .037 |
| Obedience inculcated | 55 | .26 | .053 | 53 | .12 | — |

[a]Based on a composite subsample combining several measures comparing adolescents and adults for antisocial behavior.

[b]Indicates not only the mode of training but also the intensity with which it is administered, that is, frequent ceremonies or gift-giving.

girls are given a high evaluation, suggesting that fathers concern themselves more with daughters' misbehavior when the daughters are valued and that girls in such societies feel freer to misbehave.

## Running Away

Reversing the pattern of information on antisocial behavior and, indeed, on almost all other topics, there is more information for girls than for boys on running away, that is, escaping from difficult situations. It was coded present for girls in 22 societies and absent in 14, whereas for boys it was present in 17 societies and absent in 14 (Table 8.9). These figures imply that running away is resorted to more by girls than by boys. For most cases, there is information about both sexes rather than about only one, and the correlation between the sexes is very high.

Running away is highly correlated with other antisocial behavior; when one was coded absent, the other was seldom coded present. But in many societies, one was coded present or absent while there was insufficient information to code the other. Table 8.10 excludes those variables that are as strongly associated with regular antisocial behavior as with running away. In many

*Table 8.9* Societies with Information on Running Away

| Present[a] (N = 23) | Absent[a] (N = 15) |
| --- | --- |
| Bemba (G) | !Kung Bushmen |
| Hadza (G) | Luguru |
| Mbuti | Ashanti |
| Tiv | Azande |
| Tallensi | Kenuzi |
| | |
| Fur | Uttar Pradesh |
| Rwala Bedouin | Garo (G) |
| Gheg Albanians (G) | Tiwi |
| Kurds | Kimam (B) |
| Santal | Yapese |
| | |
| Burmese | Ifugao |
| Alorese (B) | Comanche |
| Kapauku (G) | Zuni |
| Siuai | Mundurucu |
| Tikopia | Aweikoma |
| | |
| Manchu | |
| Chukchee | |
| Ingalik | |
| Klamath | |
| Huichol (G) | |
| | |
| Quiche | |
| Abipon (G) | |
| Mapuche | |

[a]Unless otherwise indicated, coding applies to both sexes. Where indicated for one sex only (G = girls; B = boys), there is no information for the opposite sex.

*Table 8.10* Running Away

|  | Boys | | | Girls | | |
|---|---|---|---|---|---|---|
|  | N | r | p | N | r | p |
| *Antecedent socialization* | | | | | | |
| Infant and mother sleep apart | 25 | .42 | .073 | 28 | .54 | .006 |
| Inclusion in adult activities in early childhood | 29 | .49 | .009 | 33 | .28 | — |
| Responsibility inculcated in later childhood | 28 | .40 | .040 | 32 | .26 | — |
| Industry inculcated in later childhood | 30 | .38 | .038 | 35 | .24 | — |
| *Characteristics of adolescence* | | | | | | |
| Sharp break from childhood | 31 | .30 | — | 33 | .38 | .034 |
| High degree of separation from family | 31 | −.60 | .001 | 34 | −.21 | — |
| Adolescents take on new roles in family | 13 | .92 | .001 | 9 | .94 | .008 |
| Adolescents take on new roles in community | 25 | .45 | .079 | 18 | .71 | .004 |
| Adult character is established in adolescence | 30 | .51 | .009 | 31 | .55 | .005 |
| Adolescence ends later | 31 | −.49 | .008 | 36 | .02 | — |

cases, running away is what adolescents do to escape the consequences of their misbehavior.

As we have no information about children's running away, we do not know whether socialization results in a pattern of running away that is established prior to adolescence. It would not be surprising to find such a pattern. Girls are generally socialized for industry and responsibility; boys are to a lesser degree. Boys are less often under direct parental surveillance. When industry and responsibility are emphasized for boys, as indicated in Table 8.10, it appears that the boy is under more than usual constraint to meet a high level of performance, and he may be punished, reprimanded, or shamed if he fails to do so. Flight is one response as an escape from either restrictions or punishment.

Running away was observed by the first author among the Hopi in 1968. In earlier times, Hopi boys as young as four were given important duties, such as watching the donkey to keep it from getting into the cornfield. In more recent years, as well, there has been training for industry and responsibility throughout childhood. The following account is from Schlegel's 1968 field notes.

I had only been in the village a couple of days when a distraught neighbor came to ask if I had seen her eight-year-old son, with whom my son had been playing. Taking flashlights, we searched the village without success. The boy turned up safe the next day, having hidden in an outbuilding. His mother told me that this is not uncommon for young boys to do.

By adolescence, a Hopi boy has so much freedom of movement that there is no incentive to run away. He frequently sleeps away from home, and in times of family tension he can eat with kin without having to return home. For an adolescent girl, however, running away is a response to conflict with her mother, usually over restrictions placed on her. She typically takes refuge with a kinswoman, who encourages her to return home when all tempers have cooled down.

Adolescents in this sample are more likely to run away when adolescence is sharply differentiated from childhood or they are burdened with adult responsibilities. These features are associated with expected deviance in adolescence for boys (Table 8.3). Boys are unlikely to run away when there is considerable separation from the family, probably because they can readily absent themselves from stressful situations. Family conflicts that initiate flight may have to do with the assumption of new roles and the establishment of adult character, as family members exert pressure for conformity.

In a recent survey of psychological research on adolescence, Petersen (1988) cited studies linking running away in modern society with pervasive parent-child conflict. We find no such linkage, indicating that running away, in most of the communities in our sample, is a response to an immediate need rather than to long-standing bad feelings. For most of these adolescents, to run away is to absent themselves for a short time from the home, not to escape into anonymity. The meaning and consequences of running away differ in small-scale societies and large ones, in which escape can be permanent and can put the runaway into danger.

Fleeing is a sure way to avoid punishment in the short term. It helps in the longer term, too, if the adolescent can remain away until adult anger subsides. The close association of running away with the variables correlated with antisocial behavior suggests that flight is a measure taken to avoid punishment. It is also a way to avoid embarrassment. If the adolescent does not perform well in the new roles taken on in the family or the community, shame can impel the boy or girl to flee.

———

Antisocial behavior is not expected of adolescents in most societies of this sample; in fact, adulthood rather than adolescence appears to be the time in life when norms are more commonly violated. When such social deviance is expected, we have no way to know how common it is. As in Western society, it is likely to be a minority of adolescents who seriously misbehave.

Exceptions might be cases like the Gros Ventre, among whom antisocial behavior (in this case, theft) seems to be socialization for raiding, even though its victims are not happy about it. Societies in which antisocial behavior is expected socialize adolescents in ways different from the majority of societies in this sample. Thus, regular antisocial behaviors and their associated features appear in atypical preindustrial societies.

A feature associated with all forms of expected antisocial behavior is the removal of adolescent boys from the company of adult men. There are several ways of accounting for the regular occurrence of good behavior when boys are much involved with men and misbehavior when they are not. One explanation might be that boys, being marginal to adult activities, feel frustrated by their exclusion and act out their frustration aggressively. However, as we have seen, not all antisocial behavior is aggressive. While adolescent misbehavior of all kinds results from the failure to control impulses, these impulses can be acquisitive or sexual rather than aggressive. Furthermore, there is no independent evidence from this study that antisocial behavior expresses hostility toward the family or the community.

Another explanation is that adolescents, being imperfectly socialized, are predisposed to misbehave, and the supervision of adults keeps them in line. A variation of this explanation suggests not that adult supervision thwarts antisocial behavior but rather that adolescents who are often in the company of adults are motivated to control their impulses in order to win the approval of their principal companions and significant figures.

Neither of these latter two explanations is completely satisfactory. Expected antisocial behavior is not a feature only and always of societies in which boys are free from much adult supervision; furthermore, the association of misbehavior with other features of child and adolescent life indicates that the social setting is not the only influence. Although child socialization practices in many societies predispose some adolescents to antisocial acts, they will be committed only in social settings conducive to deviance.

An important feature of the social setting, reflected in various measures, is the nature of the boys' peer groups. When these groups are institutionalized or adolescents perform important activities with peers rather than with adults, there is likely to be regular antisocial behavior. We have seen in Chapter 5 that both cooperation and competition are characteristic of boys' peer groups. Boys compete with one another for scarce resources in the present and the future: positions of leadership, the attention of girls, eventual wives. At the same time, the group must cooperate in its daily activities and learn the balance of private interests with public good that characterizes harmonious adult relationships. Peer groups vary in accentuating competition and cooperation. When competition has the edge, antisocial behavior is likely to appear, violence rather than theft being the more usual form that such behavior takes. This is not surprising, since theft can be a cooperative group enterprise.

Another feature is the distinctiveness of adolescence. Adolescents who are sharply set off are discouraged from free interactions with adults (cf. Gadpaille 1984).

The stage for adolescent antisocial behavior is set in childhood, even as early as infancy. Greater than usual separation of mother and infant characterizes the fighters, but not the stealers, and also the runaway girls. These findings suggest that the early bonds of child and mother are weaker than they are in the majority of societies.

Generally lower permissiveness toward infants and children is associated with adolescent misbehavior, particularly physical aggression. It is possible that training primarily by lecturing, setting examples, or rewarding with gifts are not effective in dealing with children's misbehavior and do not redirect them toward more constructive forms. Rewarding with gifts characterizes the childhood socialization of stealers rather than fighters; this has been explained by the value on reward that is instilled without a concomitant value on earning it.

Unsurprisingly, antisocial behavior occurs among adolescents when it occurs among adults. Part of the adult character established in adolescence in these societies is a tendency toward misbehavior. Adolescent violence, a physically impulsive form, is likely to be found along with adult sexual license, also physically impulsive. While violence, primarily fighting with peers, is impulsive, theft in these societies may be instrumental as well as impulsive. Sexual deviance in adolescence is socialization for sexual license in adulthood.

There is little evidence that adolescent antisocial behavior is expressive of strong alienation from or hostility toward adults, either the family or the community at large. There is no evidence that conflict with parents accompanies regular antisocial behavior. Conflict exists, however, in societies in which adolescents commit more misbehavior than do adults, most of these being cases in which antisocial behavior is not an expected pattern. We have interpreted this conflict as a response to misbehavior rather than a cause of it.

Antisocial behavior, while generally deplored, may be tolerated for various reasons. We commented in Chapter 5 on how adolescents may be designated as enforcers of community norms, even when this includes harassment of adults or destruction of property. Antisocial behavior is redefined when it is in the service of community welfare. The same can be said about some parental reactions to antisocial behavior: fighting or stealing may be privately tolerated or even condoned if it serves family interests, such as fighting with the child of an enemy or stealing from a disliked or envied neighbor. Furthermore, it would be hypocritical of adults to take adolescent misbehavior too seriously if they themselves are delinquent.

Our findings are consonant with conclusions of other researchers on antisocial aggression in adolescence. In their classic study, Bandura and Walters (1959) viewed aggression as a reaction to frustration engendered by the family. As they stated (p. 29): "It appears that frustration arising from a lack of affectional nurturance and a punitive attitude on the part of one or both of the parents is an essential condition for the occurrence of generalized antisocial aggression." Whether or not one wishes to accept their inference of a motivational predisposition, their conclusions parallel our finding of an association between violence and a lesser degree of early contact with both the mother and the father than usual for the sample. Severe punishment also characterizes the societies in which violence is expected of at least some adolescent boys.

The same authors discovered through their interviews with aggressive and nonaggressive boys that the aggressive boys spent "considerably less time in their fathers' company than did the control boys" (Bandura and Walters 1959: 54), echoing our finding of reduced contact with men when there is expected antisocial behavior. Like the boys in our sample who behave antisocially, the aggressive boys in the Bandura and Walters study expressed aggression more outside the home than in it; however, there is no evidence from our study that boys are resentful or critical of their fathers as were the aggressive boys in their study.

Bandura and Walters viewed aggression as resulting from child-training practices and family interrelationships. Savin-Williams (1987), who discussed aggression within the context of dominance and altruism in adolescent groups, was concerned with the structure of the peer group. In our view, features of the family and child socialization must be combined with features of the social settings of adolescence, as both contribute to an understanding of adolescent behavior.[3]

Earlier theories of aggression linked it to frustrated sexuality: this was the basis for Stone's (1977) explanation of youths' aggressive behavior in the 18th century (see p. 120). The more recent theorizing by sociobiologists about male-male competition over females in much of the animal kingdom contains a corollary, that males—including men and boys—are predisposed to act aggressively. With this in mind, we looked at the relation between antisocial behavior and sexual permissiveness, hypothesizing one of two possible outcomes: either antisocial behavior is positively related to sexual restrictiveness, indicating that boys are sexually frustrated and more likely to commit antisocial acts, or it is positively related to sexual permissiveness, indicating that boys are competing for the favors of girls and therefore will aggress against one another as do males in the so-called "promiscuous" species of animals. We found no association.

In this chapter, we have presented evidence of more antisocial behavior on the part of boys than of girls, a finding consistent with the evidence of a sex difference in modern society.[4] It is also consistent with observations of the disruptive behavior of some other primates. Speaking of subadult male baboons, DeVore (1971:306) stated:

In the savanna baboon, the young juvenile male, as he matures, must fight his way up through the female-dominant hierarchy until he reaches a kind of limbo above all the females but still below any of the adult males, much less the ones in the central hierarchy. There is, in other words, a kind of delayed social maturity in the young male baboon which is, I submit, the classic opportunity for frustration and, indeed, we find in such groups that the most aggressive animals are these young subadult males constantly quarrelling with the females and constantly being put down by the adult males. In some respects they are totally disruptive—the juvenile delinquents of the primate world. Not only are they unable to get into the establishment, they are literally into the hair of all the adults in the baboon group.[5]

Here too, there is diminished involvement with adults for the young male baboon (DeVore 1971:306):

During this period of life, he often becomes spatially quite peripheral to the group. In some species of macaque, the young males simply leave. They go off into young all-male groups together. In species like the savanna baboon where no animal leaves the group at any time during his lifetime unless he is changing groups, they become socially marginal.

We have already observed the difference between the settings that adolescent girls and boys inhabit. Along with whatever else may differentiate the sexes, there is clear evidence that girls are more involved with same-sex adults and less with peers than are boys. The opportunity to behave in socially inappropriate ways is greater for boys; it is our position that the stimulus for boys to do so is also greater.

Another sex difference may be the nature of the control that the peer group has over its members. Whereas the boys' peer group may encourage antisocial behavior, there are suggestions that the girls' peer group does not. There are too few cases of expected antisocial behavior of girls to permit statistical testing, but we were able to determine that when there is greater contact with peers, adolescent girls exhibit less deviant behavior than do women. This may be because a fair amount of girls' contact with peers takes place in the company of adult women, as mothers and female kin bring daughters, nieces, and granddaughters along to work or take their leisure with other women. It is also possible that girls' peer groups themselves tend to reinforce conformity to social norms. We will consider this possibility in Chapter 10, in conjunction with other sex differences.

# 9

# The Adolescent Self

In recent years, the concept of the self has again become a central one in psychological and symbolic anthropology. Earlier studies of personality, heavily influenced by Freudian theory, attempted to find resonances between personality and culture, often through the use of projective tests like the Rorschach. Dissatisfaction with constructs such as basic personality type (Kardiner 1945), modal personality (DuBois 1944; Wallace 1952), and national character (Gorer and Rickman 1949) led researchers to divert their attention from psychological interpretations of culture to studies of child rearing and its effects. As a result, researchers have conducted a number of single-case and comparative studies. Beatrice B. and John W. M. Whiting, with colleagues and students at Harvard University and elsewhere, were leaders in this development in anthropology.

The renaissance of interest in the self is expressed in two somewhat different, although overlapping, approaches: the interpretive and the behavioral. Both utilize the concepts and methods of the psychoanalytic school, but in different ways. Interpretive psychological anthropologists are more likely to use Freudian symbolism (e.g., Gregor 1985) or to be influenced by it in their analyses of ritual, myth, and action. Behavioral psychological anthropologists turn to the emphasis on early childhood socialization and the assumption that the expressive aspects of culture are in part projections of conflicts and anxieties engendered during this time. An early version of this position is associated with Abram Kardiner and Ralph Linton (Kardiner 1939). Currently, it is associated with the Whitings (cf. Whiting and Whiting 1978), among others.

The interpretive mode of studying the self has received impetus from a new way of thinking about cultures, as though they were texts requiring interpretive reading. The "text" contains not only the elements of culture, such as discourse, ritual, and patterns for action but also the actors through which it comes into being and is preserved or rewritten. This reconceptualization has led to an interest in emotion (e.g., Rosaldo 1974; Lutz 1988), a subject that has appeared with some regularity, since about 1979, in *Ethos,* the journal of the Society for Psychological Anthropology. The interpretive approach depends upon an intimate knowledge of the culture in order to link analytically the elements of the culture and these in turn to the selves of the actors.

In this study, we take the behavioral approach, drawing from both psychoanalytic and social learning theory to ask questions and interpret the answers. In Whiting and Whiting's (1978) model for psychocultural research, maintenance systems—which include subsistence patterns, social structure, and division of labor, among others—affect the child's learning environment, to which personality and behavior are adaptive. Read as a linear model, maintenance systems→child's environment→personality and behavior. However, they asserted, and we agree, that causation does not move in only one direction. In studying behavior and personality in humans, who create their environment while they adapt to it, an interactive model is more plausible than a linear, unidirectional one.

We begin this chapter by looking at character traits inculcated in adolescents. We next consider training for adult skills. Work skills are primary for this sample. Schooling as we know it is seldom represented, although our study has implications for societies in which schools are principal settings of adolescent life. Finally, we consider how adolescents are perceived by adults and what the consequences may be, in adolescence and later, of favorable or unfavorable perceptions.

## Character Traits

The 12 traits selected for the assessment of adolescent character as it varies across cultures derive from a series of cross-cultural studies of personality by psychologists and anthropologists. The first of these, begun in 1952 under the direction of Irvin L. Child, and assisted by Herbert Barry III and Margaret K. Bacon, was applied to a sample of 110 preliterate societies. The purpose was to study the modification in childhood of the original dependent behavior of infants. Six measures were rated separately for girls and boys: responsibility, nurturance, self-reliance, general independence, achievement, and obedience. Concurrent projects of research on related issues were directed by John W. M. Whiting, on identification of the child with the parents and the development of superego, and by William W. Lambert, on aggressive behavior of children.

In several resulting publications, these traits have been related to other variables, e.g., social organization (Barry, Bacon, and Child 1957), subsistence economy (Barry, Child, and Bacon 1963), adult crime (Bacon, Child, and Barry 1963), and consumption of alcoholic beverages (Bacon et al. 1965). These 6 traits, with the exception of nurturance and independence, were later coded for the Standard Sample of 186 societies. Added to the four original traits were several others that included fortitude, aggressiveness, competitiveness, sexual restraint, and trust. The code is reported in Barry et al. (1980a).

For the purpose of our study, traits were sorted into pairs of opposite or contrasting traits: trust and competitiveness, responsibility and achievement, and aggressiveness and obedience. Impulsiveness was added to contrast with fortitude; conformity, with self-reliance; and sexual expression, with sexual restraint. The 12 traits are given quantitative scores on a scale from 0 to 10. The principal criterion is indoctrination by the society, especially authority figures, who are in most cases parents. The behavior of adolescents themselves is a secondary criterion for these scores (Table 9.1).

Among these 12 traits, sexual expression and sexual restraint were rated in more than 80 percent of the 186 societies. Obedience and conformity were rated in more than 50 percent. The remaining variables were rated in fewer societies, the smallest number for girls being 35 (19 percent) with information on fortitude and for boys 63 (34 percent) with information on trust.

These data allow us to assess cross-cultural variability in the inculcation of character traits, part of the adolescent self. Most of the societies in our sample had also been coded previously for early and late childhood by a different group of coders (Barry et al. 1980a). This allows us to determine

**Table 9.1**   The Inculcation of Character Traits in Adolescence

|  | Number of societies [a] | Average intensity [b] | |
|---|---|---|---|
|  |  | Boys | Grls |
| *Measures of Compliance* |  |  |  |
| Sexual restraint | 149 | 4.1 | 4.8 |
| Obedience | 91 | 6.9 | 7.2 |
| Responsibility | 67 | 6.7 | 6.7 |
| Conformity | 103 | 7.5 | 7.6 |
| Trust | 61 | 5.8 | 5.8 |
| *Measures of Assertion* |  |  |  |
| Sexual expression | 149 | 5.2 | 4.5 |
| Self-reliance | 56 | 6.3 | 4.8 |
| Competitiveness | 56 | 4.0 | 3.2 |
| Aggressiveness | 45 | 4.2 | 3.4 |
| Achievement | 69 | 5.0 | 4.8 |

[a]Includes only societies with a score on both boys and girls for the designated measure.

[b]Intensity score is the average of individual society scorings on a scale of 0–10.

whether there is continuity or discontinuity in the socialization for these traits. Here we report those traits that show significant associations with selected measures of the social setting.

## Obedience

Obedience rises with social stratification, that is, the average inculcation of obedience is higher in societies that stratify by wealth and even higher in societies with social classes (Table 9.2). One interpretation of this finding is that as social structures become more complex they become more coercive, the advanced chiefdom and the state demanding greater compliance from its members. At the same time, wealth and property rights are greater considerations in more complex societies than in simpler ones, and children have to be trained to submerge their private wishes to the good of the family in the management of its estate. The implication for modern societies of training children to manage the family estate is that classes that do not own property are less likely to stress obedience than those that do. There might seem to be little reward to parents who do not own property for the effort expended in the discipline necessary to produce obedient children.

Contrary to our expectation that girls generally are socialized more for docility, that is, obedience, than boys, the mean scores for the two sexes are very close (Table 9.1). Obedience is negatively correlated with matrilocal residence for both sexes. Male authority declines when families live in the household of the mother, even in those cases in which the in-married husband is the acknowledged household head. Women have greater authority in this household type, often equalling or exceeding that of men. Obedience appears to be less of an issue in such households, in which subordination to the father is low (cf. Table 4.5) and persuasion (intimacy) rather than coercion (subordination) is used to motivate and coordinate family activities.

The size of the peer group is positively related to the inculcation of obedience for both sexes, although for girls it is only a trend. Larger peer groups are found in permanent communities that have higher levels of political integration (cf. Table 5.6). Thus, this finding replicates the finding that obedience is associated with higher levels of social stratification.

*Table 9.2* Obedience as an Inculcated Trait

|  | Boys | | | Girls | | |
|---|---|---|---|---|---|---|
|  | N | r | p | N | r | p |
| Social stratification | 102 | .47 | < .001 | 95 | .35 | .001 |
| Matrilocal residence | 95 | − .29 | .005 | 87 | − .32 | .003 |
| Size of peer group | 47 | .47 | .002 | 37 | .30 | .066 (trend) |

## Achievement

The inculcation of achievement is another character trait significantly related to social stratification. As stratification increases, the mean score for inculcation of achievement rises (Table 9.3). The more complex societies contain a larger variety of adult roles with more diversity of reward than do the simpler ones, thus encouraging efforts to succeed as an individual. The association is particularly strong for girls, suggesting that advanced chiefdoms and states offer females, in particular, markedly more opportunities for individual advancement than do the simper societies.

Inculcation of this trait is somewhat lower for boys in societies having extended families than in those having other family forms, possibly because the boy is trained to coordinate his activities with those of the group rather than to succeed as an individual (Table 9.3).

Achievement and competitiveness in boys are related in a linear fashion: societies with stronger inculcation of achievement also inculcate competitiveness more strongly. These variables are not related in girls. Achievement is reliably associated with peer competition in boys (Table 9.3) but not in girls. As Table 9.1 shows, girls' score on inculcation of achievement is comparable to boys', but there is a fairly large difference in the rating of competitiveness.

## Competitiveness

The inculcation of competitiveness in boys is significantly associated with achievement, but it is independently related to other features as well. It is positively associated with the size of the peer group (Table 9.4), an association not found for girls. This finding implies that status within the group is more of an issue for boys than for girls. Competitiveness is correlated with peer competition for both sexes (Table 9.4).

Inculcation of competitiveness is also associated with the structure of the household. Competitiveness tends somewhat to be low for boys in societies having the stem-family household, and it tends more to be high in those

*Table 9.3* Achievement as an Inculcated Trait

| | Boys | | | Girls | | |
|---|---|---|---|---|---|---|
| | N | r | p | N | r | p |
| Social stratification | 79 | .27 | .017 | 74 | .31 | .007 |
| Extended family | 79 | −.20 | .079 (trend) | 74 | −.12 | — |
| Inculcation of competitiveness | 51 | .34 | .016 | 31 | −.03 | — |
| Competitiveness within the peer group | 46 | .51 | .001 | 28 | .21 | — |

*Table 9.4* Competitiveness as an Inculcated Trait

|  | Boys | | | Girls | | |
|---|---|---|---|---|---|---|
|  | N | r | p | N | r | p |
| Size of peer group | 52 | .29 | .036 | 28 | .05 | — |
| Competitiveness within the peer group | 79 | .84 | < .000 | 40 | .87 | < .001 |
| Stem family household | 94 | − .18 | .087 (trend) | 57 | − .19 | — |
| Nuclear family household | 94 | .20 | .052 | 57 | .24 | .076 (trend) |

having the nuclear-family household (Table 9.4). There is also a trend for competitiveness to be higher for girls who live in nuclear-family households. The nuclear family is the classic setting of the Oedipus complex, which rests on the assumption that boys compete with the father for the attention of the mother. A more general interpretation is that with a small number of adults in the household, siblings compete for their attention more than in other household forms.

The stem family, on the other hand, is structured in a way that minimizes competition. It contains three generations: the older couple, the heir and his (or her) spouse plus the heir's unmarried sisters and brothers who still live at home, and the children of the younger couple. With several adults of both sexes in the household—parents, grandparents, and unmarried uncles and aunts—the child need not focus all of its efforts to gain attention on one or two adults. Competition among siblings is also likely to be muted in most stem families, for the rules of inheritance are usually dictated and have little to do with parental preference. In most cases, primogeniture is the norm, the oldest son (in the patrilocal stem-family household) inheriting the bulk of the family estate. There are cases of ultimogeniture as well, the form in which older siblings leave and the youngest of the appropriate sex remains in the natal household with his or her spouse. The Hopi are a society with matrilocal ultimogeniture, the youngest daughter and her husband remaining with her mother and father until she inherits the house. When the cultural basis for competition is absent, it is unlikely to be a significant feature of socialization.[1]

The extended-family household falls in between. This category is more diverse than the other two forms, nuclear and stem. Competition has been widely observed between sets of siblings in patrilocal extended-family households, the children of the different brothers who constitute the older household members. This competition is often found when the extended family lives in anticipation of eventual fission of household and property. It also occurs between half-siblings, children of the same father but different mothers, when there is nonsororal polygyny, that is, the co-wives are not sisters. In both of these cases, a sibling set constitutes an interest group whose benefits, especially from inheritance, are likely to be at the cost of another sibling set. The prospect of inheriting tangible property such as animals or land or intangible property such as titles or high-status positions promotes competition for future advantage and makes it a fixture of the older child's and adolescent's life. However, when there is little property to inherit, there is little to compete over.

## Aggressiveness

Inculcation of aggressiveness also co-varies with the household structure. For boys, the difference between the lower mean inculcation of aggressiveness in six societies with stem families and the higher mean in 63 societies with nuclear or extended families is significant (Table 9.5). For girls, the trend in the same direction is small and not significant. Without detailed case studies, any interpretation of this finding must be tentative, but it is associated with a higher ratio of adults to children in stem families, as we have suggested in the association between the stem family and low inculcation of competitiveness.

Assuming four living children per woman, in the nuclear-family household the ratio is 1:2. In the extended-family household, in which virtually every adult is married, the ratio is likely to be similar or even lower, particularly in polygynous households, in which the husband-to-wife ratio is lower than it is when marriage is monogamous. The stem-family household, however, consists of four married adults, the children's parents and grandparents, plus unmarried adult siblings of the parents. Thus, given four living children, the adult-to-child ratio with just parents and grandparents is 1:1, and with uncles and aunts present it is higher. Extensive involvement with adults seems to dampen adolescent boys' aggressiveness.

Although the stem family is a distinctive form for boys, the nuclear family stands against the other two forms for girls. Girls' aggressiveness is higher in nuclear families than in other forms. A weak association in the same direction for boys is not significant. We explain this in the following way. The relation of girls to women is somewhat different from that of boys to men. In both the stem- and the extended-family households, the mother shares her

*Table 9.5* Aggressiveness as an Inculcated Trait

|  | Boys | | | Girls | | |
|---|---|---|---|---|---|---|
|  | N | r | p | N | r | p |
| Stem family household | 69 | − .26 | .031 | 46 | − .11 | — |
| Nuclear family household | 69 | .10 | — | 46 | .35 | .020 |
| Peer competitiveness | 44 | .54 | < .001 | 20 | .62 | .007 |
| Peer contact | 51 | .30 | .036 | 30 | .04 | — |

work with other women and has time to relax with her adolescent daughter. Mothers are more burdened in nuclear-family households; they have less time to pay attention to their daughters, and they are likely to demand more help with housework, shifting some of the burden onto the girl. In the other household forms, women and girls work together, but this is less likely or occurs less frequently in nuclear families, resulting in diminished contact for the adolescent with other girls and women. Restraints on the aggressiveness of adolescent girls are thus weakened. (There are, of course, variants of the nuclear-family household in which girls do have continuous contact with other girls and women. This happens when unmarried female relatives live with the married pair and their children or when girls work alongside female servants, as often in the farms and villages of preindustrial Europe.)

We have seen in Chapter 8 that boys' contact with men is inversely related to antisocial behavior. Contact with men is inversely related to aggressiveness also, but the trend is weak and not statistically significant. Judging from the finding that aggression is lower in households with a higher adult-child ratio, it seems that it is not mere contact with men that inhibits aggression (as it does antisocial behavior) but rather level of involvement. It stands to reason that men will not tolerate aggressive boys if they have to be involved with them a good part of the time. The argumentative adolescent is very tiring in large doses. However, there is a trend toward an association between high inculcation of aggression in adolescence and infrequent contact with the father in childhood ( $p = .07$ ). This association supports the position (Burton and Whiting 1961) that aggression can be a form of masculine protest, engaged in by boys as a way of asserting a masculinity about which they are in doubt. Their weakness of masculine identity results from an absent or uninvolved father in childhood.

Aggressiveness in boys is significantly correlated with high peer competition and high peer contact (Table 9.5). The peer contact variable is especially interesting in light of the absence of a significant correlation between aggressiveness of boys and contact with men. It suggests that the peer group is more instrumental as a determinant of aggressiveness than the family or other adult structures, once boys reach adolescence.

Aggressiveness in girls is significantly correlated with high peer competition (Table 9.5) but, unlike in boys, not with high peer contact. Like the household, the peer group can have different effects depending on the sex of the adolescent.

## Sexual Restraint

Socialization for sexual restraint and its converse, sexual expressiveness, varies by social stratification. Restraint is lowest when stratification is absent, intermediate when stratification is by wealth only, highest when there are class divisions (Table 9.6). As we saw in Chapter 7, marriage in tradi-

*Table 9.6* Sexual Restraint as an Inculcated Trait

|  | Boys | | | Girls | | |
|---|---|---|---|---|---|---|
|  | N | r | p | N | r | p |
| Social stratification | 154 | .26 | .001 | 158 | .27 | .001 |
| Matrilineal descent | 154 | −.18 | .022 | 158 | −.26 | .001 |

tional stratified societies serves to maintain or enhance family status. We presented our rationale there for why the virginity of girls is valued in such societies and for why, if girls are sexually restrained, boys tend also to be restrained.

It is widely observed that sexual restraint is less in matrilineal societies, the rationale being that all children belong to the matrilineage of the mother regardless of paternity. The findings in Table 9.6 support this.[2]

## Self-Reliance

Boys are trained to be self-reliant under a very large variety of conditions, as it is most often men who go to battle and on long-distance trading expeditions or take other kinds of risks. There is a trend for greater self-reliance in foraging societies, in which men are often alone or in small groups out hunting or deep-sea fishing (Table 9.7). The association is significant for girls, who are less sheltered as foragers than in other economies (Table 9.7). The girl or woman who is gathering wild foods miles from home must be self-reliant in case of injury or threat from enemies or predatory animals.

Adolescents are being socialized to take their place in the adult world; at the same time, they are being socialized by it. We have seen a general distinction between those societies with simpler technologies and social structures and those with more complex ones. The simpler societies emphasize high self-reliance and lower obedience, achievement, and sexual restraint. The more complex societies emphasize lower self-reliance and high obedience, achievement, and sexual restraint. Competitiveness and aggressiveness do not follow this track, however; they respond to other cultural influences.

*Table 9.7* Self-Reliance as an Inculcated Trait

|  | Boys | | | Girls | | |
|---|---|---|---|---|---|---|
|  | N | r | p | N | r | p |
| Subsistence economy[a] | 79 | −.19 | .102 (trend) | 55 | −.28 | .040 |

[a]The same three ordinal categories of economy were tested in Table 5.4.

## Variations in Character Traits by Sex and Age

The principal setting for adolescent socialization in this sample is the household. Two forms that emerge as significantly associated with opposite character traits are the nuclear and the stem. The nuclear-family household is related to high inculcation of competitiveness and aggressiveness, while the stem-family household is related to low inculcation of these traits. The middling position of the extended-family household is probably due to the fact that this form characterizes so many societies, of so many types, in this sample. Character traits are correspondingly varied. The differing effects that family structure and relations have on girls versus boys are illustrated in the findings on these two variables.

In this sample, the nuclear-family household is the one associated with competitiveness, and it is likely that this trait is inherent in a social unit with a low adult-to-child ratio. In such a setting children compete with one another for the time and attention of the significant adults. This explanation seems particularly plausible when we consider that societies with the stem-family household, where there is the highest adult-to-child ratio, have the lowest score on competitiveness. Inculcation of aggressiveness is strongest in the nuclear family for girls but not for boys. This was interpreted as resulting from the girl's more problematic relation to her mother in that family form and to a reduction in her contacts with other girls and women.

The stem-family household has the lowest average score for socialization for aggressiveness in boys as well as competitiveness, possibly for the same reason of high adult-to-child ratios in these families. The stem family also appears to be a form in which there is likely to be high trust and low responsibility, although the association does not reach significance: of five stem-family cases with information on trust, four are well above the mean and one is below but close to the mean; and of the six cases with information on responsibility, five are below and one above the mean. When there are one or more adults per child, the child's needs are likely to be quickly met, but he or she will not have to assume much responsibility for the household.

Character traits were generally more highly correlated with cultural variables for boys than for girls. In this section, the data were the mean scores for girls and boys on the character traits at three stages: early childhood, late childhood, and adolescence. We looked for continuity or discontinuity by age and by sex. Table 9.1, divided into traits that measure compliance and traits that measure assertion, gives the mean scores for the two sexes in adolescence.

Mean scores for girls and boys on many traits are very close, a reminder that individuals are socialized to be members of their society as well as members of their gender class. For the compliance scores the difference in each case is not significant, although for each variable the score is slightly higher for girls than for boys. However, boys are more strongly socialized for assertion—self-reliance, aggressiveness, and competitiveness, the difference between the sexes reaching significance.

The similarity in socialization for achievement between the sexes, both in late childhood and in adolescence, calls into question the belief that girls in modern society tend to be socialized less than boys for this character trait, at least in the sense that we apply it, success in the public domain. This one-sided view of achievement recognizes only one type of success, that identified with men, and ignores social skills associated with coordinating and administering productive tasks when the household is the dominant unit of production or behind-the-scenes management of status-related activities such as the couple's social life (cf. Papanek 1979). In this sample, the gender roles in most societies are clearly defined, and girls and boys are socialized to similar degrees for achievement within their own adult roles.

The changes from early childhood to late childhood to adolescence, assessed by measures coded for all three stages, indicate some differences between compliance and assertion (Fig. 9.1). Mean scores on the compliance measures—sexual restraint, obedience, and responsibility—increase or at least do not decrease at each stage. Barry, Bacon, and Child (1957), in their study of traits in children, found that girls are socialized more strongly for responsibility than are boys. As seen in Figure 9.1, this difference does appear in late childhood. By adolescence, however, the two sexes are similar, indicating that pressure for responsibility may be weaker for boys in childhood but is increased during adolescence. Mean scores on the assertion measures—self-reliance, competitiveness, aggressiveness, and achievement—increase from early childhood to late childhood but then decrease from late childhood to adolescence. The decrease is more marked for girls than for boys.

The distribution of compliance and assertion means by age and sex indicates that both sexes are socialized for greater compliance and less assertion during adolescence, but the pressures are greater on girls than on boys. The cheeky ten-year-old becomes the more restrained teenager. The increase in socialization for compliance comes at a time when adolescents, with their more adultlike bodies and capabilities, are straining against the confining bonds of discipline. Probably for this very reason the pressures increase, and the behavior that is tolerated and considered amusing, or at least harmless, in the child is disapproved and possibly punished in the adolescent.

## Childhood and Adolescence

Figure 9.1 illustrates the direction and degree of change of measures of compliance and assertion, showing that compliance tends to rise or remain level, whereas assertion declines in adolescence. The degree of continuity from early childhood to adolescence is indicated in Table 9.8.[3] For both

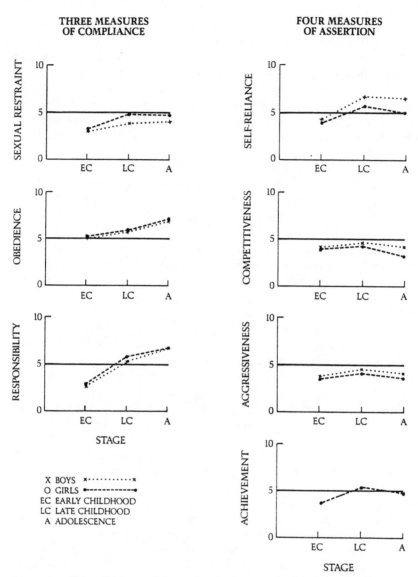

*Figure 9.1* Compliance and Assertion in Boys and Girls from Early Childhood to Adolescence

sexes, there is greater continuity of compliance between early childhood and adolescence than of assertion. Only responsibility in girls is not continuous. Among the traits measuring assertion, however, only competitiveness is continuous, although there is a trend for self-reliance to be continuous for girls. Figure 9.1 shows that there is a drop in the traits measuring assertiveness.

*Table 9.8* Continuity in Inculcated Traits from Early Childhood to Adolescence

| | Boys | | | Girls | |
|---|---|---|---|---|---|
| | $N^a$ | r | $p^b$ | r | $p^b$ |
| *Measures of compliance* | | | | | |
| Sexual restraint | 124 | .38 | < .001 | .52 | < .001 |
| Obedience | 80 | .41 | < .001 | .40 | < .001 |
| Responsibility | 59 | .28 | .036 | .11 | — |
| *Measures of assertion* | | | | | |
| Competitiveness | 41 | .33 | .039 | .37 | .020 |
| Aggressiveness | 28 | .23 | — | .29 | — |
| Self-reliance | 51 | .06 | — | .25 | .074 (trend) |
| Achievement | 57 | −.11 | — | .02 | — |

[a]Only societies with scores for both sexes are included for each measure.

[b]Calculated by the Mantel-Haenszel test and the cross-tabulation program.

This drop indicates socialization for control of assertive behavior, that is, greater maturity.

The settings in which adolescents act, whether the family or a group of age-mates, are concordant in some aspects with childhood settings. Contact with parents in infancy is positively related to contact with parents in adolescence for girls (Table 9.9) but not for boys. Girls experience greater continuity than boys in family relations generally, for they remain more tied to the home than do boys, whose activities may take them out of contact with family members.

For both sexes, there is continuity between the authority figure in childhood and adolescent subordination. When the mother has authority equal to or greater than the father in childhood, subordination to the father tends to be below the median in adolescence. When he is the principal authority figure in childhood, his control persists into adolescence and subordination is above the median. Maternal authority is a counterweight to paternal authority rather than a reinforcement.

In most societies, the principal companions of children are parents or siblings rather than other children. When this is not the case for girls, that is, when other children are the principal companions of the younger girl, adolescent girls are likely to have a high degree of contact with their peers (Table 9.10). For girls, but not for boys, there is continuity between childhood and adolescence in contact with age-mates. Boys' peer contact, like their contact with parents, appears to be determined more by what adolescent boys do than by patterns established in infancy or childhood.

*Table 9.9* Continuity in Relations with Parents

| | Contact with mother by adolescent girls | | |
| --- | --- | --- | --- |
| | Low | High | %High |
| *Nonmaternal caretakers in infancy for girls* | | | |
| infrequent | 16 | 48 | 75 |
| frequent | 34 | 28 | 45 |
| $\chi^2 = 10.50$ | | $p = .001$ | |

| | Contact with father by adolescent girls | | |
| --- | --- | --- | --- |
| | Low | High | %High |
| *Contact with father in infancy for girls* | | | |
| rare | 26 | 5 | 16 |
| occasional | 33 | 13 | 28 |
| frequent | 18 | 12 | 40 |
| Mantel-Haenszel $\chi^2 = 4.27$ | | $p = .039$ | |

| | Subordination of adolescent boys to father | | |
| --- | --- | --- | --- |
| | Low | High | %High |
| *Authority figure of young boys* | | | |
| mostly father | 22 | 60 | 73 |
| mother equal or more | 28 | 21 | 43 |
| $\chi^2 = 10.69$ | | $p = .001$ | |

| | Subordination of adolescent girls to father | | |
| --- | --- | --- | --- |
| | Low | High | %High |
| *Authority figure of young girls* | | | |
| mostly father | 11 | 47 | 81 |
| mother equal or more | 35 | 38 | 52 |
| $\chi^2 = 10.68$ | | $p = .001$ | |

*Table 9.10* Continuity in Contact with Peers for Girls

| | Contact with peers by adolescent girls | | |
|---|---|---|---|
| | *Low* | *High* | *%High* |
| *Principal companions of young girls* | | | |
| parents or siblings | 46 | 20 | 30 |
| other children | 13 | 21 | 62 |
| | $\chi^2 = 7.93$ | $p = .005$ | |

## Training for Adult Skills

For almost all of the societies in this sample, adolescence is a time for the individual to prove himself or herself in ways that will affect the individual's future social position and attractiveness as a potential spouse or child-in-law. This challenge goes beyond the mere expectation of a minimum level of competence; there is pressure to excel, with an eye on the future.

For the majority of societies, the skills that are emphasized for adolescents of both sexes are primarily in the area of productive work: for boys, in 62 percent of 152 societies; for girls, in 73 percent of 141 societies. The second most important area of excellence for boys is physical skills, which are number one for boys in 8 percent of the societies and in 4 percent for girls. For girls, the second most important area is sexual attributes, which for girls is number one in 5 percent of societies and in 2 percent for boys.

### Work

Few ethnographies discuss the work of adolescents, simply indicating that adolescent boys work alongside their fathers and girls alongside their mothers, unless boys have some specialized task like herding cattle. Balikci (1970:105, 107) had the following to say about Netsilik Eskimo boys and girls (similar to the Copper Eskimo in the sample):

> By the time he was ten or eleven, the boy had become his father's helper. On the migration track, he no longer sat on the sledge, but tried to push and pull with the others. He accompanied his father on hunting and fishing trips, performing various light but useful tasks. He rarely asked questions. Instead his father would briefly instruct him before or after a task, when necessary. This always took place in context and in reference to the particular situation at hand. During adolescence the authority of the father remained very strong, and the boy undertook no hunting trips on his own without his father's approval. His attitude was one of complete sub-

missiveness. It was only very gradually that the son acquired autonomy of action. . . .

Already at the age of seven or eight a girl began to interrupt her play in order to participate in her mother's activities. First she collaborated with the mother, accompanying her while cutting fresh ice, getting water, or gathering moss. Gradually she began to perform many of the women's tasks by herself whenever asked to do so by her mother. Soon her functions as household helper became very important. Often young girls were seen carrying infant siblings on their backs. Sewing and skin work were learned somewhat later. After a girl reached the age of eleven or twelve, just as father and son began to collaborate closely, so mother and daughter worked on similar tasks.

The Eskimo adolescent works alongside his or her parent doing the same tasks. Such a distribution of work is likely to be the case in a society in which tasks are fairly repetitive and within the physical capacity of the child.

If a higher level of skill is required, the adolescent might be considered an apprentice of the parent or whatever adult is teaching him or her productive skills. Until the transformation of production in Europe from handwork to industrial manufacture, the large majority of adolescent boys living in cities and towns were in apprenticeships (Gillis 1974:17–18, 51). Apprenticeships also have their place in the tribal world, where a talented young person learns carving or weaving or another skilled craft under the guidance of a recognized master.

Warfare can be an important economic activity, and then specialized training for war can be considered a type of apprenticeship. The young pages of the Middle Ages were in training for the time when it would be necessary to win or defend their fortunes by means of arms. We meet their tribal counterparts on the Great Plains of North America, where raiding for horses was a principal economic activity. Among the Mescalero Apache (similar to the Chiricahua Apache in the sample), boys began their military training at 13 or so, accompanying war parties as what Opler (1969:64), quoting his informant, called "novices":

Novices training for raiding wore one feather in the hair. It was easy to recognize them by this, one eagle tail feather, that's all. A novice does not scratch himself with his fingers; he has to use a stick. The rules that the novice follows hold around camp as well as in raid or war. He is required to do the jobs, to build fires in camp when they are out on a raid. He takes the water bag made from intestines and fills it. Whether or not it is rainy or dark or dangerous he has to do it. They tell him that the way he acts as a novice is the way he is going to be through life. If he minds and is prompt, that's the way he will be. In the old days a boy had to be a novice whether he wanted to or not.

The industrialization of Europe brought with it the rise of a domestic servant class, including persons of all ages. Previous to that, household help at all class levels was most frequently recruited from among the young. Gillis (1974:15–16) described this among the peasantry:

> The number of live-in servants required by particular families depended on both the size of the holding and the age of the household's own off-spring. The more well-to-do peasants were able to hire more servants than their poorer neighbors; and it was the case in most parts of Europe that the wealthier a household, the larger it was in terms of numbers, due to the number of servants who could be brought under its roof. Most of these servants were teen-aged boys and girls recruited by the wealthier households from the poorer, a practice which thus served the function of providing relief to those families who found themselves overburdened by surplus children. Paid in terms of room and board, and subordinate to the authority of the head of the household in which they were employed, these youths were effectively provided for, both economically and so-cially.

Many of these young people were eventually to marry. From the meager wages they earned during their adolescence and youth, boys whose families could not help them might be able to acquire a small farm, and girls without dowries could assemble a trousseau to bring into the marriage. The Irish maid earning her trousseau was a stock character in London or New York into the 20th century. The young girl from the country who worked as a do-mestic in town before her marriage was a common feature in Europe and America, even as late as the years just before the Second World War, and she is only now beginning to disappear from those areas of Latin America and Asia, like northern Mexico and Malaysia, that are rapidly industrializing.

The large majority of adolescents in preindustrial societies work, and through their diligence and skill they are judged as worthy of serious consid-eration by adults of their community. In state societies, schooling has been available for the elite, but until recently most adolescents have not been in school. We will consider schooling later in the chapter.

## Physical Skills

Physical skills are the principal ways by which boys prove themselves in a number of societies, primarily foraging or pastoral ones. Indeed, in socie-ties of these types that rely so heavily on physical endurance and agility, it is difficult to separate physical skill from productive activity, as the former is a prerequisite for the latter.

The Masai of Kenya are a pastoral society in which males are assorted into three age sets: uncircumcised boys, circumcised but unmarried adoles-cents and youths from about 15 to about 30, and married elders. The adolescents and youths, known as *moran,* were described by Llewelyn-Davies (1981:349) as follows:

> For example, moran are expected to be very brave. They live in the forests, hunt lions, and face death on raids. Opportunities for the display of courage are, indeed, actively sought. For example, moran hunt buffalo for sport because raiding is very difficult to organize. A cowardly moran is utterly despised by his fellows and although he will acquire a wife if his economic prospects are good enough, he is unlikely to find any girlfriends. The importance of bravery to the moran may be demonstrated by the use of the word *osuuji. Osuuji* describes bad qualities in persons. In the case of a girl or a woman, it implies that she is slovenly or a poor housewife; in that of an elder, it usually means that he is poor. But in the case of a moran, it almost always means that he is a coward. I have personally never heard a man referred to as cowardly, except in jest. The insult is too serious to be used lightly and the imputation of cowardice to any member of an age set would disgrace the age set as a whole. Physical courage is thus an important element of moranhood and mothers exhort their small sons to be brave "like little moran."

As in many societies in which physical skills are highly esteemed, the period of adolescence and youth is the time when the individual reaches his or her peak of selfhood. As Llewelyn-Davies (1981:332—333) explained:

> [I]t would be hard to exaggerate the importance of the institution of moranhood to the Maasai. . . . moranhood is also a fundamental to the way in which Maasai think about themselves as Maasai. . . . elders look back upon their own period of service with pride and nostalgia; women ostentatiously express admiration for the courage and beauty of the young men and compare them favorably, as lovers, to the elders to whom they are married.

In all societies that we know of, adolescent boys gain the attention of girls and adults through displays of strength and grace in such activities as games or dancing. This is taken seriously when much of a man's success in life depends on his physical skills, including skill in combat among the elite. When that is the case, one way, if not necessarily the principal one, that the boy proves himself is likely to be through some form of athletic endeavor.

When physical skills are particularly admired in boys, they are often admired in girls as well. An example comes from the Abkhasians, a Caucasus Mountains ethnic group today located in the Abkhasian Autonomous Republic of the U.S.S.R. (Benet 1974:72):

> At puberty, the young people become intensely involved in sports, dancing, and courting, but they never touch those of the opposite sex whom they are eligible to marry. The boys show off as sportsmen (there is com-

petition on this level) and the girls sit around and admire them. Their courtships are quite prolonged and very romantic, with a great deal of fantasy. Little things are exaggerated—a glance, a chance encounter on the street—for it's a long, long way from courtship to the marriage bed.

Young women are not always passive spectators, however. They are expected to have a great deal of stamina and endurance. To be a really good dancer, a girl should be able to wear out three male partners since the steps he is required to perform are more strenuous. Physical fitness and beauty are important for both sexes.

Although the Abkhasians practiced agriculture for centuries, pastoralism was traditionally the major source of subsistence and trade. Raiding and fighting were a part of this economy, as they so often are for pastoralists, and skill at horsemanship for both sexes was extolled where the occasional woman might go to battle on horseback (Benet 1974:42; Schlegel's data collected in 1990). Strength, endurance, and agility were expected of everyone, and those who excelled in these qualities were highly esteemed.

## Sexual Attributes

Sexual attributes include both sexual attractiveness and sexual capacity. Attractiveness to the opposite sex, whether or not young people sleep together, is one way that adolescents can be judged as successful by their peers and adults. This is particularly true, although not exclusively so, of girls when the girl's attractiveness can be a major factor in determining how good a marriage she makes.

Sexuality is given a great deal of cultural elaboration in many parts of the Pacific. (New Guinea rituals that require semen, sometimes obtained through homosexual practices, have been discussed in Chapter 7.) There is widespread tolerance, and sometimes even encouragement, of adolescent sexual adventures, but these are not merely for the amusement of the young. Weiner (1988:71), who has analyzed adolescent sexuality in the Trobriand Islands, a Melanesian society, stated:

> Attracting lovers is not a frivolous, adolescent pastime. It is the first step
> toward entering the adult world of strategies, where the line between in-
> fluencing others while not allowing others to gain control of oneself
> must be carefully learned. The procurement of magic spells "that de-
> stroy someone's mind" leads to dangerous actions because effective
> spells collapse a person's autonomy and establish control over the other
> person's thoughts. Sexual liaisons give adolescents the time and occasion
> to experiment with all the possibilities and problems that adults face in
> creating relationships with those who are relatives. Individual wills may
> clash, and the achievement of one's desires takes patience, hard work,
> and determination. The adolescent world of lovemaking has its own dan-

gers and disillusionments. Young people, to the degree they are capable, must learn to be both careful and fearless.

When sexual attractiveness can lead to status improvement, it is serious business. The story of Cinderella only thinly veils the desire to marry up, using beauty to attract a superior husband. This tale, first recorded by Charles Perrault in 1697, reflects the fantasy of upward female mobility through marriage. Although the likelihood of this happening was remote in 18th and 19th century Europe, the possibility was a resonant theme in popular culture, worthy of adult drama; for example, the opera "La Cenerentola," composed by Jacapo Ferretti in 1817, is still performed.

Sexual attractiveness as a vehicle for social improvement through marriage is not limited to women. We saw in Chapter 7 how the value placed on virginity is patterned across cultures by type of marriage transaction, and we interpreted this value in gift-exchanging and dowry-giving societies as an expression of parental concern that their daughter not be seduced by an unwelcome suitor who then claims her and her child. The other side of that coin is the possibility that an ambitious and lucky young man can do just that.

Interest in seducing virgins is probably present whenever virginity is valued: many boys and men may be tempted to seduce virgins just for the challenge, which adds an element of uncertainty and even danger to an already highly charged act. In some societies boys and youths are obsessed with the possibility and go to great lengths to achieve it. This has been noted again and again in Polynesia, where the seduction of a virgin of high rank is a special coup. It is not only the spice of the forbidden; when status considerations enter strongly into marriage and the marriage of a low-status boy with a high-status girl is virtually impossible to negotiate, the interest in defloration has as much to do with social mobility as with pleasure.

Winning the heart of a higher-status woman as a path to a better life may be a male fantasy in all societies that are divided by rank or class, or at least in those in which men will not be killed or severely punished for the attempt. Adolescent boys have nothing to lose and much to gain if they can make a paternity claim on the child of a high-status girl. In such a setting, where only a few can succeed, all boys will be tempted to refine their skills with virgins of their own rank, while hoping for their big chance with a *taupou* (the Samoan "village princess") or her equivalent.

It is well recognized that some women use their sexual attractiveness to try to improve their position through a socially advantageous marriage or liaison. It should not surprise us that men and adolescent boys do the same if the opportunity exists. When sexual success can be translated into social success, it is predictable that men and boys not only make themselves attractive to women but also make sexual exploits a major topic of discussion, teasing, and boasting. In such cases, male competitiveness is channelled into overt sexual competitiveness (Schlegel 1991).

## Schooling

One important avenue to success in modern society is schooling. This opportunity, or burden as the case may be, is not part of adolescent life in the large majority of societies in this sample. Education for adult skills comes through working alongside parents and other adults and through apprenticeships to master craftsmen. Understanding of tribal lore, inculcation of beliefs and values, ritual knowledge, and the like come to the adolescent through participation and informal explanation. Cautionary tales are probably a universal way of conveying lessons in morals and etiquette. Opler's Mescalero Apache informant reminisced about this form of education in earlier times (Opler 1969:63):

> Old Man Luntso and his wife . . . were good storytellers too. . . . We used to get these old people to tell us about Goose. I'd go to their camp and say, "Uncle and Aunt, tell us stories." They were not relatives to me, but I'd call them this just so they wouldn't refuse. . . . If they were willing, a whole bunch of us would come to their camp. Then they'd begin the story and take turns telling it. They would often stop right in the middle of a story to explain the meaning and give a lesson. . . . They would tell stories till dawn.

Slightly more formal instruction, to groups of young people, was given in the so-called "bush schools" of sub-Saharan Africa (cf. Watkins 1943). Societies in which these schools are prominent in the sample include the Mende, Wolof, Songhai, and Tallensi. They were held at sites at some distance from the village, and boys entered them for a period of several months to several years. Age of entry varied, usually being in late childhood to early biological adolescence. Schools for girls were similar, but their period of schooling usually did not last as long as the boys'. During this time, children and adolescents were given training in specific gender-linked tasks such as warfare (boys) or cooking (girls), as well as general instruction in tribal life and lore. Small groups of children and adolescents had intensive contact with a number of adults of the same sex. This was considered to be a time of spiritual transformation, and when the young people emerged from the school, they were reborn. While in the bush school, children were expected to eliminate undesirable traits and to perfect themselves through diligence and the endurance of hardship. Weaklings and deviants might not be reborn; if they failed to appear at the end of schooling, their parents were expected not to grieve.

The Aztec city of Tenochtitlan had something like a bush school (but without the seclusion) for most boys, as well as a special school, more like the traditional schools of Eurasia, for the chosen sons of nobles and a few especially talented young commoners. The following description is drawn from Peterson (1959).

It is not clear how early boys entered these schools, but they were participants during their adolescence if not before. The boys in the ordinary
school, the Telpochcalli (House of Youth), got moral training along with
instruction in religion, history, music, and martial arts. The purpose was
to turn them into good citizen-soldiers. They slept at the school but were
released for part of each day to go home to eat and to work with their
families. Punishment for infractions of discipline was severe: an illustration in the *Codex Mendocino* shows a disobedient boy who is being punished by a man sticking maguey spines into his naked body while his
hands and feet are tied. The curlicue indicating speech emanates from
the punisher's mouth, and we can imagine that the young victim must lis-
ten to a lecture while he endures the pain of his corporal punishment.

The more selective school, the Calmecac (Row of Houses), gave boys
training in cognitive skills as well as in history and the arts. In a monas-
tery-like setting, they learned how to calculate the calendar, serve the
gods, read and write, and do arithmetic. In addition, they were given
moral, civic, and military instruction. It was from this school that the
priests and the higher political officials were drawn.

Schools, in the sense of special institutions for the inculcation of cognitive skills as well as large bodies of knowledge, are confined to states among
the preindustrial societies. Their students are drawn primarily from the aristocracy and the urban mercantile and professional classes, although in many
cases in both Europe and Asia in earlier times an intelligent and ambitious
son of peasants or the urban poor could advance himself through education.
One reason that the Catholic Church in Europe was open to clergy drawn
from lower-status sectors may have been that through its educational system
it was able to use the talents of these boys and men; at the same time, clerical
celibacy avoided the embarrassing question of marriage for such persons of
humble origin who nevertheless occupied high positions.

Our coding schedule included questions about the importance of teachers as socializing agents and the opportunity, choice, and frequency of
schooling available to adolescents. Although a fair number of societies were
coded for these variables, the terms *teachers* and *schooling* have different
meanings in the code from these terms as commonly used in the modern
world. *Teachers* includes masters in a master-apprentice relationship, the instructors in the bush school, ritual instructors, and even minstrels, who in
Armenia are the voice of morality. In some cases, as among the Kurds of
Iran, only a small number of adolescent boys are in school; in other cases, as
among Turkish villagers, boys attend a mosque school for a few hours in the
week. The variety of meanings of these codings makes them unusable for
drawing comparisons with modern schooling.

Even though few of the societies in the sample have schools as we know
them for adolescents, there are data from which inferences can be made

about the effects of schooling. In most of the societies, adults of the same sex are the principal companions of adolescents (in 66 percent of 161 cases for boys and in 84 percent of 160 cases for girls). Peers are the principal companions in most of the remaining cases. This latter group of societies most closely resembles those in which adolescents are in the classroom. The adolescents are with other adolescents more waking hours of the day than they are in one-to-one or small-group relations with adults, as they would be in a master-apprentice relationship or a bush-school setting. Table 9.11 shows the significant associations for boys. When women are not the principal companions of girls, only one variable, sexual permissiveness, is significantly associated at the .05 level. Girls away from adult female control have greater sexual freedom (cf. Table 7.6).

Adolescence in such societies is more sharply set apart from both childhood and adulthood, as these young people are not so tightly integrated into the family as are the persons of other ages, nor are they integrated into the community, as are adults. A considerable amount of contact with the peer group is self-evident. Opportunity for productive property is a result of the economic activities of these societies, many of them pastoral ones in which adolescent boys are beginning to assemble their own herds. Sexual freedom for boys and permissiveness for girls relate to the generally lower level of control by adults over adolescents' activities. The lower valuation of boys in this set of societies may result from the tension between the desire of adults to control adolescent boys and their inability to do so, along with a general distrust of what boys are up to away from adult supervision.

These findings suggest that a society increases its difficulties with adolescents by putting them in the classroom. The common complaint among modernizing societies that young people are not as they used to be is very likely more than just a nostalgic longing. The transformation of the adolescent social setting from one of apprenticeship to a parent or other adult to one composed primarily of peers has marked effects on how adolescents behave. These changes are not always perceived by adults as salutary.

*Table 9.11* Where Men Are Not the Principal Companions of Boys

| Variable | N | r | $p^a$ |
| --- | --- | --- | --- |
| Differentiation from childhood | 154 | .19 | .020 |
| Differentiation from adulthood | 151 | .19 | .020 |
| Amount of contact with peer group | 120 | .22 | .018 |
| Opportunity for productive property | 89 | .23 | .028 |
| Sexual freedom | 137 | .22 | .009 |
| Lower valuation of adolescents | 104 | .19 | .048 |

[a]Calculated by the Mantel-Haenszel test and the cross-tabulation program.

## Adult Perceptions of Adolescents

Adolescents are perceived by adults in various ways—sometimes favorably, sometimes less so, often ambivalently. From the information the coders were able to find, virtually all societies in the sample have friendly perceptions of adolescents. Yet, we know from some of the more recent studies of the self or of cultural perceptions of gender and age categories that alongside these positive attitudes may go less favorable ones. The Hopi mother, for example, finds her adolescent daughter's resistance as tiresome as the daughter finds her mother's intensified discipline oppressive. As we have seen in Chapter 4, this undercurrent of tension casts a shadow on the mother-daughter relationship during this period; later, both agree that the discipline was necessary and smile about the daughter's protests. Ambivalence may extend toward actions that are deplored; the Gros Ventre boys will be scolded for their meat raids while the daring ones are admired for the skill that they will later transfer to raiding enemies for horses (see Chapter 7).

Kirkpatrick (1987) depicted the ambivalence felt toward adolescents, particularly boys, in the Marquesas Islands of Polynesia. The following sketch is drawn from his account. It refers to the mid-1970s, but probably similar patterns were present in the precolonial period.

> After leaving school at 14, girls become absorbed into the domestic economy, working alongside their mothers on tasks they have already learned. Boys may also work alongside the adult men of their households, but they do so less diligently, since adults are likely to claim credit for any work done for the household and give little reward to adolescent helpers. Instead, boys may be spending their time away from home in such productive activities as fishing, horticultural or agricultural paid work, or other kinds of wage labor. In order to be perceived as successful workers, therefore, they may have to leave home and join the company of other adolescent boys, where they are out of parental supervision and seen as being up to no good. The term *taure'are'a,* defined by Kirkpatrick as "errant youth," describes the behavior believed to characterize adolescents, particularly boys. It includes laziness, sexual license, irresponsibility, self-absorption, and devotion to pleasure. At the same time, boys represent their communities in intervalley sports and dance competitions, where their beauty and grace and physical prowess are much admired.

Modern parents are often dismayed at the change that comes over their children at adolescence, and it is not uncommon for them to reevaluate their attitude toward their children as a result. "I still love him, but I don't like him" is the guilty admission of many parents in response to unexpected rudeness or thoughtlessness. Adolescents often believe that they are not perceived in a friendly fashion, whether or not this is true: in a small sample of German

*Table 9.12* Continuity in Cultural Attitudes toward Childhood and Adolescence

|  | $N^a$ | Boys | | Girls | |
|---|---|---|---|---|---|
|  |  | *r* | $p^b$ | *r* | $p^b$ |
| Permissiveness | 122 | .32 | < .001 | .34 | < .001 |
| Affection | 83 | .24 | .028 | .33 | .003 |
| Evaluation | 109 | .14 | — | .38 | < .001 |

[a]Only societies with scores for both sexes are included for each measure.

[b]Calculated by the Mantel-Haenszel test and the cross-tabulation program.

adolescent responses collected by the first author in 1989, informants maintained that they were often viewed negatively by adults. This is in a country where children and adolescents are valued, as indicated by general acceptance in public places and by the resources allocated by the state to meet their maintenance, intellectual, and recreational needs.

There is little evidence in this sample for a sharp contrast between attitudes toward children and attitudes toward adolescents. Table 9.12 shows that permissiveness and affection toward children carry over toward adolescents of both sexes. Evaluation, whether high or low, is continuous from childhood to adolescence for girls but not for boys. Whether the lack of continuity for boys is due to a drop in evaluation at adolescence or a rise, or both, is not clear. As in earlier measures of continuity reported in this chapter, contact with parents and contact with age-mates, there is greater disjuncture between childhood and adolescence for boys than for girls.

When the perception of adolescents by adults is less than favorable, adolescents have to cope with that burden while at the same time preparing to enter the adult society that stigmatizes them. How they cope and how they make the transition from disapproved adolescent to disapproving adult are questions for further psychological and cultural examination. Is the failure to make a successful transition to adulthood more widespread in disapproving cultures than in those in which adolescents are regarded more favorably? Is disapproval, or strong ambivalence, more likely to be found when adolescents, particularly boys, are more segregated from adults in schools or work groups of peers? These questions concern not only the quality of life of adolescents but also the chances they have to move into successful adulthood.

# 10

# Gender Differences:
# Final and Proximate Causes

THE discussion in Chapter 2 and the ethogram that illustrates it (Fig 2.1) present what we believe to be the fundamental difference between girls and boys in adolescence and a contributing factor to the other differences we have identified. Across the societies in the sample, girls have more contact and greater intimacy with mothers than boys do with parents of either sex. Brought along with their mothers into the company of women, girls participate in multigenerational groups. Boys, even when they work alongside their fathers, have less contact and intimacy with them and other men than do girls with women. Leisure hours—and sometimes working hours as well—are spent in the company of age-mates.

This sex difference cuts across a wide range of societies. As it occurs in sexually egalitarian as well as male-dominant societies and among informally organized foragers as well as in traditional states, it is unlikely to be strictly "cultural," that is, a pattern that each culture or each cultural tradition invents for itself or borrows from its neighbors. We suggest that the difference is a feature of our species and predict that analyses of adolescence in modern industrial societies would find a like pattern, in spite of massive changes such as coeducation and the increasing similarity in the socialization of girls and boys.

To explain this sex difference, we offered a final cause argument. We proposed that the practice of drawing girls into the company of women and directing boys toward peers until they are accepted by adult men is a variant method of achieving sexual separation, found in other species as well, that functions to prevent close inbreeding. Every species has its own evolutionary history, and each has evolved to minimize inbreeding in its own way. The evolution of human social behavior is a topic much debated at present, and we do not intend to enter the fray. However, we do point out that what is accomplished in other primates by leaving the troop at puberty, or sequester-

182

ing females in harems by unrelated males, or expelling both young males and young females from the territory of the parental couple, is accomplished in *Homo sapiens* by psychological inhibitions to close mating and the cultural reinforcement of the incest taboo. In addition, after puberty there is some measure of sexual separation, so that girls are somewhat withdrawn from male kin and the attention of boys is displaced outside the home. These tendencies toward sexual separation do not arise *de novo* at adolescence but already appear in childhood, as even quite young children have been shown generally to prefer the company of children of their own sex, even when there are no barriers to mixed-sex play (Whiting and Edwards 1988).

## Similarities and Dissimilarities Between the Sexes

There are more commonalities in the behavior and treatment of girls and boys than there are distinctions. On most measures in this study, the contrast within any particular society is not very great. When self-reliance is inculcated for boys, so it is for girls; when one sex is denied sexual freedom, the other is also; treatment of boys and girls is likely to be similarly harsh or gentle. We find no evidence that socialization differences are so great as to produce, for example, aggressive boys and passive girls (or vice versa).

Having said that, we can examine further those areas in which there are gender differences. Here we build on the findings presented in earlier chapters. While we link gender differences to the fundamental contrast between girls and boys in their relation to adults versus peers, we do not propose that this difference in allocation of time and intensity of relationship is the only contributing factor. However, we hope to demonstrate that it should not be overlooked in any comparisons between the sexes.

We should note that the amount of information available on the two sexes is different, in part because there are more male than female ethnographers and men have more opportunities to observe boys or take more notice of them. It is also probably the case that boys' activities appear more exotic to Western observers than girls': girls seemingly do much the same things in many places, whereas what boys do in one society may be very different from what they do in another. This seems to be a real difference rather than an effect of observer bias; for even with adequate information, the variation across cultures is greater for boys than it is for girls. If cross-cultural understanding is based on closer affinities and shared experiences, such understanding may be easier for women than for men to achieve.

Adolescent girls and boys differ in the degree of continuity and change from childhood in the nature of their social settings. Childhood is characterized by hierarchy in day-to-day activities, the child subordinate to the adults of the family. Children make very few decisions that will affect their lives in significant ways. Adults, unless they are slaves and thereby classed as social minors, do make important decisions about their lives, no matter how much they may have to defer to senior men or women of the kin group or community. Within their own gender and social rank or class, adult life is characterized by relative equality.

Adolescents are midway between the hierarchy of childhood and the relative equality of adulthood. The sexes experience this transitional period in different ways, however. Through their relations with their mothers and other adult women, girls continue within the hierarchy of childhood more than do boys.[1] Even when a puberty ceremony at or around menarche marks the girl's new adolescent status, the social setting of her daily life differs little from that of earlier years. In fact, in those cases in which her freedom is more restricted and she cannot roam about with age-mates as she could as a younger child, her setting becomes even more hierarchical. The greater involvement of boys in the peer group provides more of a disjuncture from childhood, as the equality of peer group relations prepares them for the egalitarian interactions of adult male life.

As a result, we propose, girls in our sample ease into adolescence more gently than do boys. The separation from the family and particularly from her mother is less for the girl than for her brother. Contrary to those who believe that the close identification with the mother makes the girl's assertion of autonomy more of a struggle than the boy's, we believe that this identification in fact makes autonomy less of a critical issue and a struggle unnecessary. One can become one's own person gradually.

Girls are placed in a hierarchical setting more often than are boys, and the setting itself is also somewhat different for the two sexes. Boys, too, are in a subordinate position vis-à-vis adults, particularly men, and therefore in a hierarchical setting in many of their daily activities. However, the hierarchy of girls and women is ameliorated by the greater involvement they have with one another and, as a result, the greater ease that adolescent girls feel with adult women than boys feel with adult men. Girls are accepted by women much more than boys are by men.

We do not intend to exaggerate the extent of involvement of boys in their peer groups, even as we draw a contrast between the sexes. As boys grow into later childhood and adolescence, they often spend time with their fathers and other related men on the men's work that supports the family. Thus, it is common for boys to work alongside their fathers as girls work alongside their mothers, and in this matter there is similarity between the sexes. However, the boy does not usually accompany his father to events unrelated to the household, as the girl accompanies her mother. When he does, or when he interacts with men outside the home, the boy and his age-mates are likely to be relegated to the periphery of the men's group, both literally, in that they are placed behind or at the edge of the men's cluster or on the other side of the room, and metaphorically, as they are rarely asked for their opinion nor would they be so bold as to offer it.

Boys are more likely to find their voice in the peer group. These groups become not only the setting within which age-related concerns and interests are expressed, as they are for girls, but also structures that compensate boys for the diminished attachment to the home and the refusal of men to absorb them into their activities.

The peer group is different in character from the family. While the family is hierarchical, the peer group is egalitarian. It is not usual for even the hierarchy of a society divided by rank or class to be reflected in peer group hierarchy. A young prince, by nature of his exalted social status, would be the arbiter of the boys' social circle at court, and Fijian boys of high rank are the leaders of the peer groups to which they belong as long as they have the other qualifications (see Chapter 5), but such ascribed hierarchies tend to be uncommon. (Out of 29 societies with information on boys, only seven have ascribed leadership.) The positions of recognized leaders are more usually achieved on merit than ascribed by class or rank.

A consequence of the boy's attachment to the peer group is that he is committed to two structures of quite different character. At the same time that he is asserting himself in the peer group, learning to compete and to compromise, he remains subordinate within the family. It is reasonable to suppose that the boy is tempted to carry over into the family the new skills that he is perfecting in the peer group and to resent the imposition of discipline associated with a childhood that he is leaving behind. The conflict between assertion and compliance is greater for the boy than for the girl, and it can lead to strained family relations and to social awkwardness.

The greater disengagement of boys than girls from the family usually results in boys taking a greater part than girls in community activities. Boys, not girls, are sometimes the enforcers of community norms on adults (see Chapter 5). There may be some exceptions; in some European peasant villages, girls and boys seem to take equal parts in the production of certain village festivities. It may also be the case in modern states that girls are more engaged than boys in community projects sponsored by churches and charities.

The fact that boys are involved in peer groups more than girls gives boys some advantages at the same time that it may make adolescence a more difficult time. As we have already indicated, the boys' peer group prepares its members for the more egalitarian relations of adult community life, in which competition over resources and status must coexist with cooperation to achieve goals perceived as beneficial to all. For boys, but not for girls, high competitiveness and high cooperativeness occur within the same setting, and boys are socialized by the peer group both to compete and to cooperate. Boys' peer groups are more often task- or goal-oriented than are girls', whether the goal be to arrange an event or to organize a competitive game (Schlegel and Barry 1989). Girls are more likely to engage in noncompetitive activities that are not goal-oriented, such as conversation or cooperative play. There is a good deal of talk lately about putting girls into team sports to teach them goal-oriented skills. For many girls, as for many boys, competitive athletics hold little interest. Sports are only one way of training for the cooperative-competitive skills that facilitate successful political behavior. These skills can just as readily be learned in other kinds of goal-oriented peer group activities.

The greater expectation of assertion and training for it that boys experience means that the control of impulses is generally less reinforced for boys than it is for girls, among whom the weight of socialization is toward compliance. This is seen in the large gender difference in antisocial behavior, as apparent in this sample as in industrial nations. The aggressiveness of boys within their peer groups can lead to violence, fighting with other boys or using violent means to assert their masculinity. When boys feel the need to prove themselves to each other, fighting or stealing is often the result in tribes as well as in modern states.

This study suggests that girls' peer groups may reinforce rather than challenge social norms. Girls who have more contact with other girls are less likely to be deviant than are women (see Table 8.8). High levels of peer contact are correlated with high aggressiveness for boys, but not for girls (see Table 9.5). Girls in nuclear families are more likely to be aggressive than girls in stem or extended families (see Table 9.5), a finding that we have interpreted as due both to the girl's more strained relations with her mother and to a decrease in intimate contact with other girls and women in the home.

While girls certainly compete with one another for the most desirable boyfriend or future spouse and for status (popularity) within the group, this competitiveness does not appear to lead to antisocial behavior, as it does for boys. Girls' misbehavior is most often what is known in legal terminology as status offenses, that is, acts that are not delinquent when committed by adults, such as sexual misbehavior and running away. Boys also commit these offenses, but in addition they commit the more serious delinquent acts, both in our sample and in modern society (cf. Miller 1979). Both sexual activity (in societies in which it is not permitted to adolescents) and voluntarily leaving the home are adult privileges. Girls who claim them are to some degree asserting their maturity. From this sample, the evidence of girls fighting or stealing is very sparse, and the proportion that does in modern nations is small compared to boys. Fighting or stealing may be replicating the antisocial behavior of the women whom they imitate, for deviant children are often the product of deviant adults.

One reason for greater compliance, we believe, is that girls, having close relations with women, are more accepting of adult norms; in other words, adolescent girls are more socially mature than adolescent boys. Another reason may be a greater tolerance for boys' deviance; because boys are somewhat disengaged from the family, they may have greater freedom to break rules in ways that do not affect the family. We believe, however, that the compliance of girls is largely the result of their wish to keep their mothers' love and approval. It seems to reflect an unspoken contract between mothers and daughters that good behavior is the payment for close contact and intimacy.

## The Origin of Gender Differences in Adolescence

The differences we have found in adolescence have their roots in childhood. Many studies of younger children have shown that girls are more likely to form attachments to older girls and women to get what they want, whereas boys tend to rely more on aggression and strength for access to resources. Boys seek out the company of age-mates more than do girls. Additional differences, found in both human and primate juveniles, are that young females are more sociable and nurturant, whereas young males are more active, exploratory, and interested in objects, that is, in nonsocial stimulation (Hall 1985).

The search for origins leads us to ask what determines these gender differences early in life. Are there precursors in infancy that are later elaborated? The literature on infant attachment to the mother does not indicate much difference between boys and girls. In their investigation of attachment behavior through the responses of infants to unfamiliar situations, Ainsworth et al. (1978:81) found no significant sex difference in the behaviors of babies and toddlers. It appears, thus, that the sex difference in individuation between child and mother is a silent process, working itself out in ways that are not readily observable and measurable in the interaction between mother and very young child. Because the mental products—the dreams, fantasies, perceptions—of the infant cannot be recorded and analyzed, when or how or by what steps this process occurs is unknown. Inferred rather than observed, the process is reconstructed from the fantasy material of older children and adults.

The individuation process is underway by the second year of life. Children are weaned by mothers, generally between two and three (Barry and Paxson 1980). Well before this, babies and toddlers are frequently turned over to older children to be cared for while the mother gets on with her tasks (Weisner and Gallimore 1977). These behaviors are observable and measurable. It is not clear whether treatment differs according to the sex of the child. There is no evidence we know of to suggest that weaning practices are different for boys and girls or that one sex is left with child-minders more than the other. All the cross-cultural data on infancy and early childhood suggest that, at least until weaning, treatment of girls and boys is very similar; if any sex difference can be detected, it is in such things as whether a tiny bow and arrow or a doll are tied to the cradleboard or some very minor distinction in clothing. However, the available published data reflect only gross measures and do not allow for fine-grained analyses of infant socialization. For both sexes, the mother pushes the child into independence as she teaches it skills and responds less to its demands as it gets older. (Mother surrogates, such as nannies, do the same.)

These cross-cultural observations receive support from studies on infant-mother interaction conducted in industrial nations, reviewed in Maccoby and Jacklin (1974). Most of the findings, particularly for such measurable features of early child socialization as smiling at, holding, and touching, reveal either no sex difference or inconsistent differences among the studies. There are suggestions, however, that differences do exist. In four of the studies cited that relied on interviews with older children about how much affection they have received from their parents, girls reported more. Maccoby and Jacklin (1974:313) stated:

> Since observational studies of parent behavior when the children are younger do not usually report differential parental warmth to children of the two sexes, the differences reported by the children themselves may either reflect selective perceptions on the children's part or indicate that differentiation in parental warmth to the two sexes does develop but only some time after the children reach school age.

To these alternatives we can add a third, that there is a tone to the interaction that cannot be measured by techniques currently used but is perceived by the infant, the content of the interaction conveying more maternal attachment to the girl than to the boy. Observations of behavior may leave much undetected: in their studies of very young children, Jacklin and Maccoby (1978) found that these children gravitated to same-sex companions significantly more than expected by chance even when the observers could not tell the sex of the children by dress, behavior, or any other visual clues. Subtle differences in the treatment of girls and boys may be equally inaccessible to observers.

In spite of the lack of clear confirmation from observational studies, the possibility is still open that the mother pulls away from the infant son to a greater degree than from the daughter. Putting it another way, the boy is extruded more than the girl. We do not use the term *reject* because this implies coldness and insensitivity to the child, whereas some degree of extrusion is both necessary and desirable for normal social development (cf. Cohen 1964). In our view, the extrusion process that begins in infancy with the mother separating herself from her infant is of greater magnitude for boys than for girls.

Several possible theoretical explanations of the development of gender differences have been advanced. One emphasizes sex-role socialization (discussed in Draper 1985): children are held to learn their gender from those around them, that is, gender is primarily influenced by the environment in which the child is placed. Another, developed by Draper (1985), is "prepared learning": girls and boys are prepared from birth to learn differently, even if they are placed within the same environment. Draper related this preparedness to the different reproductive strategies of the sexes across many species, in that greater risk taking and keener interest in competitive and dominance activities by males are related to competition for females, while the more nurturant and affiliative behaviors of females are related to the need for females to keep their offspring alive if they are going to be reproductively successful. This explanation holds that gender differences are initiated by the child itself.

Another explanation that puts the burden of gender differentiation upon the child is the widely accepted psychoanalytic view that the child distances itself from the mother, there being a marked difference between the sexes in this process. At the earliest stage of life, the child identifies with the mother and is unable to differentiate itself from the mother. As it matures, the child perceives itself as different. The significance for gender difference is that the girl continues to identify with the mother more than the boy does, for she perceives herself to be female like her mother whereas the boy perceives himself to be other. The boy, therefore, must switch his gender identification to his father and other males. This view has been cogently summarized and related to ethnographic data by Gregor (1985).

Bischof (1975b), speaking as both an ethologist and a psychologist, also treated the individuation process as initiated by the child. He sees the proximal cause of individuation in the surfeit response of the child to overly familiar stimuli. Bischof considered the final cause for this behavior to be the prevention of incest. (This explanation, however, does not account for a sex difference in disengagement.)

As one cannot get into the mind of an infant, one cannot test whether the early identification with the mother includes gender identification or whether gender identity arises after the individuation process is well enough under way that the child's perception is not confused. We question the psychoanalytic assumption of early female gender identity for both sexes, with a necessary switch for boys. We put considerable weight on the idea that the environment, in the form of the mother, initiates both the individuation and the gender differentiation processes. We propose that it is the mother who perceives gender similarity with her daughter and dissimilarity with her son and therefore behaves differently toward children of different sexes, distancing boys more than girls. This does not mean that mothers are necessarily less warm or loving toward sons or that they respond less rapidly to the cries or actions of boys; in fact, any particular mother may show greater affection to sons than to daughters, especially in patrilocal families in which a woman's son is her guarantee of a secure position in the family when she is old. The differences we refer to can be subtle and very small, slight differences, perhaps, in length of gazing at the child, in quantity of talk to the child, or of vocal tone, which are very difficult to measure, particularly in a laboratory setting.

The result of such early maternal treatment would be to bind the daughter closer, to reward her for affiliative behavior and for compliance. The son, pushed more into the world of objects and depending more on his own resources for gratification, would develop a greater interest in exploration and in the manipulation of objects. Object manipulation, in fact, might be a compensatory form of gratification. He would learn fewer of the social skills at an early age and would be less mature than girls of his age in gaining compliance of others; he would be more likely to hit, grab, or whine—the behavior of infants—in exerting social dominance than would the girl, who has already learned to persuade and to negotiate. While the girl remains attached to her mother and the females with whom the mother interacts as she gets older, the boy would be drawn more into interaction with peers, as compensation for the diminished attachment to the mother. Although these early behaviors are modified as children mature, they would establish modes of response that can be carried into later life, particularly when these are reinforced by conditions that promote more compliance and affiliation for females and more aggression and competitiveness for males. We propose then, that very early socialization establishes patterns that are reinforced in childhood and adolescence.

This position is similar to that of Chodorow (1978), who attributed gender differences and their replication, generation after generation, to the fact that it is women who mother. She stated: "Because of their mothering by women, girls come to experience themselves as less separate than boys, as having more permeable ego boundaries. Girls come to define themselves more in relation to others" (Chodorow 1978:93). After reviewing the clinical and interview evidence, she concluded (Chodorow 1978:109):

> Because they are the same gender as their daughters and have been girls, mothers of daughters tend not to experience these infant daughters as separate from them in the same way as do mothers of infant sons. In both cases, a mother is likely to experience a sense of oneness and continuity with her infant. However, this sense is stronger, and lasts longer, vis-à-vis daughters.[2]

An important feature of Chodorow's analysis is that she emphasized the interactive nature of socialization for gender identity and behavior. Unlike many psychologists who put the burden of individuation upon the infant, she asserted that the emotional breaking away of the child is due to push from the mother as well as pull by the child itself.

The interpretations just discussed are not necessarily mutually exclusive, nor do they exclude the possibility of gender differences in behavior based on neurological or hormonal variance between the sexes, which is particularly compatible with Draper's concept of prepared learning. There is impressive evidence for biological differences in the sexes that go beyond the primary and secondary sex characteristics. Considerable research has been done on the sex-specific hormones and their effects on the central nervous systems of male and female fetuses. While human infants have not been experimentally reared in isolation from others from whom sex role learning could take place, higher primates have, and they exhibit sex-typed behavior. These observations support a conclusion that some differences between the sexes have a biological base on which social learning elaborates.

A biological base does not exclude the role of culture or setting in ameliorating these differences. In small foraging bands such as the !Kung of the Kalahari Desert (Draper and Cashdan 1988) or the Eskimo (Richard Condon, personal communication) there are rarely enough children around at any one time to permit sex-specific or age-specific play or peer groups to form. Children and young adolescents of both sexes tend to play together, although girls marry shortly after puberty and the older boys are often away practicing their hunting. In these cases, gender differences, at least in childhood, may be less than they are in societies whose population size allows for sex- and age-specific peer groups that reinforce socialization for sex roles and instill marked contrasts in behavior.

In a species such as our own, in which individuals reflect on and deliberately modify their own activities and those of others, the determination of any pervasive human difference such as gender is unlikely to have a simple or single cause. It is certainly unwarranted to take a strong stand for either sex-role learning or prepared learning to the exclusion of the other position, when there is supportive evidence for both. As Daly and Wilson (1978:251) rightly stated: "Thinking in terms of nature versus nurture is nowhere more mischievous than in the study of sex differences." Some of the determinants will be unique to our species, while others may be shared with other primates.

Although monkeys and apes are not humans with fur, there are primate behavioral analogs that can be used, with caution, in developing or supporting hypotheses about our species. One such behavior relevant to infant extrusion is the reported observation that rhesus monkey mothers embrace and clasp female infants more than males and show less threat and rejecting behavior to females than to males (Mitchell and Brandt 1970, cited in Maccoby and Jacklin 1974). Research on other species indicates that this sex difference in infant socialization is widespread among troop dwelling primates: Simonds (1977) cited studies that show similar patterns among bonnet macaques, savannah baboons, hamadryas baboons, and langurs. Among the bonnet macaques, female infants are groomed and handled more gently than males. It may be that by this means the mother binds the female to herself and her female assembly.

One observable difference among primate infants is that males more than females leave the assembly to play with other infants, and their play is rougher. The male infant savannah baboon is ejected from the female assembly by females (excluding his mother) before he is weaned, whereas female infants remain with the assembly and do not spend the long hours in play that their brothers do. Even though female hamadryas baboons spend their juvenile and adult lives in "harems" with a single male consort instead of in female assemblies, as infants they also leave the mother less often between nursings and groomings than do males. (The "harem" itself constitutes a kind of small female assembly.) Langur female infants remain close to their mothers and other females, whereas male infants begin to seek out contacts with adult males by approaching them. Simonds (1977:170) summed up the evidence by stating that "a mother monkey reacts differently to her male and female offspring, with the result that the male is forced to become independent earlier than the female and to associate with his peer play group."[3]

We would not expect any difference in treatment between the infant girl and boy to be as marked as between the female and male infant primate, because the human infant is being socialized for life in a mixed-sex family whereas the (troop-dwelling) primate infant is preparing to attach itself either to female assemblies or to male cohorts. Nevertheless, the primate data suggest a similar but much more subtle pattern in human mother-child interaction.

We come to the conclusion that the final cause of sexual separation in human society is to aid in the prevention of close inbreeding. Final causes are realized through proximal causes. The proximal cause we have identified is the greater extrusion by the mother of the boy than of the girl in the normal socialization process. This does not preclude other possible proximal causes, such as a greater propensity for boys, as a result of prenatal hormonal effects, to pull away from the mother, to explore their environment and manipulate objects, and to form attachments to age-mates rather than to older individuals. In other words, there is no conflict between sex-role learning, in the form of the mother establishing gender difference through her differential treatment of the sexes, and prepared learning, through biological differences already present at birth.

Given close female attachments, it is easy to see why mothers should incorporate their daughters into their circles, making the mixed-age associations of women and girls analogous to the primate "female assembly." But why do fathers and other men exclude adolescent boys from their "male cohorts"?

There are several possible answers. One is that men and boys have fewer interests in common than women and girls, as boys have little to offer adult men outside the home, whereas girls do domestic tasks with their mothers. This answer is not entirely satisfactory, for it presupposes a domestic domain of women and a public domain of men. Such a division does not appear in many places. In the more complex societies, boys may indeed be unprepared to interact freely with men, as they lack the skills or other criteria of adulthood, such as control over property, to be accepted. But in even the simplest societies, boys take a back seat to socially recognized adults even though they may differ very little in skills or technical knowledge.

Another possible answer is that men fear the sexual competition of adolescent boys and seek to exclude and dominate them. This argument is implied in some of the psychoanalytic literature that views circumcision (actually quite limited in worldwide distribution) as a modification of castration and evidence for hostility displaced into ritual. For most societies in this sample, though, there is a rather high degree of trust and affection between father and son, indicating that any fear or hostility is so suppressed or displaced as not to prevent friendly relations. Fathers in most cases appear to see sons as extensions of themselves and not as competitors; they promote their interests rather than impede them.

We relate the exclusion of boys by men to modes of interaction established in childhood. Boys who are extruded, as we have offered, seek social gratification in age-mates, thus establishing age-segregated associations as more of a pattern for males than for females. This pattern can emerge at any time in the life cycle when it is reinforced. In most cases, there is continual reinforcement, the childhood play group developing into the adolescent peer group, which in turn becomes the cohort of men and sometimes a further cohort of aged men. Age-exclusivity is only relative: as discussed in Chapter 8, societies with little contact between boys and men are deviant, and this type is likely to produce somewhat deviant boys. Nevertheless, it is the men of the family who have close contact with boys in most places; and no matter how frequent and close this contact may be, boys are not generally brought into the extra-domestic activities of related or unrelated men.

## Critical Issues in Gender Differences

In much of the psychological literature on gender difference there seems to be an implicit assumption that feminine personality, lacking the independence and autonomy of the masculine, or at least the masculine ideal, is disadvantaged. We are faced with a critical question: is female attachment somewhat pathological?

A second issue that must have occurred to anyone reading this chapter is the question of immutability of gender distinctions. How much of a difference can culture make?

### Is Female Attachment Detrimental?

To ask whether female attachment is detrimental is to raise another question: in what way is it detrimental? Do interconnection and emotional dependence between mother and daughter prevent either woman from becoming her own, self-actualized, person? Does such connectedness lead to mutual dependence such that neither woman is free to make her own decisions or that both suffer from some kind of blurred identity?

A physical separation between mother and daughter may or may not occur at the time of the daughter's marriage. When the husband joins the wife's household, the separation of mother and daughter does not occur. When the couple sets up its own residence, it is often in the same community as the girl's family, or alternates between the communities of each spouse. (A matrifocal tendency is also quite common for the rural proletariat and for working-class urban peoples in industrial nations, as many sociological studies of the modern family have demonstrated.) In these cases, the closeness of the young woman and her mother continues throughout the mother's life, although the interests of mother and daughter diverge somewhat. Some balance between dependence and independence of the women is achieved. Commonly, the younger woman relies heavily on her mother for help and advice when her children are young, the balance tipping as the mother ages and the daughter assumes a more parental role of care and responsibility for her mother.

The separation between mother and daughter is more sharp and severe when the girl leaves her childhood home at marriage to enter the household of the husband and his family. Frequently, the households are some distance apart. It is well recognized that the young woman misses her mother and female kin deeply, and provisions are usually made for her to make visits home at various times. These visits generally become less frequent as the wife gets older and grows more into her marriage and her husband's and children's household.

Even when the married daughter remains in her mother's household, there seems to be no problem over separate identities. The first author has been struck by the extremely strong attachments between mother and daughter and sisters among the formerly matrilocal Hopi. The women of the family used to stay together throughout their adult lives. Even today, they form intimate and supportive clusters, in contact with one another one or more times a day. (The adolescent protest of the Hopi girl described for earlier times in Chapters 4 and 9 was not a fight for autonomy but a response to increased discipline and the pressure to find a husband. Once she was married, and particularly after she had given birth, the young Hopi woman resumed her close and affectionate relation to her mother, and the women coordinated their activities and consulted one another on important matters.) Although it would be unrealistic to suppose that disagreements do not arise or that there are never personality incompatibilities, every ethnographer who has spent time with the Hopi has remarked on the closeness of female kin. The antagonisms expressed in myths and ritual are not between women but occur within the central cross-sex dyads of the social structure, the brother-sister pair of the matrilineal clan and the husband-wife pair of the household (Schlegel 1979).

Ethnographers who work in societies in which the lifelong attachments between women are extremely close have no difficulty in finding strong-minded and assertive women, realistically aware of opportunities and constraints and ready to act in the best interests of themselves and their families. The bonds between Hopi female kin, just discussed, do not appear to create an adult female personality that is dependent or infantile; the same observers who remark on close female cooperation also comment on the air of self-confidence and authority that Hopi women give off and on their readiness to take charge and to assert their wishes and opinions. Such personalities are also to be found among women secluded in harems in male-dominated societies like those of some parts of the Middle East. From the evidence of their own eyes, ethnographers would hesitate to speak of blurred identities or constricting dependence as a general problem when mothers and daughters have close ties.

Some psychologists are questioning the assumption that a strong attachment between mother and adult daughter is a sign of emotional immaturity. Gilligan (1982) delineated the moral outcome of female connectedness as a morality of caring and responsibility. Cohler and Grunebaum (1981:334–335) illustrated this shift away from the earlier view in their conclusions drawn from a study of Italian-American women and their mothers:

> As this book shows, many adult women may not have become fully differentiated or psychologically separate from their own mothers. This statement sounds at first pejorative—a most unfortunate conclusion for two men to make—particularly since we have tried to avoid making any judgment regarding the significance for adjustment of this flexible differentiation that characterizes the mode of relationship between women and their relatives. Clearly, it is time to re-examine traditional views of the supposed ideal mode of adult interpersonal relationships and to recognize the degree of interdependence that is far more characteristic of adult relationships than the "autonomy" described by theorists such as Goldfarb.

They noted that women learn to be responsive to the needs of others and suggested that a cognitive style that is responsive to context be relabelled from "field-dependence" to "environmentally sensitive." With this we concur.

An acceptance of close female attachment as normal and conducive to emotional health does not mean that it is necessarily free of problems. With both the greater attachment of the girl and woman and the lesser attachment of the boy and man, some balance must be struck. For either sex, attachment can become an emotional choke-hold on the fulfillment of the individual's ability to make his or her decisions. On the other hand, a too early or too great push into independence can leave the individual, of either sex, with a hunger for unfulfilled closeness or the fear that this human need is unfulfillable, and thus it is safer to avoid intimacy.

The findings from this study lead to the conclusion that the affiliative needs of girls can be satisfactorily met through close attachments to mothers and other women, while the affiliative needs of boys more than girls can be satisfied through peer group relations. Many girls in modern societies may suffer from the lack of close ties to women, particularly if the relationship with the mother is disturbed. This may account for the observation of Offer and Sabshin (1984:97) that "it has been our finding that adolescent girls find the high school years more taxing psychologically. Hence they have more signs and symptoms, have more problems with their affect than boys, and do not cope as well with life." In the unusually highly peer-oriented settings of contemporary adolescence, girls would seem to be more vulnerable to the frustration of affiliative needs than boys and, accordingly, to show more signs of emotional distress.

Disturbances in the mother-daughter relationship may be more common in modern societies, in which both ideology and the looser ties within the kinship network, as compared to traditional societies, promote greater independence. (We earlier proffered thoughts about the mother-daugher relationship in the nuclear family, which is the characteristic family form in industrial societies.) Clinical psychologists and psychiatrists, who see disturbed patients, may wrongly assume from that evidence that difficulties are inherent in the relationship. One does not wish to romanticize the little community, and there is plenty of evidence for disturbed families in all kinds of societies; nevertheless, close ties among female kin appear, in this sample and in many ethnographic reports, to be a source of strength and comfort for women and a secure base from which they can move into the world, rather than a source of inhibition and infantile dependency.

## Are Gender Differences Immutable?

The strong version of the sex-role learning position holds that identical socialization would erase gender differences, while the strong version of the prepared learning position has it that culture can somewhat modify but not alter biological givens. A less strong version of the latter recognizes that humans, like other living beings, are evolving and that, as conditions change, so will the genetically determined attributes that permit successful adaptation. Furthermore, it has not been determined what those biological givens of sex difference actually are. Even the most fervent holder of the prepared learning position must grant that the intelligence to perceive and rationally to address needs and conditions, and the flexibility to adapt behavior in accordance with these, are species characteristics of *Homo sapiens*.

From the way we have phrased the issue, it should be apparent that we are friendly to the weaker version of the prepared learning position. The evidence suggests that there are more than trivial sex differences at birth and that differences are also established in the early treatment of the infant. These lead on to gender differences in young children.

At this point, the progression becomes murkier. Studies from life-course sociology and life-span psychology have cast doubt upon the belief that childhood irrevocably determines the course of adult personality and behavior. As Cohler and Boxer (1984:147) stated:

> Over the past twenty years, as results from pioneering longitudinal studies have been reported in the literature, earlier assumptions of development across the life course as necessarily linear and continuous have had to be qualified. Particularly in the area of personality development, it has become clear that earlier experiences are not necessarily related to later outcomes. . . . While earlier longitudinal research had focused primarily upon childhood as the central determinant of adult actions and intents, findings from longitudinal studies have suggested that no one phase of the life cycle may be identified as "primary" for later outcomes. . . .

We infer that early sex differences, while real, can be significantly modified. On this point, Ember's (1973) research is highly relevant. Ember worked in a village in Kenya, where she studied the effect of feminine tasks performed by boys on modifying typically masculine behavior, as defined by the community. She found that those boys who performed the typically feminine tasks behaved in more feminine ways than did boys who performed masculine tasks. Her explanation was that feminine tasks in this community kept girls, or boys who did them, near the home in close contact with the mother, and they frequently involved child care. As a result, boys became more compliant and nurturant. The setting as much as earlier experience was a factor in influencing the behavior of children.

It is our view that the differences between boys and girls established in infancy and early childhood can be strengthened if they are reinforced by settings in later life that impose feminine compliance and nurturance and masculine competitiveness, emotional distance, and egocentric achievement. They will be counteracted in settings that encourage young women to participate in task-oriented groups and young men to put less emphasis on power and more on building alliances through helping and caring. Gender differences are unlikely to disappear, but they need not disadvantage one sex or the other. There does not seem to be any sex difference in the capacity to learn.

# 11

# Review and Prospect

W E have taken a universalistic rather than a relativistic approach to adolescence. We see adolescence as a social stage in all human societies, intervening between nonreproductive childhood and reproductive adulthood. Our purpose has been to uncover the commonalities of this stage and to account for the variations.

The adolescents in most of the societies in our study are quite young, as marriage often takes place earlier in tribal groups than in the modern industrial nations. We identified a further stage when marriage and full adulthood are delayed, a youth stage, although we did not investigate it in detail. When such a stage exists, it is distinguished from adolescence by greater responsibility and freedom (although not necessarily sexual freedom for young women) and more serious attention to work and marital prospects (unless youths are young married people who will move into adulthood at some later point).

We are working within the tradition of life-course and life-span research. The concept of life as periodized into named or unnamed stages is found in many cultures. That it is a cultural product does not mean that it is arbitrary, however; for even though a human life is continuous, its developmental peaks have profound cultural consequences.

The most significant of these peaks in early life is the acquisition of language, a feature unique to our species. Although language is not essential for social interaction—the communication of information, intentions, and dispositions—as indicated by the many animal species whose lives are lived in social groups, it is essential for the invention of and reflection upon culture. The culturally constructed person does not exist apart from language.

Puberty, the change to a biologically reproductive being, is another such dramatic transition. Although the precise timing of the beginning of adolescence as a social stage varies, it is everywhere associated with pubertal events such as menstruation, the appearance of secondary sexual features like the girl's breasts or the boy's facial hair, or general changes in body conformation.

We have drawn from research in child development, ethology, and primatology to explain some of the universal, generic features of adolescence, in particular the gender differences. We have proposed a human ethogram, or model of social organization by sex and age, that locates adolescent peer groups among the other significant types of social groups, the single-sex adult groups and the group within which biological and social reproduction take place—specifically the family but in many societies including the kin group. Adolescents, unlike children, are capable of reproducing but, unlike adults, are not yet incorporated into reproductive relationships. This model, we maintain, is universal for boys but not necessarily so for girls, who may lack a social adolescence or have only a very short one, depending on the speed with which girls are moved into marriage or motherhood. The key points that the model illustrates are (1) the imposed or self-segregation of the sexes that commonly occurs in preindustrial societies by adolescence if not before and (2) the greater extrusion of boys than girls from close relations with same-sex adults and, consequently, the greater salience of peer groups for boys than for girls.

The final cause for this social arrangement, we maintain, is the avoidance of close inbreeding. In this, our species behaves like most other animals and has evolved social mechanisms to guard against incest. A complicating factor in human social organization is the continuity over time of the mixed-sex family, which provides abundant opportunity for incest. By some degree of separation of the sexes and by drawing the attention of the adolescent away from the family toward peers, the likelihood of incest is reduced. Psychological inhibitions and the incest taboo also aid in inhibiting incest. Although these factors do not prevent incest altogether, parent-child and sibling matings in adolescence are infrequent and do not endanger the viability of the species.

The final cause argument does not, however, tell us how these social arrangements actually come into being generation after generation. For proximal causes, we have looked to adult social roles and to child socialization. Adolescents, particularly boys, are excluded from adult activities and thus encouraged to associate with peers. In complex societies, adolescence may be a time when the more elaborated roles of adult life are learned in ways not possible for the immature child. But even in the simplest societies, boys take a back seat to socially recognized men even though they have learned adult skills.

We have discussed early child socialization as a major factor in the development of gender difference. We propose that mothers treat boys and girls differently, extruding boys more than girls. The result is that boys seek out age mates for social affiliation more than do girls. This difference in extrusion establishes a pattern whereby throughout childhood and into adolescence, boys are involved more with peers and less with the mother than are girls. Boys are likely to be more involved with their fathers than are girls, but the total involvement with the parent of the same sex is less for boys. In other words, there seems to be greater extrusion both from the family and from same-sex adult company for boys and consequently greater reliance on peers.

At the same time that we have attempted to establish universal or generic patterns of adolescence, we have also looked at differences among cultures and the factors that explain them. We have seen that the behavior and treatment of adolescents varies according to subsistence needs and constraints, property ownership or its absence, the structure of the family and the community, and anticipations of adult life.

In looking for explanations, we have considered both antecedent and situational factors, particularly in our discussions of disposition toward antisocial behavior (Chapter 8) and of character traits (Chapter 9), in which we identify several features of infancy and early childhood associated with later outcomes in adolescence. The debate between antecedent and situational factors as causes is a lively one and cannot be settled by simply looking at correlations.

The strong version of the "antecedent" position is that character is formed when the child is very young and can be modified only slightly. As we discussed in Chapter 10, in which we considered the modification of sex-typed behavior established early in life, this position has been called into question by the results of longitudinal studies of personality. The strong version of the "situational" position says that the same cultures that produce adolescent personality and behavior through the settings in which they place adolescents also produce the treatment of children, so that even statistically significant associations between variables of childhood and adolescence are coincidental rather than causally related.

A weaker version of the "situational" position is that early socialization results in proclivities that can be reinforced or counteracted later in life. This version seems the best fit with the data, which indicate situational features consonant with antecedent ones.

The cases in this sample represent a world that has vanished. However, researchers are beginning to undertake studies of adolescence in modernizing societies, formerly traditional peoples who are undergoing a transition to industrial production and experiencing massive social changes that this brings in its wake. The most extensive project in anthropology has been the Harvard Adolescence Project of the early 1980s, under the direction of Beatrice B. and John W. M. Whiting, in which ethnographic studies were conducted in seven field sites. Four of the resulting ethnographies have appeared (Burbank 1988; Condon 1987; Davis and Davis 1989; Hollos and Leis 1989). In addition to the results of the project, a number of reports on other societies have also appeared or are in progress. It is to such studies that we can turn to learn what becomes of adolescents who reach this transitional stage in life in a context of rapid cultural change.

## Adolescence in Modernizing Societies

For the last few centuries, the center of economic and technological innovations and the accompanying social transformations has been the nations of Europe and European settlers, lumped together as "Western" society and culture. There is a tendency to think in terms of polarities, of "Western" as opposed to "other." This is dangerous. We cannot ignore the immense variety of non-Western societies, from the descendants of ancient civilizations of Asia and the Middle East to the remnant groups of foragers that until recently lived in pockets or on the fringes of more complex societies. The effects of modernization, of transformations to industrial states or of accommodations to them, vary along with the nature of the transforming society. The process of transformation varies also according to the nature of the first contact: precolonial trading partnerships, colonial rule, or the sudden absorption of tribes into present-day states. It is extremely difficult, if not impossible, to generalize about adolescence in modernizing societies. The experience of adolescents in a formerly foraging-band society now located as a special-status group within a modern nation, like the Inuit of Canada (Condon 1987), is very different from that of adolescents in Morocco (Davis and Davis 1989), heirs of an old civilization that was in the recent past a colony of France.

A common feature of adolescence in all modernizing societies, however, is an educational system grounded in the humanistic and scientific traditions of the West. For better or for worse, within the last century Western culture has become a global culture, more so than any competing set of knowledge and values. Almost everywhere, adolescents are learning the scientific view of the world, often as they learn to read a European language. Some benefit by broadening their horizons to include two cultural traditions, the ablest attaining a kind of cross-cultural sophistication that few Westerners do. For others, the end result is confusion and loss: having inadequately learned their own culture, they fail to become adept in the one they encounter in school.

Western culture affects more than the educational system. Whether directly in the form of music, films, videotapes, television, and imported or translated literature or indirectly through local copies of these media, young people are learning new ways of thinking and behaving. The Indonesian magazine *Topchords,* which features guitar chords and lyrics of Indonesian and Western popular music and information about musicians and clothing (Siegel 1986), is communicating to its teenage readers the same message for success (of the popular musicians it writes about) that one finds in the American popular press: talent, some work, and a good deal of luck. (A strong weight on luck is, of course, not foreign to Indonesian tradition, in which gambling is a popular form of recreation.) Rock musicians, film stars, and sports heroes are the idols of adolescents worldwide, personifying adolescent fantasies of wealth and freedom.

Many elements around which adolescent recreation revolves in the West and increasingly in other parts of the world—music, videos, video games, sports facilities—are not the product of adolescent imagination or organization but are rather commodities produced by adults for the teenage market. If there is an adolescent "culture," it is largely one manipulated by adults who provide what they believe adolescents will buy. One rarely hears of European or American teenagers composing their own songs or organizing village festivities, like some of the adolescents we met in Chapter 5. Given little responsibility to society and little authority over certain, albeit small, domains of social life, modern adolescents seldom act as autonomous groups in constructive, socially meaningful ways. If young people are successful during their adolescent years, it is as talented individuals or in activities organized by adults for adolescents like school sports, not through peer groups who plan their own actions and are rewarded by appreciative adults. Opportunities for adolescents are constrained and their scope of activities determined by adults in all societies, but in many parts of the world, peer groups seemed to play larger social roles before their transitions to modern and modernizing societies than they do today.

Ironically, adolescents are losing incentives to plan and act at the same time that they are becoming increasingly emancipated from the control of parents and other adult authorities. Over and over, the decline in adult authority over adolescents is reported as a cause of grave concern and distress. Of the many contributing factors, it would not be fair to blame only the winds of cultural change blowing from the West.

One factor is education, valued by modernizing countries and needed by them to raise productivity. It removes adolescent children from home and kin and places them in peer settings for much of the day. When family and school cooperate and reinforce one another, as in present-day China where children are scolded and shamed at home if their schoolwork is deficient, the school setting does not diminish parental authority. If there is a discordance of values, parental values do not necessarily triumph. Adolescents who do remain true to the values of their elders can fail to learn the skills and attitudes that lead to effective participation in modern life. Ausubel (1965) believed that this accounts for some of the difficulties faced by Maori youth of New Zealand, contrasting them with Polynesian counterparts in Western Samoa, Cook Islands, and Fiji. When parents insist that children assume the same level of household responsibility that earlier generations did, the adolescent may be caught between the demands of household tasks and the demands of schoolwork. This happens to Ijo girls of Nigeria (Hollos and Leis 1989), leading to conflict with the mother.

Another factor in the decline of parental authority is the delay in marriage, caused by increasing opportunities for both sexes to pursue education and by expanding employment of young women. The older a person gets, the less amenable he or she is to parental dictates. Nevertheless, girls and their parents resist early marriage when girls can get jobs, as both the daughter and her family benefit from the wages she brings in.

Opportunities for wage labor remove control over the individual's economic future from the hands of the adults, primarily kin, who controlled it in most societies in times past. (An important exception is the foraging groups where, in the absence of property, young people created their own opportunities and, as we have seen, were not so obedient as adolescents in property-owning societies.) Employment not only delays marriage for girls; it also increases the independence of adolescents and youths of both sexes. As the factory replaced the field as the dominant locus of production in Europe, adolescents and youths were able to find better jobs and free themselves from parental control. Emancipation is possible when there is a shortage of labor and young people can choose among alternatives. However, when jobs are scarce and one must use influence to get them, independence does not flourish. As Hollos and Leis (1989:83-84) related for the Ijo:

> What is important now is that most of the youngsters want to continue schooling and intend to secure good jobs and positions. For this they need help, and for this help they are dependent on either their parents or their parents' siblings. . . . Because usually there are far more children in a family than potential sponsors, school-age children are often kept in line by competition for the goodwill of kinsmen who are successful or influential men.

They gain this goodwill by being obedient and deferential. In such cases, adults and adolescents develop a sort of patron-client relationship.

Delaying the marriage of girls in societies in which adolescents formerly had sexual freedom can result in a high number of premarital pregnancies if there is no concomitant change in sexual mores or practices. Pregnancy need not raise barriers to the girl's successful completion of her education or pursuit of employment if there are adults willing to care for or adopt the child. Adolescent pregnancy does not seem to have adverse effects for Ijo girls (Hollos and Leis 1989) or for the Inuit girls of Canada (Condon 1987). For the Australian Aboriginal community studied by Burbank (1988), unmarried pregnancy is a new phenomenon, as in former times girls were married before menarche. Burbank cited cases of girls using their pregnancies to push through marriage to young men of their choice rather than to men preferred by their parents, thus upsetting their parents' plans for social alliances. For these contemporary Aborigines, absence of control over a daughter's sexuality threatens loss of control over the marriage she will make.

The Moroccan girls studied by Davis and Davis (1989) have been put into a dilemma by the increased freedom of movement and the opportunities to meet boys in the classroom. The old prohibition of any intimation of sexuality on the part of girls is still intact, contradicting the messages of romantic love that enter through films, television, and popular literature. Former levels of propriety are difficult to maintain under modern conditions, and it may even be that girls who are more daring are more likely to end up with a husband. In a society in which control over female sexuality is an important feature of male control over women, the possibility of a daughter or sister becoming pregnant endangers men's self-esteem as well as their honor and the reputation of their families. It is not easy for girls to balance the propriety demanded by kin and community with the possibility that this propriety will impede the highest goal to which most of them aspire, marriage to a good husband.

Decline in adult authority over adolescents is usually framed in terms of parental authority, but that is too narrow a view. Parents do not control adolescents unaided by community norms and sanctions; boys in particular, as we have seen, are likely to behave well when they are much in the presence of men. These men do not necessarily have to be their fathers.

The greater freedom of young people causes distress to adults who feel that they are losing authority within their households, but it can open new possibilities to adolescents to seek happier lives. It is easy to forget that the often well-regulated systems of other times and places contained individuals with blighted hopes and frustrated expectations, not because of any deficiencies on their parts but because they were the pawns of family strategies that overlooked their needs. The adolescent Hopi boy who obeyed his father's request to return home to help with the farm when he wanted to pursue his education still expressed his disappointment sixty years later as he sadly recalled that time of his life to the first author.

Freedom to succeed also means freedom to fail. One effect of schooling in modern and modernizing societies is to sort out those who are and are not academically able. Every class-stratified society has its processes for recruiting people into the different classes, and education has increasingly become a major means for this recruitment throughout the world. It is not surprising that fantasies of success, wealth, and fame should be so prominent in class-stratified societies as an escape from the prospect of completing school—to many adolescents, dreary or unattainable. These fantasies may change in their cast of characters from earlier times, the movie queen becoming the new Cinderella and the rock star or sports hero replacing the poor boy who marries the princess (and the equivalents of Cinderella and the poor boy in other mythologies), but the mechanism of success in these fantasies is the same, good fortune. For most of today's adolescents, however, failure at school can mean the loss of opportunity or even downward social mobility.

Studies of adolescence in the West often deal with self-perception and the attitudes adolescents have toward their bodies. Adolescents all over the world are conscious of their appearance: one notes with some amusement reports of young people running off to the river to bathe and beautify themselves when their parents would rather have them home working in the gardens, or the careful attention given to body painting and decoration before some village festivity. It does seem, however, that Western adolescents, and perhaps American adolescents in particular, are inordinately conscious of their appearance and overwhelmingly dissatisfied with it. The Western, and especially American, emphasis on youth and beauty has often been blamed, and we do not deny the importance of this glorification of the superficial. However, there is another factor. Adolescents not only compare their changing bodies with some impossible ideal, but they also compare them with the bodies of their contemporaries. Those who mature too quickly may be embarrassed, while the late maturers may harbor doubts and fears about their attainment of physical adulthood. Adolescents in societies in which children are not grouped by chronological age but rather by observable level of physical maturity, as in most societies in our sample, do not suffer from invidious comparisons of themselves with others, at least not when level of maturity is being compared. As grouping by chronological age becomes more common worldwide, we anticipate that anxieties over their bodies will spread among adolescents.

Researchers have failed to find the *Sturm und Drang* that supposedly characterizes adolescence in Western society, nor does it generally seem to characterize adolescence in modernizing societies either. For all the uncertainties about the future that adolescents in these societies feel and the discrepancies in experience between themselves and their parents and grandparents, ethnographic reports do not indicate general apathy, despair, or serious rebellion. As Davis and Davis (1989:182) found:

> Erikson's account of an adolescent identity beleaguered by contradictory role expectations sounds like it would work well in the rapidly changing Moroccan setting, but in fact we have not seen much of the "role confusion" of which Erikson writes. Zawiya youth seem to us surprisingly good at negotiating the twists and turns of daily life.

In communities that remain intact, adolescents are likely to find their own way through the generation gap and into an adult society that will welcome their new skills.

## Some Implications for Modern Adolescence

Our exploration of gender differences has been of central importance to our effort. A major finding, mentioned throughout this book and discussed in some detail in Chapter 10, has been the different social settings of the sexes: girls are involved more with same-sex adults, while boys are involved more with peers. We have already explored some of the ramifications of this behavior of adolescents. Here we would like to consider implications for understanding adolescence in Western society. Industrial Western communities were not included in our sample, and therefore we are limited to presenting hypotheses and suggestions for research.

We proposed in Chapter 10 that boys, more than girls, find social satisfaction in relations with peers. In peer-oriented settings like the modern school, girls may be vulnerable to loneliness and unhappiness if their attachments to their mothers or other adult females are disturbed. They may be less able than boys to substitute peer relations for family attachments.

In general, it appears that girls are more dependent than boys on relations with family members, while by adolescence boys enter the larger world more through their peer groups. Thus, boys may respond more strongly to breakdown of community organization while girls may be more sensitive to disruption within the home. We propose that when the mother-daughter bond or another attachment to an adult female is strong, girls are protected from adverse community influences in ways boys are not. On the other hand, close peer ties and the feeling of belonging in the community help boys more than girls to weather a troubled home.

These insights may help to explain why boys from "good homes" can become delinquent. Our data show that, in general, antisocial behavior is more common for boys than for girls. For the most part, the antisocial behavior committed by adolescents in the sample is more of a nuisance than serious delinquency: their violence rarely kills or maims, and most theft could be likened more to the petty shoplifting of Western children than to the theft of a car or significant amounts of goods. The antisocial behavior found in European and American communities, as well as in many cities of modernizing nations, can be of a different order. The adolescent crime of the urban slums is the result, we believe, more of community than family breakdown. Boys' delinquency, acted out in groups more than as individuals, is not necessarily a product of family failure. In such crime-ridden quarters as East Los Angeles or its equivalent, the best home socialization is helpless in the face of gangs of adolescents and youths unconstrained by community sanctions. In these parts, if one does not join, one is an enemy. The community structures that evolve to regulate behavior crumble in the face of massive migrations into the cities; they cannot even develop when constant turnover in the neighborhood population creates social anonymity. (For a similar picture of adolescence in the urban slums of 19th century America, see Kett 1977.)

To illustrate, the low rate of delinquency in American Chinese communities was often credited to the tight control of the Chinese family over its members. Yet, as the ethnographic sketch in Chapter 5 reveals, boys and youths were under the authority of men in Chinatowns, executing their wishes and receiving rewards from them. These men controlled the resources on which the boys depended for future success, and the boys were their social apprentices. New opportunities and waves of (often illegal) immigration into Chinatowns have shaken that hierarchy. We propose that the rise in male delinquency in such communities is due to changes in the authority of the male hierarchy more than to changes in the Chinese family.

The ways to help antisocial or troubled adolescents may differ according to sex. For both sexes, friends and family are important for social support and the enjoyment of life. Girls might be helped more by programs designed to strengthen the ties they have with mothers and individual women, whereas boys might respond more to efforts involving groups of boys and men, not necessarily their fathers (particularly when father-son relations are distant or strained), engaged in goal-oriented activities. Our findings on competitiveness and antisocial behavior, in Chapter 8, suggest that these activities should not be competitive but rather cooperative in nature. Building something together is more likely to lead to desired behavior than are competitive games.

Another issue that is receiving a good deal of attention currently is teenage motherhood. As we have seen, child-bearing need not doom the young mother to loss of schooling and good opportunities for employment. When she turns over the infant to kin to rear, she has become a mother biologically but not socially. In her eyes and the eyes of the community, she can remain an adolescent, and her chances in life need not be affected by her biological motherhood. This way of handling adolescent maternity has considerable merit. The young adolescent mother is not a woman and should not be expected to take on a woman's responsibilities.

While this way of handling adolescent maternity appears to be satisfactory in the cases discussed earlier in this chapter, communities in which women are not employed outside the home, it is questionable whether it works as well in industrialized economies. The mother of the adolescent, a woman in her thirties or forties, is likely to be employed and unwilling to quit her job in order to care for her daughter's child. Other female kin, like grandmothers and aunts, are also employed, or they have moved into another phase of their lives that does not accommodate the demands of infant care. Although the family may pressure a grandmother, for example, to take on her granddaughter's baby, she may well resent the imposition. The agents of the state who deal with pregnant adolescent girls must realize that the care of the future child is a family matter. For the girl who does not want an abortion, her female kin, who may be left with the responsibility of caring for the child, should be involved in any decisions concerning the infant.

---

We have proposed that social adolescence is a response to sexual development in humans. Social recognition is given to the growth of reproductive capacity as marking the end of childhood and the prelude to adult life. Sexual separation, as one barrier to inbreeding, is initiated or intensified.

By focusing on reproduction, we place human society within the framework devised by ethologists for the study of other species. We consider that kinship and marriage, the system of human biological and social reproduction, carries as great a weight as the system of production, which for a long time has held first place in many anthropological accounts as a determinant of human social organization.

The societies in our sample are very different today from what they were when the first ethnographic reports on them were made. Many important aspects of life have changed, and the experience of adolescence has altered in irrevocable ways. Are the patterns we have established for this preindustrial sample characteristic only of the "other" and not the West and the industrializing societies following its lead? We think not.

# Notes

## Chapter 1 / The Anthropological Study of Adolescence

1. A useful summary of these differing approaches, in this case to the study of games as an aspect of expressive culture, is provided by Avedon and Sutton-Smith (1971), who cited primarily the works of psychologists and sociologists.

2. The usual way of phrasing this discrepancy is to talk about "real" versus "ideal" culture. There is, however, a distinction between the concepts of real versus ideal culture and tradition versus cohort effect, for there can be a long-term "real" culture that is nevertheless responsive to short-term variations (cohort effect) due to time-specific conditions.

3. We have to remember that the societies in this study consist of face-to-face communities. Even in large cities, for example, Rome (Romans) or Tenochtitlan (Aztecs), people lived out their daily lives within wards that functioned as smaller communities, where adolescent behavior was monitored by adults. The adolescents considered here could not escape into anonymity.

4. Old age may vary from being a social stage marked by significant changes, as among Japanese village elderly given license to behave foolishly, to being simply a time in adulthood when physical capacities are diminished but roles, except for female reproductivity, are not altered in any socially significant way, as among the Hopi.

5. In cases of marriage occurring before puberty, the wife usually does not have sexual relations until menarche, at which time she is generally given adult status.

6. The coding manuals, codes, and tables of frequency distributions have been compiled in HRAF Cross-Cultural Data Series, vol. 4, *Adolescence,* by Herbert Barry III and Alice Schlegel (1990). This book is available from Human Relations Area Files Press, Box 2054 Yale Station, New Haven, Connecticut 06520.

## Chapter 2 / An Ethological Approach to Human Social Organization

1. This chapter grew out of a paper by the first author read at the Institute of Psychology, University of Zurich, to a seminar conducted by Professor Dr. Norbert Bischof.

2. The term *ethogram* is an adaptation of *biogram,* used by Count (1958) to mean

an animal's anatomy and physiology, or its structure and processes, along with its characteristic way of living. This configuration is a consequence of evolution. We use *ethogram* similarly, to mean the evolved structure and behavior of a human set. The set in this case is human beings restricted by two parameters, age and sex, and the relations among age-sex classes.

### Chapter 3 / Looking at Adolescent Socialization Across Cultures

1. As we could not find data on the age of puberty for boys in traditional societies comparable to that available on menarche, we do not know whether the sex differ-ence in age of reproductive capacity is constant (allowing for individual differences within populations) or varies according to diet, environmental factors, or other causes. If boys' puberty is less variable than girls', that is, if 13 to 15 is a fairly con-stant age range for this event, then in some cases we have underestimated the length of adolescence for boys.

2. We did not consider the highlands New Guinea populations in arriving at our estimate, as they seem to represent a deviant cluster of societies.

### Chapter 4 / Adolescents and Their Families

1. *Parents* includes stepparents, adoptive parents, and foster parents as well as nat-ural parents. In societies with a high mortality rate for young and middle-aged adults, there is no guarantee that the mother and father to whom the child was born will be alive when it reaches adolescence. A relatively high rate of stepparenthood, increas-ing with the increasing age of child, is indicated for a foraging society, the Aka Pyg-mies of Africa, in Hewlett (1990).

### Chapter 5 / Peer Groups and Community Participation

1. The view that females are innately less competitive than males received a blow in the widely acclaimed research of Hrdy (1981) on female primates. She presents a con-vincing argument for female competitiveness among related species. The goals and form of competition among females, both human and other primate, may differ from those of males, but activities to promote self-interest at the expense of others occur within both sexes.

### Chapter 6 / Mating, Marriage, and the Duration of Adolescence

1. We doubt that patrilineal descent *per se* is the determinant of paternity concern. In Gaulin and Schlegel (1980), a number of societies rated as having low paternal confidence are patrilineal. We consider it more likely that property considerations are the determinant: when men invest heavily in the wife's children, they want to make sure that these children are their own.

2. Bridewealth is the gift of goods, of either productive or symbolic value, given in exchange for a bride to her kin. Token bridewealth refers to a small gift of this sort, usually of symbolic value. Bride service is the groom's payment of labor instead of goods for a wife to her family, lasting from a period of several months to several years or even the lifetime of the wife's parents. Gift exchange refers to a more or less equal exchange between kin of bride and groom. Women exchange occurs when the marriage of a woman from one kin group entails the return of a bride to her kin

group. Dowry is the transfer of goods from the bride's kin to the bride and her new household; it is not the mirror image of bridewealth, as the groom's kin do not receive it. Indirect dowry takes two forms: either the groom's kin give goods to the bride's kin, who in turn give all or a substantial part to the bride herself, or the groom's kin give goods directly to the bride to take into her marriage. More information on these types of marriage transactions and on their cultural concomitants can be found in Schlegel and Eloul (1987, 1988).

3. Frayser (1985:350) found an association between the prospective bride's or groom's consent to a marriage and the residence pattern. In societies with patrilocal residence, both girls and boys are less likely to be consulted and to give consent to a prospective marriage than in societies with other forms. Patrilocal societies have a much higher proportion of property-giving transactions than societies with other forms of residence, the latter more commonly giving bride service, exchanging women, or having no transaction beyond the giving of small gifts (cf. Schlegel and Eloul 1988, Table 6).

## *Chapter 7 / Adolescent Sexuality*

1. We did not code for bestiality, but we assume that it is much less widespread than the other forms and practiced, if at all, as a novelty or as a form of cruelty to animals rather than as a regular manner of releasing sexual tension.

2. We found no association between accessibility of caretaker and sexual permissiveness in our sample, although our measure of permissiveness and restrictiveness is associated with Broude and Greene's (1980) measure of attitudes toward premarital sex for girls at a probability level of < .0001.

3. The following discussion relies heavily on a related study by Schlegel (1991), using a different code for premarital sex norms, one that codes for ideology rather than behavior.

4. There is a discrepancy in the findings on gift exchange between this study and a related one (Schlegel 1991). The other study is concerned with the value placed on virginity, while this one is concerned with behavior. Virginity may be valued and be prescribed for elite adolescent girls whose marriages involve status negotiations and are accompanied by an exchange of substantial amounts of goods, at the same time that common people, who give and receive much less, are more relaxed regarding their daughters' sexual activities. This argument is developed in Schlegel (1991). A society may be coded as permissive for this book even though virginity is valued, if the majority of adolescents are given sexual freedom. The code here differs somewhat from that used in Schlegel (1991).

5. Socially condoned and medically safe abortions were, however, widely used in southeast Asia. See the discussion in Schlegel (1991).

6. Cf. Fay et al. (1989) for data on male homosexuality in the United States.

## *Chapter 8 / Violating Cultural Norms*

1. In addition to these areas, we have a fair amount of information on witchcraft. As we stated in Chapter 3, adolescents do not stand out as a class of either practitioners or victims when compared to persons of other ages. Furthermore, while witchcraft

may be used malevolently against others and thereby represents a form of antisocial behavior, it can equally well be used to protect oneself and one's property. As our measures of witchcraft are not fine-grained enough to permit interpretation with confidence, we will not consider that subject in the following analyses.

2. The testing of cross-cultural findings on intracultural samples has been called *subsystem validation* by Roberts and Sutton-Smith (1962). The use of two or more methods to study a problem is highly recommended.

3. Recently, a novel way of accounting for social deviance has been proposed by Draper and Harpending (1988) and Rowe (in press). They distinguished between two male reproductive strategies in animals: a paternal strategy, in which the male makes a large investment in offspring and mates with few females, and a mating strategy, in which he makes a small investment but mates with many. In the latter case, the females rear the offspring alone or with help from others who are not their fathers.

These researchers identified mating strategy in humans as characterizing sociopathic men, who are criminal, mobile, and promiscuous, who lack long-term bonds, and who produce illegitimate offspring and abandon them and their mothers. Rowe believes that some or all of the personality features contributing to this syndrome are genetic.

Although the evidence for the heritability of personality traits is becoming increasingly strong, a genetic explanation of crime or adolescent delinquency would have to account for the great variability across cultures. Although it is plausible that genetic factors are components in the antisocial behavior of individuals, it seems to us that they will be influential only in combination with socialization practices and social settings that reinforce them. These vary intraculturally. We have shown that they vary cross-culturally as well.

4. Although the rate of delinquency is greater for boys than for girls, delinquent girls in modern societies may commit the same kinds of acts, such as fighting and stealing, as delinquent boys, and fighting among young adolescent girls (up to about age 14 or 15) is not uncommon (Hendy 1983). Although expected antisocial behavior is very rare for girls in this sample, girls may also misbehave in ways similar to boys when it is present.

5. Here Devore assumed that aggression is a consequence of frustration, as did Bandura and Walters (1959). The evidence from this chapter cautions against applying theories of aggression directly to delinquent behavior, unless this is specifically violent behavior. As we have seen, there is theft, of the same order as white-collar crime, which is expressive of acquisitive rather than aggressive impulses and may be instrumental rather than reactive.

## Chapter 9 / The Adolescent Self

1. This finding does not imply the absence of any competition among the Hopi, for men compete with one another in the public arena where they gain their status and social recognition. However, little or no competition exists among brothers, and the sister-sister relationship is one of the greatest warmth and confidence.

2. Barry and Schlegel (1984, 1986) reported further analyses of cultural correlates with a measure of sexual freedom that includes the quantitative scale of sexual restraint.

3. Early rather than later childhood was used to insure that the childhood ratings were not influenced by information on adolescence. Later childhood, defined as ending around puberty, could overlap in some instances with social adolescence as we defined it.

## Chapter 10 / Gender Differences: Final and Proximate Causes

1. The distinction between equality and hierarchy in the experiences of boys and girls has been influenced by the work of Gilligan and her associates (Gilligan et al. 1988).

2. Chodorow's position, and ours, raises an issue of paternal care: if fathers or other males had total responsibility for infants as mothers or other women usually do, would the consequences for girls and boys be reversed, that is, would boys be drawn in and girls extruded? If adult women and men shared child-rearing equally, would this lead to androgyny? Chodorow (1978) speculated that shared parental care would minimize gender differences, but Rossi (1985) expressed doubt based on the available evidence. The question is open.

3. Information about sex-linked treatment by fathers or other adult males of infants in species other than our own is sparse and usually based on very small samples. What little is currently available can be found scattered throughout Taub (1984). In a study of stumptail macaques (Estrada 1984), female infants were subjected to more aggressive acts from male juveniles and adults than were male infants (sample size is seven infants). Among Japanese monkeys (Gouzoules 1984), males did not differentiate between male and female one-year-old infants but gave two-year-old females more carrying, grooming, and protection that the males. Chacma baboons (Busse 1984) equally carried female and male infants under one year. Lamb (1984), in his review of human fathers, remarked on the paternal preference for male infants, but to our knowledge no matrilineal or matrilocal societies, which often have a cultural preference for daughters, have been studied by psychologists for this trait. Human fathers respond more to sons, while mothers stimulate daughters more. Fathers increase their attention to sons early in the second year. Without much more evidence from primate species and from a variety of cultures, it would be difficult to generalize from these data.

# References

Aberle, David F., Urie Bronfenbrenner, Eckhard H. Hess, Daniel R. Miller, David M. Schneider, and James N. Spuhler. 1963. The Incest Taboo and the Mating Patterns of Animals. *American Anthropologist* 65:253–265.

Ainsworth, Mary D. Salter, Mary C. Blehar, Everett Waters, and Sally Wall. 1978. *Patterns of Attachment*. Hillsdale, N.J.: Lawrence Erlbaum Associates.

Aiyappan, A. 1934. Cross-Cousin and Uncle-Niece Marriages in South India. *Proceedings of the Congrès International des Sciences Anthropologiques et Ethnographiques,* 281–282. London.

Allerbeck, Klaus, and Wendy J. Hoag. 1985. *Jugund ohne Zukunft?* Munich: Piper.

Anderson, Wanni W., and Douglas D. Anderson. 1987. Thai Muslim Adolescents' Self, Sexuality, and Autonomy. *Ethos* 14:344–367.

Arensberg, Conrad. 1937. *The Irish Countryman.* New York: The Macmillan Company.

Ariès, Philippe. 1962. *Centuries of Childhood* (trans. R. Baldick). New York: Vintage Books.

Arnold, Marigene. 1978. Celibes, Mothers, and Church Cockroaches: Religious Participation of Women in a Mexican Village. In *Women in Ritual and Symbolic Roles,* ed. Judith Hoch-Smith and Anita Spring, 45–53. New York: Plenum.

Ausubel, David P. 1965. *Maori Youth: A Psychoethnological Study of Cultural Deprivation.* New York: Holt, Rinehart and Winston, Inc.

Avedon, F. M., and Brian Sutton-Smith. 1971. The Function of Games. In *The Study of Games,* ed. F. M. Avedon and Brian Sutton-Smith, 429–439. Melbourne, Florida: Krieger.

Awe, Bolanle. 1977. The Iyalode in the Traditional Yoruba Political System. In *Sexual Stratification: A Cross-Cultural View,* ed. Alice Schlegel, 144–160. New York: Columbia University Press.

Ayres, Barbara. 1967. Pregnancy Magic: A Study of Food Taboos and Sex Avoidances. In *Cross-Cultural Approaches,* ed. C. S. Ford, 111–125. New Haven: Human Relations Area Files Press.

Bacdayan, Albert S. 1977. Mechanistic Cooperation and Sexual Equality among the Western Bontoc. In *Sexual Stratification: A Cross-Cultural View,* ed. Alice Schlegel, 270–291. New York: Columbia University Press.

215

Bacon, Margaret K., Herbert Barry III, C. Buchwald, Irvin L. Child, and C. R. Snyder. 1965. A Cross-Cultural Study of Drinking. *Quarterly Journal of Studies of Alcohol,* Suppl. No. 3.

Bacon, Margaret K., Irvin L. Child, and Herbert Barry III. 1963. A Cross-Cultural Study of Correlates of Crime. *Journal of Abnormal and Social Psychology* 66:291–300.

Bakan, David. 1972. Adolescence in America: From Idea to Social Fact. In *Twelve to Sixteen: Early Adolescence,* ed. Jerome Kagan and Robert Coles, 73–89. New York: W. W. Norton and Company.

Balikci, Assen. 1970. *The Netsilik Eskimo.* Prospect Heights, Ill.: Waveland Press, Inc.

Bandura, Albert, and Richard H. Walters. 1959. *Adolescent Aggression.* New York: The Ronald Press.

Baranowski, Marc D. 1982. Grandparent-Adolescent Relations: Beyond the Nuclear Family. *Adolescence* 17:575–584.

Barnett, Homer C. 1949. *Palauan Society.* Eugene: University of Oregon Publications.

Barry, Herbert, III, Margaret K. Bacon, and Irvin L. Child. 1957. A Cross-Cultural Survey of Some Sex Differences in Socialization. *The Journal of Abnormal and Social Psychology* 55:327–332.

Barry, Herbert, III, Irvin L. Child, and Margaret K. Bacon. 1963. Relation of Child Training to Subsistence Economy. *American Anthropologist* 61:169–199.

Barry, Herbert, III, Lili Josephson, Edith Lauer, and Catherine Marshall. 1980a. Traits Inculcated in Childhood: Cross-Cultural Codes 5. In *Cross-Cultural Samples and Codes,* ed. Herbert Barry III and Alice Schlegel, 205–236. Pittsburgh: University of Pittsburgh Press.

Barry, Herbert, III, Lili Josephson, Edith Lauer, and Catherine Marshall. 1980b. Agents and Techniques for Child Training: Cross-Cultural Codes 6. In *Cross-Cultural Samples and Codes,* ed. Herbert Barry III and Alice Schlegel, 237–276. Pittsburgh: University of Pittsburgh Press.

Barry, Herbert, III, and Leonora M. Paxson. 1980. Infancy and Early Childhood: Cross-Cultural Codes 2. In *Cross-Cultural Samples and Codes,* ed. Herbert Barry III and Alice Schlegel, 161–204. Pittsburgh: University of Pittsburgh Press.

Barry, Herbert, III, and Alice Schlegel, eds. 1980a. *Cross-Cultural Samples and Codes.* Pittsburgh: University of Pittsburgh Press.

Barry, Herbert, III, and Alice Schlegel. 1980b. Early Childhood Precursors of Adolescent Initiation Ceremonies. *Ethos* 8:132–145.

Barry, Herbert, III, and Alice Schlegel. 1982. Cross-Cultural Codes on Contributions by Women to Subsistence. *Ethnology* 21:165–188.

Barry, Herbert, III, and Alice Schlegel. 1984. Measurements of Adolescent Sexual Behavior in the Standard Sample of Societies. *Ethnology* 23:315–329.

Barry, Herbert, III, and Alice Schlegel. 1986. Cultural Customs that Influence Sexual Freedom in Adolescence. *Ethnology* 25:51–62.

Barton, R. F. 1969. *Ifugao Law.* Berkeley and Los Angeles: University of California Press.

Baxter, P. T. W., and U. Almagor. 1978. Observations about Generations. In *Sex and Age as Principles of Differentiation,* ed. J. S. LaFontaine, 159–182. London: Academic Press.

Beauchamp, Gary K., Kunio Yamazaki, and Edward A Boyse. 1985. The Chemosensory Recognition of Genetic Individuality. *Scientific American* 253:86–92.

Benedict, Ruth. 1938. Continuities and Discontinuities in Cultural Conditioning. *Psychiatry* 1:161–167.

Benet, Sula. 1974. *Abkhasians: The Long-Living People of the Caucasus.* New York: Holt, Rinehart and Winston, Inc.

Bischof, Norbert. 1975a. Comparative Ethology of Incest Avoidance. In *Biosocial Anthropology,* ed. R. Fox, 37–67. New York: John Wiley and Sons.

Bischof, Norbert. 1975b. A Systems Approach Toward the Functional Connections of Attachment and Fear. *Child Development* 46:801–817.

Blos, Peter. 1979. *The Adolescent Passage: Development Issues.* New York: International Universities Press.

Bolton, Charlene, et al. 1976. Pastoralism and Personality: An Andean Replication. *Ethos* 4:463–482.

Boswell, John. 1989. *The Kindness of Strangers: The Abandonment of Children in Western Europe from Late Antiquity to the Renaissance.* New York: Pantheon.

Brandt, Vincent S. R. 1971. *A Korean Village: Between Farm and Sea.* Cambridge: Harvard University Press.

Bronfenbrenner, Uri. 1970. *Two Worlds of Childhood: U.S. and U.S.S.R.* New York: Simon and Schuster.

Broude, Gwen J. 1975. Norms of Premarital Sexual Behavior: A Cross-Cultural Study. *Ethos* 3:381–402.

Broude, Gwen J. 1981. The Cultural Management of Sexuality. In *Handbook of Cross-Cultural Human Development,* ed. Ruth H. Munroe, Robert L. Munroe, and Beatrice B. Whiting, 633–673. New York: Garland.

Broude, Gwen J., and Sarah J. Greene. 1980. Cross-Cultural Codes on Twenty Sexual Attitudes and Practices. In *Cross-Cultural Samples and Codes,* ed. Herbert Barry III and Alice Schlegel, 313–334. Pittsburgh: University of Pittsburgh Press.

Bulmer, R. N. H. 1965. The Kyaka of the Western Highlands. In *Gods, Ghosts and Men in Melanesia,* ed. P. Lawrence and M. J. Meggitt, 132–161. Melbourne: Oxford University Press.

Burbank, Victoria K. 1987. Premarital Sex Norms: Cultural Interpretations in an Australian Aboriginal Community. *Ethos* 15:226–234.

Burbank, Victoria K. 1988. *Aboriginal Adolescence: Maidenhood in an Australian Community.* New Brunswick: Rutgers University Press.

Burke, Peter. 1978. *Popular Culture in Early Modern Europe.* New York: Harper and Row, Inc.

Burton, Roger V., and John W. M. Whiting. 1961. The Absent Father and Cross-Sex Identity. *Merrill-Palmer Quarterly of Behavior and Development* 7:85–95.

Bush, Diane Mitsch, and Roberta Simmons. 1981. Socialization Processes over the Life Course. In *Social Psychology: Sociological Perspectives,* ed. M. Rosenberg and R. H. Turner, 33–64. New York: Basic Books.

Busse, Curt. 1984. Triadic Interactions among Male and Infant Chachma Baboons. In *Primate Paternalism,* ed. D. M. Taub, 186–212. New York: Van Nostrand Reinhold.

Caro Baroja, Julio. 1944. *La Vida Rural en Vera de Bidasoa (Navarre).* Instituto Antonio de Nebrija, Biblioteca de Tradiciones Populares. Madrid.

Chance, Michael R. A., and Clifford J. Jolly. 1970. *Social Groups of Monkeys, Apes, and Men.* London: Jonathan Cape.

Chodorow, Nancy. 1978. *The Reproduction of Mothering: Psychoanalysis and the Sociology of Gender.* Berkeley: University of California Press.

Cohen, Yehudi A. 1964. *The Transition from Childhood to Adolescence.* Chicago: Aldine Publishing Co.

Cohler, Bertram J., and Andrew M. Boxer. 1984. Middle Adulthood: Settling into the World—Person, Time and Context. In *Normality and the Life Cycle,* ed. Daniel Offer and Melvin Sabshin, 145–203. New York: Basic Books Inc.

Cohler, Bertram J., and Henry U. Grunebaum. 1981. *Mothers, Grandmothers, and Daughters: Personality and Childcare in Three-Generation Families.* New York: John Wiley and Sons.

Coleman, John C. 1980. Friendship and the Peer Group in Adolescence. In *Handbook of Adolescent Psychology,* ed. Joseph Adelson, 408–431. New York: John Wiley and Sons.

Coleman, James S. 1961. *The Adolescent Society.* New York: Free Press.

Collier, Jane F., and Michelle Z. Rosaldo. 1981. Politics and Gender in Simple Societies. In *Sexual Meanings,* ed. Sherry B. Ortner and Harriet Whitehead, 275–329. Cambridge: Cambridge University Press.

Condon, Richard G. 1987. *Inuit Youths: Growth and Change in the Canadian Arctic.* New Brunswick: Rutgers University Press.

Conger, John J. 1972. A World They Never Knew: The Family and Social Change. In *Twelve to Sixteen: Early Adolescence,* ed. Jerome Kagan and Robert Coles, 197–230. New York: W. W. Norton.

Count, Earl W. 1958. The Biological Basis of Human Society. *American Anthropologist* 60:1049–1085.

Creed, Gerald W. 1982. Sexual Subordination: Institutionalized Homosexuality and Social Control in Melanesia. *Ethnology* 21:157–176.

Daly, Martin, and Margo Wilson. 1978. *Sex, Evolution, and Behavior.* North Scituate, Mass.: Duxbury Press.

Davis, Natalie Zeman. 1971. The Reasons of Misrule: Youth Groups and Charivaris in Sixteenth-Century France. *Past and Present* 50:41–75.

Davis, Susan Schaefer, and Douglas A. Davis. 1989. *Adolescence in a Moroccan Town: Making Social Sense.* New Brunswick: Rutgers University Press.

Dennis, Wayne. 1940. *The Hopi Child.* New York: John Wiley and Sons.

DeVore, Irven. 1971. The Evolution of Human Society. In *Man and Beast: Comparative Social Behavior,* ed. J. F. Eisenberg and Wilton S. Dillon, 297–312. Washington: Smithsonian Institution Press.

Dibble, Charles E., and Arthur J. O. Anderson. 1961. *Florentine Codex.* Monographs of the School of American Research and the Museum of New Mexico. Santa Fe, New Mexico.

Dobrizhoffer, Martin. 1822. *An Account of the Abipones, an Equestrian People of Paraguay,* vol. 2. London: J. Murray (Latin Original 1784).

Draper, Patricia. 1985. Two Views of Sex Differences in Socialization. In *Male-Female Differences: A Biocultural Perspective,* ed. Roberta L. Hall, 5–25. New York: Praeger.

Draper, Patricia, and Elizabeth Cashdan, 1988. Technological Change and Child Behavior among the !Kung. *Ethnology* 27:339–366.

Draper, Patricia, and Henry Harpending. 1988. A Sociobiological Perspective on the Development of Human Reproductive Strategies. In *Sociobiological Perspectives on Human Development,* ed. Kevin B. MacDonald, 341–371. New York: Springer-Verlag.

DuBois, Cora. 1944. *The People of Alor: A Social-Psychological Study of an East Indian Island.* Minneapolis: The University of Minnesota Press.

Duby, Georges. 1980. *The Three Orders: Feudalism Imagined.* Chicago: University of Chicago Press.

Dumézil, Georges. 1967. *The Resting of the Warrior.* Chicago: University of Chicago Press.

Dumont, Louis. 1970. *Homo Hierarchicus.* Chicago: The University of Chicago Press.

Dunbar, Robin I. H. 1988. *Primate Social Systems.* London: Croom Helm.

Dunphy, Dexter C. 1963. The Social Structure of Urban Adolescent Peer Groups. *Sociometry* 26:230–246.

Eckhardt, Kenneth W. 1971. Exchange Theory and Sexual Permissiveness. *Behavior Science Notes* 6:1–18.

Eisenstadt, S. N. 1956. *From Generation to Generation.* Glencoe: Free Press.

Elam, Itzhak. 1973. *The Social and Sexual Roles of Hima Women.* Manchester: Manchester University Press.

Elder, Glen H., Jr. 1974. *Children of the Great Depression.* Chicago: University of Chicago Press.

Elder, Glen H., Jr. 1975a. Adolescence in the Life Cycle: An Introduction. In *Adolescence in the Life Cycle: Psychological Change and Social Context,* ed. Sigmund E. Dragastin and Glen H. Elder, Jr., 1–22. New York: John Wiley and Sons.

Elder, Glen H., Jr. 1975b. Age Differentiation and the Life Course. In *Annual Review of Sociology,* vol. 1, ed. A. Inkeles, J. Coleman, and N. Smelser. Palo Alto: Annual Reviews, Inc.

Ellis, Havelock. 1906. *Sexual Selection in Man.* Philadelphia: F. A. Davis.

Elwin, Verrier. 1947. *The Muria and Their Ghotul.* Bombay: Oxford University Press.

Elwin, Verrier. 1968. *The Kingdom of the Young.* Bombay: Oxford University Press.

Ember, Carol R. 1973. Female Task Assignment and the Social Behavior of Boys. *Ethos* 1:429–493.

Ember, Carol R. 1983. The Relative Decline in Women's Contribution to Agriculture with Intensification. *American Anthropologist* 85:285–304.

Ember, Melvin, and Carol R. Ember, 1979. Male-Female Bonding: A Cross-Species Study of Mammals and Birds. *Behavior Science Research* 14:37–56.

Erikson, Erik H. 1950. *Childhood and Society.* New York: W. W. Norton.

Estrada, Alejandro. 1984. Male-Infant Interactions among Free-Ranging Stumptail Macaques. In *Primate Paternalism,* ed. David M. Taub, 56–87. New York: Van Nostrand Reinhold.

Eveleth, Phyllis B., and J. M. Tanner. 1976. *Worldwide Variation in Human Growth.* Cambridge: Cambridge University Press.

Fay, Robert E., Charles F. Turner, Albert D. Klassen, and John H. Gagnon. 1989. Prevalence and Patterns of Same-Gender Sexual Contact among Men. *Science* 243:338–348.

Finestone, Harold. 1976. *Victims of Change: Juvenile Delinquents in American Society.* Westport, Connecticut: Greenwood Press.

Flannery, Regina. 1953. *The Gros Ventres of Montana: Part I, Social Life.* Washington, D. C.: The Catholic University of America Anthropological Series, no. 15.

Frayser, Suzanne G. 1985. *Varieties of Sexual Experience: An Anthropological Perspective on Human Sexuality.* New Haven: Human Relations Area Files Press.

Friedenberg, Edgar Z. 1973. The Vanishing Adolescent: Adolescence: Self-Definition and Conflict. In *The Sociology of Youth: Evolution and Revolution,* ed. Harry Silverstein, 109–118. New York: Macmillan.

Friedl, Ernestine. 1963. Some Aspects of Dowry and Inheritance in Boeotia. In *Mediterranean Countrymen,* ed. Julian Pitt-Rivers, 113–136. Paris: Mouton and Co.

Gadpaille, Warren J. 1984. Adolescent Aggression from the Perspective of Cultural Anthropology. In *The Aggressive Adolescent,* ed. Charles R. Keith, 432–454. New York: The Free Press.

Gaulin, Steven J., and Alice Schlegel. 1980. Paternal Confidence and Paternal Investment: A Cross-Cultural Test of a Sociobiological Hypothesis. *Ethology and Sociobiology* 1:301–309.

Gecas, Viktor. 1981. Contexts of Socialization. In *Social Psychology: Sociological Perspectives,* ed. Morris Rosenberg and Ralph H. Turner, 165–199. New York: Basic Books.

Gilligan, Carol. 1982. *In a Different Voice: Psychological Theory and Women's Development.* Cambridge: Harvard University Press.

Gilligan, Carol, Janie V. Ward, Jill M. Taylor, and Betty Bardige, eds. 1988. *Mapping the Moral Domain: A Contribution of Women's Thinking to Psychological Theory and Education.* Cambridge, Mass.: Harvard University Press.

Gillis, John R. 1974. *Youth and History.* New York: Academic Press.

Goethals, George W. 1971. Factors Affecting Permissive and Nonpermissive Rules

Regarding Premarital Sex. In *Sociology of Sex: A Book of Readings,* ed. J. M. Henslin, 9–26. New York: Appleton-Century-Croft.

Goody, Jack. 1983. *The Development of the Family and Marriage in Europe.* Cambridge: Cambridge University Press.

Goody, Jack, and S. J. Tambiah. 1973. *Bridewealth and Dowry.* Cambridge Papers in Social Anthropology 7. Cambridge: Cambridge University Press.

Gorer, Geoffrey, and John Rickman. 1949. *The People of Great Russia.* London: Cressett.

Gough, Kathleen. 1961. Nayar: Central Kerala. In *Matrilineal Kinship,* ed. David M. Schneider and Kathleen Gough, 298–384. Berkeley: University of California Press.

Gouzoules, Harold. 1984. Social Relations of Males and Infants in a Troop of Japanese Monkeys: A Consideration of Causal Mechanisms. In *Primate Paternalism,* ed. David M. Taub, 127–145. New York: Van Nostrand Reinhold.

Gregersen, Edgar. 1982. *Sexual Practices: The Story of Human Sexuality.* London: Mitchell Beazley International Ltd.

Gregor, Thomas. 1985. *Anxious Pleasures: The Sexual Lives of an Amazonian People.* Chicago: The University of Chicago Press.

Hall, G. Stanley. 1916. *Adolescence.* New York: Appleton.

Hall, Roberta L., ed. 1985. *Male-Female Differences: A Bio-Cultural Perspective.* New York: Praeger.

Hart, C. W. M., and Arnold R. Pilling. 1960. *The Tiwi of North Australia.* New York: Holt, Rinehart, and Winston, Inc.

Hendy, Leo B. 1983. *Growing Up and Going Out: Adolescents and Leisure.* Aberdeen University Press.

Henry, Jules. 1964. *Jungle People: A Kaingang Tribe of the Highlands of Brazil.* New York: Vintage Books.

Herdt, Gilbert H. 1981. *Guardians of the Sacred Flutes: Idioms of Masculinity.* New York: McGraw-Hill.

Herdt, Gilbert H., ed. 1984. *Ritualized Homosexuality in Melanesia.* Berkeley: University of California Press.

Herskovits, Melville J. 1971. *Life in a Haitian Valley.* Garden City: Doubleday and Co., Inc.

Hewlett, Barry S. 1990. Demography and Childcare of Hunter-Gatherers and Horticulturalists. Paper presented at the annual meeting of the Society for Cross-Cultural Research, Pomona, California.

Hoebel, E. Adamson. 1978. *The Cheyennes: Indians of the Great Plains.* New York: Holt, Rinehart and Winston.

Hoffer, Carol P. 1974. Madam Yoko: Ruler of the Kpa Mende Confederacy. In *Woman, Culture, and Society,* ed. M. Z. Rosaldo and L. Lamphere, 173–188. Stanford: Stanford University Press.

Hogan, Dennis P. 1980. The Transition to Adulthood as a Career Contingency. *American Sociological Review* 45:261–276.

Hollingshead, August B. 1949. *Elmtown's Youth: The Impact of Social Classes on Adolescents.* New York: Wiley.

Hollos, Marida, and Philip E. Leis. 1986. Descent and Permissive Adolescent Sexuality in Two Ijo Communities. *Ethos* 14:395–408.

Hollos, Marida, and Philip E. Leis. 1989. *Becoming Nigerian in Ijo Society*. New Brunswick: Rutgers University Press.

Hopkins, Keith. 1980. Brother-Sister Marriage in Roman Egypt. *Comparative Studies in Society and History* 22:303–354.

Howard, Alan. 1982. Interactional Psychology: Some Implications for Psychological Anthropology. *American Anthropologist* 84:37–57.

Hrdy, Sarah Blaffer. 1981. *The Woman that Never Evolved*. Cambridge: Harvard University Press.

Jacklin, Carolyn N., and Eleanor E. Maccoby. 1978. Social Behavior at 33 Months in Same-Sex and Mixed-Sex Dyads. *Child Development* 49:557–569.

Joseph, Alice, Rosamond B. Spicer, and Jane Chesky. 1949. *The Desert People*. Chicago: University of Chicago Press.

Kandel, Denise B., and Gerald S. Lesser. 1972. *Youth in Two Worlds*. San Francisco: Jossey-Bass.

Kardiner, Abram. 1939. *The Individual and His Society: The Psychodynamics of Primitive Social Organization*. New York: Columbia University Press.

Kardiner, Abram. 1945. *The Psychological Frontiers of Society*. New York: Columbia University Press.

Kendis, Kaoru O., and Randall J. Kendis. 1976. The Street Boy Identity: An Alternate Strategy of Boston's Chinese-Americans. *Urban Anthropology* 5:1–17.

Keniston, Kenneth. 1971. *Youth in Dissent: The Rise of a New Opposition*. New York: Harcourt Brace Jovanovich.

Kett, Joseph F. 1977. *Rites of Passage: Adolescence in America 1790 to the Present*. New York: Basic Books.

Kirkpatrick, John. 1987. *Taure'are'a:* A Liminal Category and Passage to Marquesan Adulthood. *Ethos* 15:382–405.

Köbben, André J. F. 1973. Comparativists and Non-Comparativists in Anthropology. In *A Handbook of Method in Cultural Anthropology,* ed. R. Naroll and R. Cohen, 581–596. New York: Columbia University Press.

Korbin, Jill E. 1987. Child Sexual Abuse: Implications from the Cross-Cultural Record. In *Child Survival: Anthropological Perspectives on the Treatment and Maltreatment of Children,* ed. Nancy Scheper-Hughes, 247–266. Dordrecht: D. Reidel Publishing Co.

Kresz, Maria. 1976. The Community of Young People in a Transylvanian Village. In *Youth in a Changing World,* ed. Estelle Fuchs, 207–212. The Hague: Mouton.

Lamb, Michael E. 1984. Observational Studies of Father-Child Relationships in Humans. In *Primate Paternalism,* ed. D. M. Taub, 407–430. New York: Van Nostrand Reinhold.

Laslett, Peter. 1965. *The World We Have Lost*. New York: Scribner's.

LeRoy Ladurie, Emmanuel. 1978. *Montaillou: The Promised Land of Error*. New York: George Braziller, Inc.

Levine, Nancy E., and Walter H. Sangree, eds. 1980. *Women with Many Husbands:*

*Polyandrous Alliance and Marital Flexibility in Africa and Asia.* Special Issue: *Journal of Comparative Family Studies,* vol. 11, no. 3.

LeVine, Robert A. 1973. *Culture, Behavior, and Personality.* Chicago: Aldine.

Levinson, David, and Martin J. Malone. 1980. *Toward Explaining Human Culture: A Critical Review of the Findings of Worldwide Cross-Cultural Research.* New Haven: Human Relations Area Files Press.

Levy, Robert I. 1973. *Tahitians: Mind and Experience in the Society Islands.* Chicago: University of Chicago Press.

Lewin, Roger. 1984. Practice Catches Theory in Kin Recognition. *Science* 233:1049–1051.

Llewelyn-Davies, Melissa. 1981. Women, Warriors, and Patriarchs. In *Sexual Meanings: The Cultural Construction of Gender and Sexuality,* ed. Sherry B. Ortner and Harriet Whitehead, 330–358. Cambridge: Cambridge University Press.

Lutz, Catherine. 1988. *Unnatural Emotions: Everyday Sentiments on a Micronesian Atoll and Their Challenge to Theory.* Chicago: The University of Chicago Press.

Maccoby, Eleanor E., and Carol N. Jacklin. 1974. *The Psychology of Sex Differences.* Stanford: Stanford University Press.

Mair, Lucy. 1977. *Marriage.* London: The Scolar Press.

Malinowski, Bronislaw. 1932. *The Sexual Life of Savages in Northwestern Melanesia.* London: Routledge and Kegan Paul.

Mannheim, Karl. 1952. The Problem of Generations. In *Essays on the Sociology of Knowledge,* ed. P. Keckskemeti, 276–322. London: Routledge and Kegan Paul.

Mantel, Nathan. 1963. Chi-Square Tests with One Degree of Freedom: Extensions of the Mantel-Haenszel Procedure. *Journal of the American Statistical Association* 58:690–700.

Mead, Margaret. 1928. *Coming of Age in Samoa.* Ann Arbor: Morrow.

Meillassoux, Claude. 1981. *Maidens, Meal and Money: Capitalism and the Domestic Economy.* Cambridge: Cambridge University Press.

Miller, Patricia Y. 1979. Female Delinquency: Fact and Fiction. In *Female Adolescent Development,* ed. Max Sugar, 115–140. New York: Brunner/Mazel.

Minturn, Leigh, Martin Grosse, and Santoah Haider. 1969. Cultural Patterning of Sexual Beliefs and Behavior. *Ethnology* 8:301–318.

Mitchell, G., and E. M. Brandt. 1970. Behavioral Differences Related to Experience of Mother and Sex of Infant in the Rhesus Monkey. *Developmental Psychology* 3:149.

Munroe, Robert L., and Ruth H. Munroe. 1989. Birth Order and Its Psychological Correlates in East Africa. In *The Contents of Culture: Constants and Variants. Studies in Honor of John M. Roberts,* ed. Ralph Bolton, 271–323. New Haven: Human Relations Area Files Press.

Murdock, George P. 1964. Cultural Correlates of the Regulation of Premarital Sex Behavior. In *Process and Pattern in Culture,* ed. Robert A. Manners, 399–410. Chicago: Aldine Publishing Co.

Murdock, George P. 1967. *Ethnographic Atlas.* Pittsburgh: University of Pittsburgh Press.

Murdock, George P., and Diana O. Morrow. 1980. Subsistence Economy and Supportive Practices: Cross-Cultural Codes 1. In *Cross-Cultural Samples and Codes,* ed. Herbert Barry III and Alice Schlegel, 45–74. Pittsburgh: University of Pittsburgh Press.

Murdock, George P., and Catarina Provost. 1980. Measurement of Cultural Complexity. In *Cross-Cultural Samples and Codes,* ed. Herbert Barry III and Alice Schlegel, 147–160. Pittsburgh: University of Pittsburgh Press.

Murdock, George P., and Douglas R. White. 1980. The Standard Cross-Cultural Sample and Its Codes. In *Cross-Cultural Samples and Codes,* ed. Herbert Barry III and Alice Schlegel, 3–44. Pittsburgh: University of Pittsburgh Press.

Murdock, George P., and Suzanne F. Wilson. 1980. Settlement Patterns and Community Organization: Cross-Cultural Codes 3. In *Cross-Cultural Samples and Codes,* ed. Herbert Barry III and Alice Schlegel, 75–116. Pittsburgh: University of Pittsburgh Press.

Musgrove, F. 1964. *Youth and the Social Order.* Bloomington: University of Indiana Press.

Muus, Rolf E. 1975. *Theories of Adolescence.* New York: Random House.

Nadel, S. F. 1967. Witchcraft in Four African Societies: An Essay in Comparison. In *Cross-Cultural Approaches,* ed. Clellan S. Ford, 207–218. New Haven: Human Relations Area Files Press.

Nag, Moni. 1962. *Factors Affecting Human Fertility in Nonindustrial Societies: A Cross-Cultural Study.* Yale University Publications in Anthropology, no. 66. New Haven.

Nakane, Chie. 1967. *Garo and Khasi: A Comparative Study in Matrilineal Systems.* The Hague: Mouton & Co.

Nerlove, Sara. 1969. Trait Disposition and Situational Determinants of Behavior among Gusii Children of Southwestern Kenya. Doctoral dissertation, Department of Anthropology, Stanford University.

Nerlove, Sara, Ruth H. Munroe, and Robert L. Munroe. 1971. Effect of Environmental Experience on Spatial Ability: A Replication. *Journal of Social Psychology* 84:3–10.

Newman, Philip R., and Barbara M. Newman. 1976. Early Adolescence and Its Conflicts: Group Identity versus Alienation. *Adolescence:* 42:261–274.

Norbeck, Edward. 1953. Age-Grading in Japan. *American Anthropologist* 55:373–383.

O'Connell, M. C. 1982. Spirit Possession and Role Stress Among the Xesibe of Eastern Transkei. *Ethnology* 21:21–37.

Offer, Daniel, and Melvin Sabshin. 1984. Adolescence: Empirical Perspectives. In *Normality and the Life Cycle,* ed. Daniel Offer and Melvin Sabshin, 76–107. New York: Basic Books.

Opler, Morris E. 1969. *Apache Odyssey: A Journey between Two Worlds.* New York: Holt, Rinehart, and Winston, Inc.

Paige, Karen Ericksen. 1983. Virginity Rituals and Chastity Control During Puberty: Cross-Cultural Patterns. In *Menarche: Transition from Girl to Woman,* ed. Sharon Golub, 155–174. Lexington: D. C. Heath.

Papanek, Hanna. 1979. Family Status Production: The "Work" and "Non-Work" of Women. *Signs* 4:775–781.

Parker, Seymour. 1976. The Precultural Bases of the Incest Taboo: Toward a Biosocial Theory. *American Anthropologist* 78:285–305.

Parsons, Talcott, and Robert F. Bales. 1955. *Family, Socialization and Interaction Process.* New York: The Free Press.

Patterson, Gerald R. 1982. *Coercive Family Process.* Eugene, Ore.: Castalia Publishing Company.

Patterson, Gerald R. 1988. Family Process: Loops, Levels, and Linkages. In *Persons in Context: Developmental Processes,* ed. N. Bolger, A. Caspin, G. Downey, and M. Moorehouse, 114–152. Cambridge: Cambridge University Press.

Pearlin, Leonard I. 1975. Sex Roles and Depression. In *Life-Span Developmental Psychology: Normative Life Crises,* ed. Nancy Datan and Leon H. Ginsberg, 191–208. New York: Academic Press.

Peter, H. R. H., Prince of Greece and Denmark. 1963. *A Study of Polyandry.* The Hague: Mouton and Co.

Petersen, Anne C. 1988. Adolescent Development. *Annual Review of Psychology* 39:583–607.

Peterson, Frederick A. 1959. *Ancient Mexico: An Introduction to the Pre-Hispanic Cultures.* New York: G. P. Putman's Sons.

Riley, Matilda W., Marilyn Johnson, and Anne Foner. 1972. *Aging and Society.* Vol. 3, *A Sociology of Age Stratification.* New York: Russell Sage.

Roberts, John M., and Brian Sutton-Smith. 1962. Child Training and Game Involvement. *Ethnology* 1:166–185.

Rosaldo, Michelle Z. 1974. *Knowledge and Passion: Ilongot Notions of Self and Social Life.* Cambridge: Cambridge University Press.

Rossi, Alice S. 1985. Gender and Parenthood. In *Gender and the Life Course,* ed. Alice S. Rossi, 161–191. New York: Aldine.

Rothman, David J. 1971. Documents in Search of a Historian: Toward a History of Childhood and Youth in America. *Journal of Interdisciplinary History* 2:367–377.

Roubin, Lucienne. 1977. Male Space and Female Space within the Provençal Community. In *Rural Society in France: Selections from the Annales,* ed. Robert Forster and Orest Ranum, 152–180. Baltimore and London: Johns Hopkins University Press.

Rowe, David C. In press. An Adaptive Strategy Theory of Crime and Delinquency. In *Some Current Theories of Crime and Deviance,* ed. David Hawkins. Newbury Park: Sage.

Sahlins, Marshall. 1962. *Moala: Culture and Nature on a Fijian Island.* Ann Arbor: University of Michigan Press.

Sanday, Peggy. 1981. *Female Power and Male Dominance: On the Origins of Sexual Equality.* Cambridge: Cambridge University Press.

Savin-Williams, Ritch C. 1987. *Adolescence: An Ethological Perspective.* New York: Springer-Verlag.

Schildkrout, Enid. 1978. Age and Gender in Hausa Society: Socio-Economic Roles of

Children in Urban Kano. In *Sex and Age as Principles of Differentiation,* ed. J. S. LaFontaine, 109–137. London: Academic Press.

Schlegel, Alice. 1972. *Male Dominance and Female Autonomy: Domestic Authority in Matrilineal Societies.* New Haven: Human Relations Area Files Press.

Schlegel, Alice. 1973. The Adolescent Socialization of the Hopi Girl. *Ethnology* 4:449–462.

Schlegel, Alice. 1975. Situational Stress: A Hopi Example. In *Life Span Developmental Psychology: Normative Life Crises,* ed. Nancy Datan and Leon H. Ginsberg, 209–216. New York: Academic Press.

Schlegel, Alice. 1977. Male and Female in Hopi Thought and Action. In *Sexual Stratification: A Cross-Cultural View,* ed. Alice Schlegel, 245–269. New York: Columbia University Press.

Schlegel, Alice. 1979. Sexual Antagonism among the Sexually Egalitarian Hopi. *Ethos* 7:124–141.

Schlegel, Alice. 1990. Gender Meanings: General and Specific. In *Beyond the Second Sex: New Directions in the Anthropology of Gender,* ed. Peggy R. Sanday and Ruth G. Goodenough, 21–42. Philadelphia: University of Pennsylvania Press.

Schlegel, Alice. 1991. Status, Property, and the Value on Virginity. *American Ethnologist,* in press.

Schlegel, Alice, and Herbert Barry III, 1980a. Adolescent Initiation Ceremonies: A Cross-Cultural Code. In *Cross-Cultural Samples and Codes,* ed. Herbert Barry III and Alice Schlegel, 277–288. Pittsburgh: University of Pittsburgh Press.

Schlegel, Alice, and Herbert Barry III. 1980b. The Evolutionary Significance of Adolescent Initiation Ceremonies. *American Ethnologist* 7:696–715.

Schlegel, Alice, and Herbert Barry III. 1986. The Cultural Consequences of Female Contribution to Subsistence. *American Anthropologist* 88:142–150.

Schlegel, Alice, and Herbert Barry III. 1989. Adolescents at Play: A Cross-Cultural Study of Adolescent Games. In *The Content of Culture: Constants and Variants. Essays in Honor of John M. Roberts,* ed. Ralph Bolton, 33–48. New Haven: Human Relations Area Files Press.

Schlegel, Alice, and Rohn Eloul. 1987. Marriage Transactions: A Cross-Cultural Code. *Behavior Science Research* 21:118–140.

Schlegel, Alice, and Rohn Eloul. 1988. Marriage Transactions: Labor, Property, and Status. *American Anthropologist* 90:291–309.

Schneider, David M. 1984. *A Critique of the Study of Kinship.* Ann Arbor: University of Michigan Press.

Sebald, Hans. 1984. *Adolescence: A Social Psychological Analysis.* Englewood Cliffs: Prentice-Hall, Inc.

Serpenti, L. M. 1977. *Cultivators in the Swamps: Social Structure and Horticulture in a New Guinea Society.* Assen, Netherlands: Van Gorcum.

Sherif, Muzafer, and Carolyn W. Sherif. 1964. *Reference Groups: Exploration into Conformity and Deviation of Adolescents.* New York: Harper and Row.

Shostak, Marjorie. 1983. *Nisa: The Life and Words of a !Kung Woman.* New York: Vintage Books.

Shweder, Richard A. 1979. Rethinking Culture and Personality Theory, Parts I and II. *Ethos* 7:255–278 and 279–311.

Siegel, James T. 1986. *Solo in the New Order: Language and Hierarchy in an Indonesian City.* Princeton: Princeton University Press.

Simonds, Paul E. 1977. Peers, Parents, and Primates: The Developing Network of Attachments. In *Attachment Behavior,* ed. T. Alloway, P. Pliner, and L. Krames, 145–176. New York: Plenum.

Skinner, Elliott P. 1961. Intergenerational Conflict among the Mossi: Father and Son. *Journal of Conflict Resolution* 5:55–60.

Socolow, Susan M. 1978. *The Merchants of Buenos Aires 1778–1810.* Cambridge: Cambridge University Press.

SPSS, Inc. 1988. SPSSX User's Guide, 3rd ed. Chicago: SPSSX, Inc.

Stinchcombe, Arthur L. 1964. *Rebellion in a High School.* Chicago: Quadrangle.

Stone, Lawrence. 1977. *The Family, Sex and Marriage in England 1500–1800.* New York: Harper and Row.

Sudarkasa, Niara. 1973. *Where Women Work: A Study of Yoruba Women in the Marketplace and in the Home.* Ann Arbor: The University of Michigan Press.

Taub, David M., ed. 1984. *Primate Paternalism.* New York: Van Nostrand Reinhold.

Titiev, Mischa. 1944. *Old Oraibi: A Study of the Hopi Indians of Third Mesa.* Papers of the Peabody Museum of American Archaeology and Ethnology, Harvard University, vol. 22, no. 1. Cambridge, Mass.

Trumbach, Randolph. 1978. *The Rise of the Egalitarian Family.* New York: Academic Press.

Turnbull, Colin. 1962. *The Forest People.* Garden City: Doubleday and Co., Inc.

Wallace, Anthony F. C. 1952. *The Modal Personality of the Tuscorora Indians, as Revealed by the Rorschach Test.* Bulletin 150, Bureau of American Ethnology. Washington, D. C.: Smithsonian Institution.

Ware, Helen. 1978. *The Economic Value of Children in Asia and Africa: Comparative Perspectives.* Papers of the East-West Population Institute, no. 50. Honolulu: East-West Center.

Watkins, Mark Hanna. 1943. The West African "Bush" School. *American Journal of Sociology* 48:1666–1675.

Weiner, Annette B. 1988. *The Trobrianders of Papua New Guinea.* New York: Holt, Rinehart and Winston, Inc.

Weisner, Thomas S. 1982. Sibling Interdependence and Child Caretaking: A Cross-Cultural View. In *Sibling Relationships: Their Nature and Significance Across the Lifespan,* ed. Michael E. Lamb and Brian Sutton-Smith, 305–328. Hillsdale: Lawrence Erlbaum Associates.

Weisner, Thomas S., and Ronald Gallimore. 1977. My Brother's Keeper: Child and Sibling Caretaking. *Current Anthropology* 18:169–190.

White, Douglas R. 1989. Focused Ethnographic Bibliography: Standard Cross-Cultural Sample. *Behavior Science Research* 23:1–145.

Whiting, Beatrice B. 1980. Culture and Social Behavior: A Model for the Development of Social Behavior. *Ethos* 8:95–116.

Whiting, Beatrice B., and Carolyn P. Edwards. 1988. *Children of Different Worlds.* Cambridge, Mass.: Harvard University Press.

Whiting, Beatrice B., and John W. M. Whiting. 1975. *Children of Six Cultures: A Psycho-Cultural Analysis.* Cambridge: Harvard University Press.

Whiting, John W. M., Victoria K. Burbank, and Mitchell S. Ratner. 1986. The Duration of Maidenhood across Cultures. In *School-Age Pregnancy and Parenthood: Biosocial Dimensions,* ed. Jane B. Lancaster and Beatrix A. Hamburg, 273–302. New York: Aldine De Gruyter.

Whiting, John W. M., Richard Kluckhohn, and Albert S. Anthony. 1958. The Function of Male Initiation Ceremonies at Puberty. In *Readings in Social Psychology,* ed. Eleanor E. Maccoby, Theodore M. Newcomb, and Eugene L. Hartley, 359–370. New York: Holt, Rinehart and Winston.

Whiting, John W. M., and Beatrice B. Whiting. 1978. A Strategy for Psychocultural Research. In *The Making of Psychological Anthropology,* ed. George D. Spindler, 41–61. Berkeley and Los Angeles: The University of California Press.

Wilson, Monica. 1963. *Good Company: A Study of Nyakyusa Age Villages.* Boston: Beacon Press.

Worthman, Carol M. 1986. Development Dysynchrony as Normal Experience: Kikuyu Adolescents. In *School-Age Pregnancy and Parenthood: Biosocial Dimensions,* ed. Jane B. Lancaster and Beatrix A. Hamburg, 95–112. New York: Aldine De Gruyter.

Young, Frank W. 1965. *Initiation Ceremonies: A Cross-Cultural Study of Status Dramatization.* Indianapolis: Bobbs-Merrill.

Youniss, James, and Jacqueline Smollar. 1985. *Adolescent Relations with Mothers, Fathers, and Friends.* Chicago: University of Chicago Press.

Zingg, Robert Mowry. 1938. *The Huichols: Primitive Artists.* Contributions to Ethnography, I, University of Denver. New York: G. E. Steckert and Company.

*Appendix*

# I

---

# Societies in the Sample

---

The 186 societies of the standard sample are listed alphabetically by name followed by serial number from 1 to 186. One or more alternative names are given for some societies. Location of each society is specified by the present-day country, or state for those in the United States. The geographical coordinates are followed by the focal date for each society and by the historical context for some societies. A summary statement about the type of culture classifies its fixity of settlement, political integration, and subsistence economy. Affiliation with an international religion is also noted. The information on some societies indicates that the local community is not representative of the entire culture, such as a peasant village within a class-stratified state.

Bibliographic references for these societies are included in articles reprinted by Barry and Schlegel (1980a) and in an article by White (1989). Fixity of settlement and political integration were coded by Murdock and Provost. Subsistence economy was coded by Murdock and Morrow. These articles are reprinted in Barry and Schlegel (1980a). Some of the information on subsistence economy is from the Ethnographic Atlas (Murdock 1967).

The five categories of fixity of residence are nomadic, seminomadic, semisedentary, sedentary but impermanent, and sedentary. Variations in political integration include independent groups, independent communities, chiefdoms, kingdoms, small states, nations, and empires. Chiefdoms, small states, and nations usually have respectively one, two, and three administrative levels above the local community. A few large nations containing multiple ethnic populations are designated as empires. The six categories of subsistence economy are agriculture, animal husbandry, hunting of large animals, fishing, gathering of edible flora or fauna, and intercommunity trading.

The categories of subsistence economy listed are those that contribute more than 10% of the total food supply. When two or more categories are listed, the adjective "primarily" precedes the first one if it contributes the majority of all food. The information on agriculture usually specifies one of three types of cultivation: cereal grains, root crops, or tree crops. Cereal grains include wheat, millet, rice, and corn. Root crops include yams, cassava, and potatoes. Tree crops include plantains, coconuts, and bananas. Additional information when applicable specifies that cultivation is on permanent fields, with irrigation, or with plow animals.

Abipon 183 or Mepene, the Chaco, northeastern Argentina, 27° to 29°S, 59° to 60°W, 1750, after having acquired horses introduced to South America by the Spaniards. Raiders of Spanish settlements, nomadic, independent communities, Christian influence, hunting, also gathering and cattle husbandry.

Abkhaz 55, Russian Caucasus, 42°50′ to 43°25′N, 40° to 41°35′E, 1880. A sedentary chiefdom, some are Christians or Moslems, primarily cattle herding, secondarily cultivating cereal grains.

Ahaggaren 41 or Tuareg, Algeria, 21° to 25°N, 4° to 9°E, 1900, prior to French occupation. A small state of nomadic bands, Moslems, herding sheep, goats, and camels, also cultivating cereal grains and trading.

Ainu 118 or Saru Ainu, southeastern Hokkaido, Japan, 42°40′ to 43°30′N, 142° to 144°E, 1880, prior to Japanese colonization. Dispersed, independent communities, technologically primitive, fishing, also hunting and gathering.

Ajie 103, New Caledonia and Loyalty Islands, east of Australia, 21°20′S, 165°40′E, 1845, prior to European influence. A small chiefdom of sedentary villages, cultivating root crops, also fishing and trading.

Aleut 123, Aleutian Islands, Alaska, 53° to 57°30′N, 158° to 170°W, 1778, prior to pervasive Russian influence. Chiefdom, fishing.

Alorese 89 or Abui, island of Alor, Indonesia, between Java and New Guinea, 8°20′S, 124°40′E, 1938, under Dutch rule. A small chiefdom of sedentary small communities in the mountains, cultivating cereal grains and root crops.

Amahuaca 170, eastern Peru, 10°30′S, 72° W, 1960, almost completely unacculturated. Independent groups in small sedentary but impermanent communities, primarily cultivating cereal grains, secondarily hunting.

Amhara 37, central Ethiopia, 11° to 14°N, 36° to 38°45′E, 1953. A large nation of sedentary villages, Coptic Christians, cultiving cereal grains with plow animals, also milking cows and trading.

Andamanese 79, islands east of India, 11°45′ to 12°N, 93° to 95°10′E, 1860, prior to disruption by a penal colony established in 1858. Small nomadic independent communities on the seacoast, technologically primitive, fishing, also gathering and hunting.

Aranda 91 or Arunta, central Australia, 23°30′ to 25°S, 132°30′ to 134°20′E, 1896. Small nomadic independent communities, technologically primitive, hunting, also gathering.

Armenians 56, Russian Caucasus near Turkey, 40°10′N, 44°30′E, 1843, ruled by Russia, prior to political disruption in the late nineteenth century. A numerous ethnic minority, Christians, primarily cultivating cereal grains with plow animals, secondarily milking cows. Focus is the city of Erivan and surrounding villages.

Ashanti 19, Ghana, West Africa, 6° to 8°N, 0° to 3°W, 1895, prior to conquest by the British. A large kingdom ruling several tribes, sedentary but impermanent settlements, primarily cultivating root crops, secondarily hunting and husbandry of sheep or goats.

Atayal 113, north central Taiwan (Formosa), 23°50′ to 24°50′N, 120°20′ to 120°50′E, 1930, when aboriginal culture was relatively intact. A chiefdom of sedentary but impermanent settlements in mountainous terrain, primarily cultivating cereal grains, secondarily hunting.

Aweikoma 180 or Caingang or Skokleng, southern Brazil, 28°S, 50°W, 1932, Indians hunted by Brazilian and German settlers. Small nomadic independent groups in the mountains, technologically primitive, primarily hunting, secondarily gathering.

Aymara 172, southern Peru, 16°S, 70°W, 1940, subjected to social disorganization and acculturation, formerly a portion of the Inca state. Ethnic minority, a large population of sedentary villages, Christians, cultivating root crops, also husbandry of sheep or goats and fishing.

Azande 28, southern Sudan, 4°20′ to 5°50′N, 27°40′ to 28°50′E, 1905, after British conquest broke up a large kingdom but prior to complete subjugation. A kingdom with sedentary villages, cultivating cereal grains, also hunting and gathering.

Aztec 153 or Tenochca, Mexico City (Tenochtitlan), 19°N, 99°10′W, 1520, immediately preceding the Spanish conquest under Cortez. Urban capital of a technologically complex empire, cultivating cereal grains with irrigation, also hunting, tending small animals, and trading.

Babylonians 45, Iraq, 32°35′N, 44°45′E, 1750 B.C. Capital of a technologically complex empire, primarily cultivating cereal grains, secondarily milking cows and fishing.

Badjau 86 or Tawi-Tawi Badjau or Sea Gypsies, the Tawi-Tawi islands, east of Malaysia, 5°N, 120°E, 1963. Small nomadic independent communities, technologically primitive, primarily fishing, secondarily trading.

Balinese 84, Bali island Indonesia, 8°30′S, 115°20′E, 1958. Sedentary villages, technologically complex, Hindus, cultivating cereal grains, also tending pigs and trading.

Bambara 22, southern Mali, 12°30′ to 13°N, 6° to 8°W, 1902, shortly after the beginning of French rule. Large sedentary villages, primarily cultivating cereal grains with plow animals, secondarily milking cows.

Banen 15, western Cameroon, 4°35′ to 4°45′N, 10°35′ to 11°E, 1940, ruled by France but only slightly acculturated. Sedentary, cultivating root crops.

Basques 50, the Pyrenees, northeastern Spain, 43°18′N, 1°40′W, 1940. Ethnic minority, large sedentary villages, technologically complex, Christians, primarily cultivating cereal grains with plow animals, secondarily milking cows.

Basseri 58, southwestern Iran, 27° to 31°N, 53° to 54°E, 1958. Confederacy of small nomadic groups, Moslems, primarily husbandry of sheep and goats, secondarily cultivating cereal grains and trading.

Bellacoola 132, western British Columbia, Canada, 52°20′N, 126° to 127°W, 1880, at an early stage of intensive acculturation. Small sedentary autonomous community, primarily fishing, secondarily hunting and gathering.

Bemba 7, northern Zambia, 9° to 12°S, 29° to 32°E, 1897, prior to British occupation. A large chiefdom, cultivating cereal grains with plow animals, also hunting, fishing, and gathering.

Bogo 38 or Belen, northern Ethiopia, 15°45'N, 38°45'E, 1855, at the time they were being converted from Christianity to Islam. A small semisedentary tribe, primarily herding cattle, secondarily cultivating cereal grains with plow animals.

Botocudo 178 or Aimore, eastern Brazil, 18° to 20°S, 41°30' to 43°30'W, 1884, relatively unacculturated. Small nomadic independent groups, technologically primitive, primarily hunting, secondarily fishing.

Bribri 157 or Talamanca, southern Costa Rica, 9°N, 83°15'W, 1917. Small sedentary autonomous communities, cultivating cereal grains, also hunting.

Burmese 71, central Burma, 21°58'N, 95°40'E, 1960. Peasant village in a technologically complex nation, Buddhists, cultivating cereal grains with irrigation and plow animals, also fishing and trading.

Burusho 64, Hunza state, northern India, 36°20' to 36°30'N, 74°30' to 74°40'E, 1934. Ethnic minority in small sedentary communities, Moslems, primarily cultivating cereal grains with irrigation and plow animals, secondarily husbandry of sheep and goats.

Callinago 161 or Island Carib, Dominica island, Windward Islands, 15°30'N, 61°30'W, 1650, shortly after European occupation. Independent sedentary but impermanent communities, cultivating root crops on permanent fields, also fishing and hunting.

Carib 164 or Barama River Carib, northwest Guyana and northeast Venezuela, 7°10' to 7°40'N, 59°20' to 60°20'W, 1932, when acculturation was slight. Small nomadic autonomous communities, fishing, also cultivating root crops and hunting.

Cayapa 168, southwestern Colombia and northern Ecuador, 0°40' to 1°15'N, 78°45' to 79°10'W, 1908, prior to acculturation. Independent sedentary communities, cultivating tree crops, also fishing and hunting.

Cayua 181 or Caingua, southern Brazil and Paraguay, 23° to 24°S, 54° to 56°W, 1890, only slightly acculturated. Small independent nomadic groups, hunting, also cultivating cereal grains and gathering.

Chinese 114 or Chekiang Chinese, northern Chekiang province, eastern China, 31°N, 120°05'E, 1936, prior to Japanese invasion. Densely settled communities in a technologically complex nation, primarily cultivating cereal grains with irrigation, secondarily fishing and trading. Focus is a peasant village.

Chiricahua Apache 148, southeast Arizona, 32°N, 109°30'W, 1870, prior to being placed on a reservation. Small nomadic bands, frequently engaged in raiding, technologically primitive, gathering, also hunting.

Chukchee 121 or Reindeer Chukchee, northeastern Russia, 63° to 70°N, 171°W to 171°E, 1900, unacculturated. Small seminomadic independent groups, primarily reindeer herding, secondarily hunting.

Comanche 147, Texas, Oklahoma, and southern Kansas, 30° to 38°N, 98° to 103°W, 1870, more than a hundred years after they acquired horses, shortly before settlement in a reservation and disappearance of the buffalo herds. Independent nomadic bands, frequently engaged in raiding, primarily equestrian hunting, secondarily gathering.

Copper Eskimo 124, northern Northwest Territories, Canada, 66°40' to 69°20'N, 108° to 117°W, 1915, prior to first settlement of European descendents. Small seminomadic independent groups, primarily fishing, secondarily hunting.

Creek 145 or upper Creek or Muskogee, eastern Alabama, 32°30' to 34°20'N, 85°30' to 86°30'W, 1800, while a member of a confederacy of tribes independent of the United States. Semisedentary villages, cultivating cereal grains, also hunting and fishing.

Cubeo 167, eastern Colombia, 1° to 1°50'N, 70° to 71°W, 1939, when partially acculturated. Small sedentary independent communities, cultivating root crops, also fishing and hunting.

Cuna 158 or Tule, eastern Panama, 9° to 9°30'N, 78° to 79°W, 1927, shortly after they massacred all resident Panamanians and declared political independence under United States protection. Sedentary villages, Christians, primarily cultivating tree crops, secondarily fishing and hunting.

Egyptians 43, south central Egypt, 24°45'N, 33°E, 1950. Peasant village in a technologically complex nation, Moslems, primarily cultivating cereal grains with irrigation and plow animals, secondarily trading.

Eyak 130, southern Alaska, 60° to 61°N, 144° to 146°W, 1890, shortly before complete acculturation and detribalization. Small semisedentary village, primarily fishing, secondarily hunting.

Fijians 102, the island of Mbau, southwest of Samoa, 18°S, 178°35'E, 1840, 40 years after the first European contact. Chiefdom of sedentary villages, primarily fishing, secondarily cultivating root crops.

Fon 18 or Dahomeans, Dahomey, 7°12'N, 1°56'E, 1890, before conquest by the French. Focus is capital of an empire, large sedentary settlements, exporting slaves, cultivating cereal grains with plow animals, also tending pigs, hunting, and trading.

Fulani 25 or Wodaabe Fulani, southern Niger, 13° to 17°N, 5° to 10°E, 1951, 48 years after arrival of the British. Chiefdom of Moslems, nomadic, primarily cattle herding, secondarily cultivating cereal grains.

Fur 29 or For, western Sudan, 13°30'N, 25°30'E, 1880, prior to British conquest. A large state of Moslems, with sedentary settlements, cultivating cereal grains, also milking cows, fishing, and hunting.

Ganda 12 or Baganda, Uganda, 0°20'N, 32°32'E, 1875, prior to subjugation by the British. Kingdom of sedentary large settlements, cultivating tree crops on permanent fields, also hunting and fishing.

Garo 69, Assam, eastern India, 26°N, 91°E, 1955. Group of sedentary villages, practicing shifting cultivating of cereal grains, also husbandry of sheep or goats and trading.

Gheg Albanians 48, northwestern Albania, 41°20' to 42°40'N, 19°30' to 20°30'E, 1910, while under Turkish rule. Semisendentary peasant communities in mountainous terrain, Moslem majority, Christian minority, cultivating cereal grains on permanent fields, also milking cows.

Gilbertese 107 or Makin, northeast of Australia, 3°30′N, 172°20′°E, 1890, prior to colonial administration by the English. Chiefdom of sedentary villages, primarily cultivating tree crops, secondarily fishing.

Gilyak 119, Sakhalin island, eastern Siberia in Russia, 53°30′ to 54°30′N, 141°50′ to 143°10′E, 1890. Small seminomadic independent communities in an arctic environment, primarily fishing, secondarily hunting and gathering.

Goajiro 159, northern Colombia and Venezuela, 11°30′ to 12°20′N, 71° to 72°30′W, 1947, acculturation slight although cattle acquired from the Spaniards four centuries earlier. Small nomadic groups, primarily cattle herding, also gathering.

Gond 60 or Hill Maria Gond, east central India, 19°15′ to 20°N, 80°30′ to 81°20′E, 1930. Small sedentary but impermanent settlements, cultivating cereal grains, also cattle husbandry and gathering.

Gros Ventre 140 or Atsina, northeastern Montana, 47° to 49°N, 106° to 110°W, 1880, shortly before missionary activity and disappearance of the buffalo. Nomadic tribe, much warfare with other Indian tribes and with whites, primarily equestrian hunting, secondarily gathering.

Hadza 9 or Kindiga, northern Tanzania, 3°30′ to 4°10′S, 34°40′ to 35°25′E, 1930, related to the Bushmen-Hottentots of southern Africa. Small nomadic independent groups, technologically primitive, primarily gathering, secondarily hunting.

Haida 131 or Masset Haida, northern Queen Charlotte Islands, western British Columbia, Canada, 54°N, 132°30′W, 1875, shortly prior to the first Christian mission. Small semisedentary independent communities, primarily fishing, secondarily gathering.

Haitians 160, Haiti, 18°50′N, 72°10′W, 1940, descendants of slaves imported from Africa in the seventeenth century. Sedentary peasant villages, Christians, primarily cultivating cereal grains on permanent fields, secondarily cattle husbandry.

Hausa 26 or Zazzagawa Hausa, northern Nigeria, 9°30′ to 11°30′N, 6° to 9°E, 1900, just before rule by the Fulani was replaced by British occupation. Large population in sedentary villages, Moslems, primarily cultivating cereal grains, secondarily trading.

Havasupai 150, north central Arizona, 35°20′ to 36°20′N, 111°20′ to 113°W, 1918, while indigenous culture was practically intact. Seminomadic small independent groups, primarily cultivating cereal grains, secondarily gathering and hunting.

Hebrews 44 or Judah, southern Israel, 30°30′ to 31°55′N, 34°20′ to 35°30′E, 621 B.C., during a brief interval of political independence under King Josiah. A small state with a capital city and sedentary, densely populated villages, technologically complex, Judaic religion, cultivating cereal grains with plow animals, also husbandry of sheep or goats.

Hidatsa 141 or Minitari, central North Dakota, 47°N, 101°W, 1836, shortly before a smallpox epidemic. Semisedentary small independent village, primarily cultivating cereal grains on permanent fields, secondarily hunting and gathering.

Huichol 152, western Mexico, 22°N, 105°W, 1890, after more than a century and a half of acculturation. Sedentary independent communities, Christians, cultivating cereal grains, also hunting and cattle husbandry.

Huron 144 or Wendot, central Ontario, Canada, 44° to 45°N, 78° to 80°W, 1634, when the aboriginal culture was still largely undisturbed. Member of a confederacy of tribes, semisedentary large villages, cultivating cereal grains, also fishing and hunting.

Iban 85 or Sea Dayak, central Sarawak in Malaysia, 2°N, 112°30′ to 113°30′E, 1950. Most numerous ethnic group of Sarawak, small sedentary but impermanent independent communities, cultivating cereal grains.

Ibo 17 or Igbo, southeastern Nigeria, 5°20′ to 5°40′N, 7°10′ to 7°30′E, 1935, shortly after they were initially required to pay taxes to the British Protectorate. Sedentary large villages, primarily cultivating root crops, secondarily trading.

Ifugao 112, the northern Philippines, 16°45′ to 16°52′ N, 121°05′ to 121°12′E, 1910. Independent groups in sedentary communities, cultivating root crops with irrigation.

Inca 171, southern Peru, 13°30′S, 72°W, 1530, immediately prior to civil war and Spanish conquest. Focus is Cuzco, capital city of the empire, primarily cultivating cereal grains with irrigation, secondarily trading.

Ingalik 122 or Tinneh, southwestern Alaska, 62°30′N, 159°30′W, 1885, after a smallpox epidemic and establishment of a trading post but prior to missionary influence. Small seminomadic independent villages, primarily fishing, secondarily hunting.

Irish 51, County Clare, southwest Ireland, 52°40′ to 53°10′N, 8°20′ to 10°W, 1932. A peasant community in a technologically complex nation, Christians, primarily cultivating root crops on permanent fields, secondarily milking cows and trading.

Japanese 117, Okayama prefecture, southwestern Japan, 34°40′N, 133°48′E, 1950. The small peasant village of Niiike, technologically complex, primarily cultivating cereal grains with irrigation, secondarily trading.

Javanese 83, eastern Java, Indonesia, 7°43′S, 112°13′E, 1955. Focus is peasant villages surrounding a town in a technologically complex nation, Moslems, primarily cultivating cereal grains with irrigation, secondarily trading.

Jivaro 169 or Xibaro, southern Ecuador, 2° to 4°S, 77° to 79°W, 1920, only partially acculturated while still fighting against European intruders. Small independent groups in sedentary but impermanent settlements, cultivating root crops, also hunting, fishing, and tending pigs.

Kafa 33 or Kaffa or Kafficho, southwestern Ethiopia, 6°50′ to 7°45′N, 35°30′ to 37°E, 1905, eight years after conquest by Ethiopia. Small villages, primarily cultivating cereal grains on permanent fields, secondarily cattle husbandry and gathering.

Kapauku 94, western New Guinea, Indonesia, 3°25′ to 4°10′S, 135°25′ to 137°E, 1955, prior to administrative control by the Dutch and while missionary penetration was minimal. Small sedentary villages, cultivating root crops, also tending pigs and trading.

Kaska 129 or Eastern Nahani, northern British Columbia and eastern Yukon, Canada, 60°N, 131°W, 1900, prior to extensive missionary activity. Small seminomadic independent communities, technologically primitive, fishing, also hunting.

Kazak 65 or Great Horde, southeastern Russia and western China, 37° to 48°N, 68° to 81°E, 1890. Seminomadic confederation of clans, Moslems, equestrian herders of sheep, goats, some cattle.

Kenuzi Nubians 39, southern Egypt, 22° to 24°N, 32° to 33°E, 1900, immediately prior to their displacement by the first Aswan Dam. Small sedentary independent villages, Moslems, primarily cultivating cereal grains with irrigation, secondarily tending sheep or goats.

Khalkha Mongols 66, west central part of Outer Mongolia, 47° to 47°20'N, 95°10' to 97°E, 1920, at the time of the Autonomous Northern Mongolia nation, prior to becoming the Mongolian People's Republic of the Soviet Union. Small seminomadic groups, Buddhists, primarily husbandry of sheep or goats, secondarily trading.

Khmer 75 or Cambodians, northwestern Cambodia, 13°30'N, 103°50'E, 1292, in the golden age of the Khmer empire. Capital city of Angkor, technologically complex, primarily cultivating cereal grains on permanent fields, secondarily fishing.

Kikuyu 11 or Akikuyu, south central Kenya, 0°40'S, 37°10'E, 1920, at the end of relative stability of the traditional system. Small sedentary independent villages, primarily cultivating cereal grains on permanent fields, secondarily cattle husbandry.

Kimam 93, southwestern New Guinea, Indonesia, 7°30'S, 138°30'E, 1960, shortly before transfer from Dutch to Indonesian rule. Sedentary independent villages, primarily cultivating root crops on permanent fields, secondarily gathering.

Klamath 138, southwestern Oregon, 42° to 43°15'N, 121°20' to 122°20'W, 1860, 35 years after first contact with whites, shortly prior to intense acculturation. Small seminomadic independent communities, technologically primitive, primarily fishing, secondarily gathering.

Konso 35, southwestern Ethiopia, 5°15'N, 37°30'E, 1935, 38 years after conquest by the Ethiopian kingdom. Sedentary towns, primarily cultivating cereal grains on permanent fields, secondarily milking cows.

Koreans 116, north central Korea, 37°37'N, 126°25'E, 1950, shortly after formation of the independent country of North Korea. Focus is peasant villages in a technologically complex nation, primarily cultivating cereal grains with irrigation, secondarily trading.

Kung Bushmen 2, northeastern South West Africa, 19°50'S, 20° to 21°E, 1950, unacculturated, intermarrying bands. Small nomadic independent groups, technologically primitive, primarily gatherers, secondarily hunters.

Kurd 57, northeastern Iraq, 35°30'N, 44°30'E, 1950. Numerous ethnic minority, Moslems, cultivating cereal grains with irrigation, also husbandry of sheep or goats and trading. Focus is the town of Rowanduz.

Kutenai 139 or Lower Kutenai or Kootenay, northern Idaho and southern British Columbia, Canada, 48°40' to 49°10'N, 116°40'W, 1890, when still relatively autonomous, prior to intensive acculturation. Small seminomadic independent communities, fishing, also hunting and gathering.

Kwoma 95, northeastern New Guinea, 4°10′S, 142°40′E, 1937, when relatively un-acculturated and prior to missionary contact. Sedentary small independent villages, cultivating root crops, also gathering.

Lakher 70 or Mara, southern Assam state of India, western Burma, and eastern Bangladesh, 22°20′N, 93°E, 1930, while under British rule. Ethnic minority in sedentary villages, Moslems, primarily cultivating cereal grains, secondarily cattle husbandry.

Lamet 72, northwestern Laos, 20°N, 100°40′E, 1940. Small semisedentary independent villages, cultivating cereal grains, also cattle husbandry and hunting.

Lapps 52 or Könkämä Lapps, northern Sweden, 68°20′ to 69°05′N, 20°05′ to 23°E, 1950. Small nomadic independent bands, Christians, primarily reindeer herding, secondarily fishing.

Lengua 182, central Paraguay, 23° to 24°S, 58° to 59°W, 1889, prior to the acculturation that began with a Christian mission. Nomadic small independent communities, hunting, also fishing, gathering, and cultivating root crops.

Lepcha 68 or Rong, western Bhutan, in the state of Sikkim and Darjeeling district of eastern India, 27° to 28°N, 89°E, 1937, while under British rule. Small sedentary villages, Buddhists, cultivating cereal grains on permanent fields, also cattle husbandry and gathering.

Lesu 97, New Ireland, south of Hawaii, 2°30′S, 151°E, 1930, while an Australian protectorate. Sedentary independent villages, cultivating root crops, also fishing and gathering.

Lolo 67 or Nosu, Szechwan province, south central China, 26° to 29°N, 103° to 104°E, 1910, ten years after onset of Chinese control and initial encounter with Europeans. Ethnic minority of sedentary independent villages, highly stratified society, owning horses, primarily cultivating cereal grains on permanent fields, secondarily husbandry of sheep or goats.

Lozi 4 or Barotse, southwestern Zambia, 14° to 18°20′S, 22° to 25°E, 1900, a component of the Barotse nation during its maximum expansion. Semisedentary villages, cultivating cereal grains on permanent fields, also tending cattle and fishing.

Luguru 10 or Waluguru, eastern Tanzania, 6°25′ to 7°25′S, 37°20′ to 38°E, 1925, with the traditional political organization in spite of British and previously German rule. Sedentary independent villages, cultivating cereal grains.

Manchu 115 or Aigun Manchu, northeastern Manchuria district of China, 50°N, 125°30′E, 1915. Small sedentary villages, in a technologically complex nation, primarily cultivating cereal grains on permanent fields, secondarily tending pigs.

Manus 96, Admiralty Islands, southwest of Hawaii, 2°10′S, 147°10′E, 1929, governed by Australia. Sedentary independent villages, primarily trading, secondarily fishing.

Mao 32 or Northern Mao, western Ethiopia, 9°5′ to 9°35′N, 34°30′ to 34°50′E, 1939. Small, relatively independent and unacculturated tribe, in sedentary independent villages, primarily cultivating cereal grains, secondarily hunting and fishing.

Maori 104, northern New Zealand, 35°10′ to 35°30′S, 174° to 174°20′E, 1800, shortly after settlement by Europeans, prior to extensive acculturation. Small chiefdom, frequent warfare with other Maori chiefdoms, sedentary villages, cultivating root crops, also fishing and hunting.

Mapuche 184 or Araucanians, south central Chile, 38°30'S, 72°35'W, 1950, following extensive contact with whites and settlement in a reservation 64 years earlier. Small sedentary villages, primarily cultivating cereal grains on permanent fields, secondarily husbandry of sheep or goats and fishing.

Marquesans 105, Nuku Hiva Island, southeast of Hawaii, 8°54' to 8°58'S, 140°08' to 140°12'W, 1800. Small chiefdom of small sedentary villages, primarily cultivating tree crops, secondarily fishing.

Marshallese 108 or Jaluit, south of Hawaii, 6°N, 165°30'E, 1900, during German protectorate, after almost a century of contacts with Europeans. Sedentary villages on small atolls, primarily fishing, secondarily cultivating tree crops.

Masai 34, northeastern Tanzania, 1°30' to 5°30'S, 35° to 37°30'E, 1900, eight years after severe smallpox epidemic, at the onset of German and British colonial occupation. Independent nomadic bands, primarily cattle herding, secondarily trading.

Massa 27 or Bana, southwestern Chad, 10° to 11°N, 15° to 16°E, 1910, shortly after German colonial occupation. Sedentary independent villages, cultivating cereal grains, also fishing and milking cows.

Mbundu 5 or Ovimbundu, 12°15'S, 16°30'E, central Angola, 1890, prior to occupation by the Portuguese. Kingdom of small sedentary villages, primarily cultivating cereal grains, secondarily cattle husbandry.

Mbuti 13 or Mbuti Pygmies or Bambuti, northeastern Zaire, 1°30' to 2°N, 28°15' to 28°25'E, 1950. Small nomadic independent bands in tropical forest, technologically primitive, gathering, also hunting.

Mende 20, Sierra Leone, 7°50'N, 12°W, 1945. Sedentary villages, primarily cultivating cereal grains, secondarily trading.

Micmac 126 or Souriquois, Maine and southeastern Canada, 43°30' to 50°N, 60° to 66°W, 1650, after 40–45 years of European settlement and missionary contact. Small seminomadic independent communities, primarily hunting, secondarily fishing.

Miskito 156 or Mosquito, eastern Honduras and northeastern Nicaragua, 15°N, 83°W, 1920. Racial and cultural mixture for the prior three centuries. Sedentary villages, Christians, cultivating root crops, also hunting and fishing.

Montagnais 125, west central Quebec, Canada, 48° to 52°N, 73° to 75°W, 1910, following three centuries of acculturation. Small seminomadic independent communities, technologically primitive, primarily hunting, secondarily fishing and trading.

Mundurucu 166, central Brazil, 6° to 7°S, 56° to 57°W, 1850, after substantial acculturation but prior to assimilation into Brazilian culture. Small sedentary independent villages, cultivating root crops, also hunting and fishing.

Nama Hottentot 1 or Namaqua, central South West Africa, 23°30'S, 17°E, 1860, the last year when they collected tribute from other groups, prior to the devastating German-Hottentot war. Nomadic bands, milking cows, hunting, and gathering.

Nambicuara 174, Southern Mato Grosso of west central Brazil, 12°30' to 13°30'S, 58°30' to 59°W, 1940, following long exposure to Europeans. Small seminomadic independent communities, gathering, also hunting, fishing, and cultivating cereal grains.

Natchez 146, south central Louisiana, 31°30′N, 91°25′W, 1718, when the first missionaries arrived. Chiefdom of sedentary villages, cultivating cereal grains, also hunting and fishing.

Negri Sembilan 82, central Malaysia, 2°35′N, 102°15′E, 1958. Large sedentary villages in a technologically complex nation, Moslems, primarily cultivating cereal grains with irrigation, secondarily fishing.

Nicobarese 78, Nicobar islands, east of Sri Lanka, 8°15′ to 9°15′N, 92°40′ to 93°E, 1870, the year after British occupation. Sedentary independent villages, primarily cultivating tree crops, secondarily fishing and tending pigs.

Nkundo Mongo 14, west central Zaire, 0°15′ to 1°15′S, 18°35′ to 19°45′E, 1930, a component of the Mongo nation. Small sedentary villages, cultivating root crops.

Nyakyusa 8, southwestern Tanzania, 9°20′ to 9°35′S, 34° to 34°10′E, 1934. Small chiefdoms of sedentary but impermanent villages, primarily cultivating cereal grains on permanent fields, secondarily cattle husbandry.

Omaha 143, eastern Nebraska and western Iowa, 41°10′ to 41°40′N, 96° to 97°W, 1854, immediately before they were granted a reservation. Semisedentary community, equestrian hunting, also cultivating cereal grains and fishing.

Orokaiva 92, eastern New Guinea, 8°20′ to 8°40′S, 147°50′ to 148°10′E, 1925, while relatively unacculturated although an Australian protectorate. Small sedentary independent villages, cultivating root crops.

Otoro 30 or Otoro Nuba, south central Sudan, 11°20′N, 30°40′E, 1930, prior to extensive migration from the hills to the plains. Sedentary independent groups, primarily cultivating cereal grains on permanent fields, secondarily husbandry of sheep or goats.

Palauans 111, Palau islands, east of the Philippines, 7°21′N, 134°31′E, 1873, when the Germans established the first trading station. Small sedentary villages, primarily cultivating root crops, secondarily fishing.

Papago 151 or Tohono O'odham, southern Arizona, 32°N, 112°W, 1910, prior to establishment of the reservation. Semisedentary independent communities, Christians, cultivating cereal grains, also gathering, cattle husbandry, and trading.

Pawnee 142 or Skidi Pawnee, north central Nebraska, 42°N, 100°W, 1867, when the aboriginal population was intact although severely reduced by disease. Semisedentary bands, cultivating cereal grains, also equestrian hunting.

Pentecost 101 or Bunlap, island west of Fiji, 16°S, 168°35′E, 1953, following heavy depopulation. Small sedentary independent villages, primarily cultivating root crops, secondarily gathering.

Pomo 135 or Eastern Pomo, north central California, 39°N, 123°W, 1850, prior to influx of white settlers. Semisedentary independent communities, gathering, also hunting and fishing.

Popoluca 154 or Sierra Popoluca, southeastern Mexico, 18°15′N, 94°50′W, 1940, after extensive acculturation and assimilation into Mexican society. Sedentary villages, Christians, primarily cultivating cereal grains, secondarily tending small animals.

Punjabi 59 or West Punjabi, northeastern Pakistan, 32°30′N, 74°E, 1952, peasant villages in a technologically complex nation, Moslems, primarily cultivating cereal grains on permanent fields, secondarily milking cows.

Quiche 155, southern Guatemala, 15°N, 91°W, 1930, descendants of the Mayans, heavily influenced by the Spanish. Sedentary villages, Christians, cultivating cereal grains.

Rhade 74, south central Vietnam, 13°N, 108°E, 1962, ethnic minority in South Vietnam, shortly after French withdrawal. Sedentary but impermanent independent villages, primarily cultivating cereal grains, secondarily tending pigs.

Riffians 42, northeastern Morocco, 34°20' to 35°30'N, 2°30' to 4°W, 1926. An ethnic minority, sedentary villages, Moslems, primarily cultivating cereal grains on permanent fields, secondarily milking cows and gathering.

Romans 49, west central Italy, 41°50'N, 12°30'E, A.D. 110, during the Early Empire, a span of two centuries of internal peace. Capital of a technologically complex empire, primarily trading, secondarily agriculture.

Russians 54, southeast of Moscow, 52°40'N, 41°20'E, 1955, early in Khrushchev's regime. Peasant village in a technologically complex nation, Christian rituals persisting in spite of government disapproval, collectivized farming, primarily cultivating cereal grains with irrigation, secondarily milking cows.

Rwala Bedouin 46, Jordan, southern Syria, western Iraq, 31° to 35°30'N, 36° to 41°E, 1913, under Turkish rule. Small groups of nomads, Moslems, primarily camel herding, secondarily trading.

Samoans 106 or Western Samoans, Upolu Island, northeast of New Zealand, 13°48' to 14°S, 171°54' to 172°3'W, 1828, prior to the first missionary settlement and the defeat of the chief of the focal group. Chiefdom of sedentary villages, primarily cultivating root crops, secondarily fishing.

Santal 62, eastern India, 23° to 24°N, 86°50' to 87°30'E, 1940. A minority non-Hindu ethnic group in sedentary villages, cultivating grain crops with irrigation.

Saramacca 165 or Bush Negroes, Surinam, 3° to 4°N, 55°30' to 56°W, 1928, descendants of refugee slaves from Africa, relatively unacculturated. Sedentary villages, cultivating root crops, also hunting and fishing.

Saulteaux 127 or Northern Saulteaux, an Ojibwa tribe in southeastern Manitoba, Canada, 51°30' to 52°30'N, 94° to 97°W, 1930, less acculturation than other Ojibwa tribes. Small seminomadic independent bands, fishing, also hunting and trading.

Semang 77 or Negritos, northern Malaysia, 4°30' to 5°30'N, 101° to 101°30'E, 1925, the original inhabitants. Small nomadic independent groups in the mountains, technologically primitive, gathering, also hunting and trading.

Shavante 179, central Brazil, 13°30'S, 51°30'W, 1958, five years after beginning of amicable relations with whites. Seminomadic independent communities, technologically primitive, primarily gathering, secondarily hunting.

Shilluk 31, southeastern Sudan, 9° to 10°30'N, 31° to 32°E, 1910, while under Anglo-Egyptian rule. Sedentary villages, primarily cultivating cereal grains, secondarily milking cows, hunting, and fishing.

Siamese 76 or Central Thai, southern Thailand, 14°N, 100°52'E, 1955. Peasant village in the technologically complex kingdom of Thailand, large sedentary village, Buddhists, primarily cultivating cereal grains with irrigation, secondarily fishing.

Siriono 173, northwestern Bolivia, 14° to 15°S, 63° to 64°W, 1942, at a time of very slight acculturation. Small seminomadic independent bands, technologically primitive, hunting, also gathering.

Siuai 99 or Motuna, Solomon islands, east of New Guinea, 7°S, 155°20′E, 1939, minimal acculturation until Australian administration beginning 20 years earlier. Small sedentary independent villages, primarily cultivating root crops, secondarily tending pigs, gathering, and trading.

Slave 128 or Etchareottine, southwestern Northwest Territories of Canada, 62°N, 122°W, 1940, prior to heavy acculturation. Small semisedentary independent communities, nominally Christians, hunting, also fishing and trading.

Somali 36, northern Somalia, 7° to 11°N, 45°30′ to 49°E, 1900, while governed by the English. Nomadic communities, Moslems, milking camels.

Songhai 24, central Mali, 16° to 17°15′N, 0°10′E to 3°10′W, 1940, under French occupation. Ethnic minority in a country dominated by the Ahaggaren Tuareg, sedentary villages, Moslems, cultivating cereal grains on permanent fields, also milking cows.

Suku 6 or Pindi, western Zaire, 6°S, 18°E, 1920, while autonomous, prior to colonial Belgian administration. Chiefdom of small sedentary but impermanent communities, primarily cultivating root crops, also gathering.

Tallensi 23, northeastern Ghana, 10°30′ to 10°45′N, 0°30′ to 0°50′W, 1934, shortly after English colonization, at a time of very little acculturation. Sedentary independent villages, primarily cultivating cereal grains on permanent fields, secondarily trading.

Tanala 81 or Menabe Tanala, eastern Madagascar, 20°S, 48°E, 1925. Semisedentary mountain villages, cultivating cereal grains and root crops.

Teda 40, northern Chad, 19° to 22°N, 16° to 19°E, 1950. Small nomadic independent communities, Moslems, primarily camel herding, secondarily trading.

Tehuelche 185 or Patagon, southern Argentina, 40° to 50°S, 64° to 72°W, 1870, prior to intense acculturation but after a severe smallpox epidemic. Horses had been acquired from the Spanish. Small nomadic independent bands, equestrian hunting.

Thonga 3 or Bathonga, northeastern South Africa, 25°50′S, 32°20′E, 1895, shortly after Portuguese colonization, which terminated subjugation by the Zulus. Sedentary but impermanent small communities, cultivating cereal grains.

Tikopia 100, northwest of Fiji, 12°30′S, 168°30′E, 1930. Small chiefdom of sedentary villages, primarily cultivating root crops, secondarily fishing.

Timbira 176 or Ramcocamecra or Eastern Timbira, east central Brazil, 6° to 7°S, 45° to 46°W, 1915 after severe disease and warfare with Brazilians. Sedentary but impermanent independent communities, cultivating root crops, also hunting.

Tiv 16 or Munshi, southern Nigeria, 6°30′ to 8°N, 8° to 10°E, 1920, after British colonization but prior to extensive changes. Sedentary villages, primarily cultivating root crops, secondarily trading.

Tiwi 90, Bathurst and Melville islands, northern Australia, 11° to 11°45′S, 130° to

132°E, 1929, shortly after onset of frequent visits by Japanese pearl fishermen. Small nomadic independent bands, technologically primitive, gathering, also hunting and fishing.

Tobelorese 88 or Tobelo, Halmahera island in the Molucca islands, northwest of New Guinea, 2°N, 128°E, 1900, after the Dutch forced them to give up piracy but prior to the missionary efforts of the principal ethnographer. Sedentary villages, primarily cultivating cereal grains, secondarily fishing.

Toda 61, southern India, 11° to 12°N, 76° to 77°E, 1900, during British rule. Mountainous non-Hindu tribe, small, semisedentary communities, primarily cattle herding, secondarily gathering and trading.

Toradja 87, Celebese, Indonesia, 2°S, 121°E, 1910, during Dutch colonial occupation. Small sedentary villages in the mountains, primarily cultivating cereal grains, secondarily hunting.

Trobrianders 98, west of Marquesas islands, 8°38′S, 151°4′E, 1914, during administration by Australia. Small sedentary villages, primarily cultivating root crops, secondarily fishing and trading.

Trukese 109, Romonum or Ulali Island, north of Trobriand islands, 7°24′N, 151°40′E, 1947, shortly after transfer from Japanese rule to United States trusteeship. Small island in a complex atoll, sedentary villages, cultivating tree crops, also fishing.

Trumai 175, French Guiana, 11°50′S, 53°40′W, 1938, after exposure to only sporadic contacts with Europeans. A small sedentary independent village, cultivating root crops, also fishing and gathering.

Tupinamba 177, eastern Brazil, near Rio de Janeiro, 22°33′ to 23°S, 42° to 44°30′W, 1550, prior to missionary influence. A large population of warring subtribes, chiefdom, sedentary but impermanent villages, cultivating root crops, also hunting and fishing.

Turks 47, central Turkey, 38°40′ to 40 N, 32°40′ to 35°50′E, 1950. Component of a technologically complex nation, peasant villages of orthodox Moslems, primarily cultivating cereal grains on permanent fields, secondarily husbandry of sheep and goats.

Twana 133, western Washington, west of Seattle, 47°20′ to 47°30′N, 123°10′ to 123°20′W, 1860, subsequent to contacts with Europeans and smallpox epidemics, prior to settlement on a reservation and influence of missionaries. Small seminomadic independent communities, primarily fishing, secondarily hunting and gathering.

Uttar Pradesh 63, north central India, 25°55′N, 83°E, 1945, during British rule. Sedentary, focus is a large peasant village in Uttar Pradesh state, culturally complex, Hindus, primarily cultivating of cereal grains with irrigation, secondarily milking cows.

Vedda 80 or Forest Vedda, Sri Lanka, 7°30′ to 8°N, 81° to 81°30′E, 1860, prior to substantial intrusion. Small seminomadic independent groups, technologically primitive, hunting, also gathering.

Vietnamese 73 or North Vietnamese, north central Vietnam, south of Hanoi, 20° to 21°N, 105°30′ to 107°E, 1930, while under French rule. A large, technologically complex state, primarily cultivating cereal grains with irrigation, secondarily fishing. Focus is the peasantry of the Red River delta.

Wadadika 137 or Paiute, Harney Valley band of Northern Paiute, eastern Oregon, 43° to 44°N, 118° to 120°W, 1870, one year after the first settlement by whites. Small seminomadic independent communities, technologically primitive, gathering, also hunting and fishing.

Warrau 162 or Guarauno, northeastern Venezuela, 8°30' to 9°50'N, 60°40' to 62°30'W, 1935, missionized but relatively unacculturated. Small seminomadic independent communities, Christians, fishing, also gathering and hunting.

Wolof 21 or Ouolof, central Gambia, 13°45'N, 15°20'W, 1950. An ethnic minority in a recently independent country. Sedentary small villages, Moslems, cultivating cereal grains on permanent fields, also trading.

Yahgan 186 or Yamana, southern Argentina and southern Chile, 54°30' to 55°30'S, 67° to 70°W, 1865, missionized but prior to extensive acculturation and severe epidemics. Small nomadic independent bands, technologically primitive, Christians, fishing.

Yanomamo 163, southern Venezuela, 2° to 2°45'N, 64°30' to 65°30'W, 1965, when only slightly acculturated. Sedentary but impermanent small independent villages, primarily cultivating tree crops, secondarily gathering.

Yapese 110, Yap island, east of the Philippines, 9°30'N, 138°10'E, 1910, while a German colony, during progressive depopulation. Small sedentary villages, primarily cultivating root crops, secondarily fishing.

Yokuts 136 or Lake Yokuts, southern California, west of Los Angeles, 35°10'N, 119°20'W, 1850, prior to heavy influx of white settlers. Semisedentary independent communities, fishing, also gathering and hunting.

Yukaghir 120, east central Siberia, 63°30' to 66°N, 150° to 157°E, 1850, while culture was still functioning, prior to marked decrease in population. Small nomadic independent communities, fishing, also hunting.

Yurak Samoyed 53 or Nenets, of the Berents Sea, Russia, northeast of Leningrad, 65° to 71°N, 41° to 62°E, 1894. Ethnic minority in the subarctic, small nomadic independent communities, primarily reindeer herding, secondarily fishing.

Yurok 134, northwest California, 41°30'N, 124°W, 1850, prior to the first influx of white settlers. Small independent groups in sedentary villages, fishing, also gathering and hunting.

Zuni 149, western New Mexico, 35° to 35°30'N, 108°30' to 109°W, 1880, after some acculturation to the Spanish but while still economically self-sufficient. Sedentary, densely populated independent village, primarily cultivating cereal grains, secondarily husbandry of sheep or goats.

---

# Variables on Adolescence

---

A total of 341 variables were coded in the study of adolescence. Only a minority of the 341 variables are reported in this book and thus included in this Appendix. The name of each variable, in capital letters, is followed by its serial numbers in parentheses. Information on a society is recorded by one of the codes specified for the variable.

Some of the variables listed designate which of several choices is ranked first. A single new variable thereby summarizes information from several variables because each of the choices is a separate variable. For example, the single new variable FARK summarizes the rank order for variables 9–14.

TERM (1). Is there a term for adolescence applied to all young people? Two codes: No or Yes.

START (3). At what age does adolescence begin, as indicated by changes in behavior and treatment? Five codes: No social adolescence recognized; Before puberty; Puberty; Post puberty; No change.

TRANS (4). Is there a form of ritualized behavior signifying the transition from childhood to adolescence? Eight codes: None; Private; Cognitive skills; Work; Military; Religious; Other; Adolescent initiation ceremony. The last code was defined and coded by Barry and Schlegel, reprinted in Barry and Schlegel (1980a).

END (5). At what age, in relation to biological adolescence, does social adolescence end? Three codes: Early; Mid-adolescence; Later.

ADULT (8). Do people move out of adolescence into full adulthood? Two codes: No or Yes. If coded No, there is an additional stage of youth.

FARK. This new variable summarizes variables 9–14, rank orders of six family agents of socialization. The agent ranked first determines one of seven codes for primary family agent: Mother; Father; Older males in household; Older females in household; Male kin outside household; Female kin outside household; Two or more primary agents.

OFRK. This new variable summarizes variables 15–22, rank orders of eight agents outside the family. The agent ranked first determines one of nine codes for primary extrafamily agent of socialization: Male teachers; Female teachers; Male religious leaders; Female religious leaders; Male community leaders; Female community leaders; Older males; Older females; Two or more primary agents.

SOCIA (27). Are adolescents significant socializers of younger children? Two codes: No or Yes.

WHRK. This new variable summarizes variables 28–33, rank orders of six allocations of waking hours. The allocation ranked first determines one of seven codes for primary allocation of waking hours: Alone; Adults same sex; Adults both sexes; Peers; Younger children; Not rankable; Two or more primary allocations.

VMC (37). Are adolescents differentiated from children by visual markers, such as new dress or ornamentation? Two codes: No or Yes.

VMA (38). Are adolescents differentiated from adults by visual markers, such as difference in dress or ornamentation? Two codes: No or Yes.

WEA (40). Do adolescents differ significantly from adults in kind or degree of work expected? Two codes: No or Yes.

LAA (42). Do adolescents differ significantly from adults in kind or degree of leisure activities? Two codes: No or Yes.

PP (50). Do adolescents have productive property of their own to manage? Three codes: No; Yes, same as younger children; Yes, more than younger children.

SKRK. This new variable summarizes variables 51–55, rank orders of five skill areas. The skill area ranked first determines one of six codes for primary skill area: Productive activities; Cognitive skills; Physical skills; Social skills; Sexual attractiveness or capacity; Two or more primary skill areas.

SEXHO (57). Homosexual activity. Four codes: Unrecognized; Prohibited; Tolerated; Expected and accepted.

SEXHI (59). Full sexual intercourse. Four codes: Prohibited; Tolerated; Expected with limited number of partners; Expected with large number of partners.

SEXHP (60). Who is the heterosexual partner likely to be? Five codes: None; Another adolescent; Young adult; Older adult; Two or more types of partner.

FSEP (61). Attachment to or separation from the natal household group. Five codes: Adolescents spend most time in or near home (no or minimal separation); Much time (more than three or four hours per day) is spent away from home but adolescent eats and sleeps at home; Adolescent spends much time away from home and sometimes sleeps or eats away from home; Adolescent frequently eats and sleeps away from home; Absolute separation.

FNEW (64). Does the adolescent take on new family or household roles involving decision-making or contributing to decision-making and in what context? Four codes: No; Household management; Family religious responsibilities; Representing the family to the community.

NEWA (66). If marriage choice is made during adolescence, at what age does it occur? Three codes: Early (up to 2 years after puberty); Middle adolescence (about 2 to 4 years after puberty); Later.

NEWD (67). If marriage choice is made during adolescence, who decides on the marriage partner? Five codes: The individual alone; The individual with advice from kin; The individual with kin having veto power; Primarily kin; Other.

PGRP (69). Degree of importance of adolescent peer groups to the adolescents. Five codes: Nonexistent; Less important than other social groups; Equal importance to other social groups; Of greater importance than other social groups; Groups exist, but importance unspecified.

PSIZ (70). What is the most common size of the peer group? Three codes: Small—about 3 to 6; Medium—about 6 to 14; Larger group.

PSTA (71). Is this a socially recognized group, i.e., an age set or group with a name? Two codes: No or Yes.

PRAN (72). What is the age range of the peer group? Three codes: Small—within three years; Medium—three to five years; Larger range.

PARK. This new variable summarizes variables 75–80, rank orders of six peer group activities. The peer group activity ranked first determines one of seven codes for primary peer group activity: Productive work; Leisure; Ceremonial; Military; Community Service; Other; Two or more primary peer group activities.

PSTR (82). Structure of the peer group. Three codes: Hierarchical—two or more levels of leadership; Non-hierarchical but with a single recognized leader; Fluid—no single recognized leader.

CRNEW (90). Do adolescents take on new community roles, and in what contexts? Seven codes: No; Production for the community; Military; Political; Community welfare; Religious; Other.

ASREG (93). Does any patterned, i.e., recognized and expected, form of antisocial behavior occur among adolescents? Two codes: No or Yes.

ASYC (94). Is antisocial behavior believed to be more characteristic of adolescents than younger children? Two codes: No or Yes.

ASAD (95). Is antisocial behavior believed to be more characteristic of adolescents than adults? Two codes: No or Yes.

AFRK. This new variable summarizes variables 102–109, rank orders of eight forms of antisocial activities. The form of antisocial activity ranked first determines one of nine codes for primary form of antisocial activity: Very little exists; Verbal; Violence; Theft; Sexual misbehavior; Destruction of property; Drunkenness or other drugs; Other.

TRAS (110). How is misbehavior treated? Three codes: Ignored or mildly admonished; Mildly punished, e.g., by tongue-lashing, restitution, or light corporal punishment; Severely punished, e.g., by beating, religious sanction, ostracism, or severe mocking.

CPAS (111). Corporal punishment. Two codes: No or Yes.

RUNAW (120). Are adolescents likely to run away? Two codes: No or Yes.

OCCUP (127). Is the adolescent expected to choose between several available occupational or community roles? Three codes: No; Yes, for some; Yes, for most or all.

.SPOUS (128). Is the adolescent expected to take the initiative in finding a spouse, whether or not the final decision is up to him or her? Two codes: No or Yes.

BREAK (129). Is there a sharp break from childhood? For example, is there a marked increase in the degree of responsibility undertaken by adolescents over that expected of younger children? Three codes: No; Yes, somewhat; Yes, a great deal.

ESTAB (130). Is adolescence a time during which the person establishes an adult character of excellence in certain areas that will determine to a large degree what occupational or social roles, or what possible spouses, will be available to him or her? Two codes: No or Yes.

Quantitative relationships on a scale of 0–10 are rated for each of four types of relationships with the adolescent: Contact, Intimacy, Subordination, and Conflict. They are rated on a scale of 0–10 for several categories of person, a rating of 0 being lowest, 10 being highest.

The categories of person rated are Mother (variables 138–141), Father (142–145), Older male sibling (146–149), Older female sibling (150–153), Grandmother (154–157), and Grandfather (158–161).

Contact refers to proportion of waking time spent together during adolescence.

Intimacy is defined as the degree of emotional affiliation between the adolescent and the category of person specified, as evidenced by behavior and expressions by the adolescent or by the other category of person or especially mutually by both. Evidence for sharing possessions, secrets, or other special affiliation is important and is necessary for a high rating. The amount of time voluntarily spent together is another indicator of degree of intimacy.

Subordination is defined as the degree to which the relationship involves the behavior of obedience and the attitude of submission or deference by the adolescent. Behavior of prompt, consistent obedience is adequate evidence, but reports on attitudes of submission or deference constitute more direct information on the variable to be measured.

Conflict is defined as the degree to which contradictory aims or expectations are expressed in the relationship between the adolescent and the specified other category of person. Reports of strife, punishments, or disobedience provide good evidence for intense conflict, but competing pressures, such as high ratings for both intimacy and subordination, provide inferential information. Conflict may be rated above medium only if overt strife, punishment, or disobedience is reported.

PCONT (207). The degree of contact with peers is rated on the same scale (0–10) as for contact as a type of social relationship with mother and other categories of persons. Peers are defined as other adolescents, usually in a social group of companions, within several years in age and without formally defined authority and submission roles.

PCOMP (208). Competition with peers is rated on the basis of the degree to which status or leadership in the peer group is determined by the strength, skill, or other personal qualities of the individuals. The degree to which status or leadership is achieved rather than determined by family rank or exact age is the most important criterion.

PCOOP (209). Cooperation with peers is based on the degree to which the peer group is cohesive, with the members contributing to group activities and goals rather than competing with each other or engaging in individual activities, regardless of whether the group has formal structure or leadership.

RECYC (213). Degree to which younger children are included in the adolescent's recreational activities. Five codes: Never; Occasionally; Often; Usually; Always.

RECAD (214). Degree to which adults are included in the adolescent's recreational activities. Same five codes as for younger children.

RARK. This new variable summarizes variables 227–231, rank orders of five types of recreational activities. The type of recreational activity ranked first determines one of five codes for primary type of recreational activity: Competitive games; Model adult activities; Patterned behavior; Free play; Nonphysical contact.

CUOR (241). Range of opportunity available for adolescents for current work. This is rated on a scale of 0–10. Work refers to all participation in duties for the household or subsistence economy.

VOCH (246). Degree to which adolescents rather than other categories of people make the choice among the opportunities available to the adolescent for vocation. This is rated on a scale of 0–10. Vocation refers to the adult occupation that the adolescent may choose or may prepare for by any method, including schooling, apprenticeship, and supervised or unsupervised practice.

PROOR (253). Range of opportunity available for adolescents for productive property. This is rated on a scale of 0–10. Property includes productive domestic animals, gardens, and other material possessions with exchange value, such as pottery or beads.

DRUOR (262). Range of opportunity available for adolescents for drugs. This is rated on a scale of 0–10. Drugs refer to all pharmacological substances that are psychoactive (affecting mood and emotion). These include alcohol, tobacco, coffee, tea, and other drugs available in the environment or by trade.

The following twelve traits inculcated in adolescence, rated on a scale from 0 to 10, are arranged into six pairs of contrasting or even opposite traits. This is done to indicate the existence of conflict by a high rating for both members of a pair of contrasting traits. A high rating for one member of the pair and a low rating for the other member indicates a consistent cultural pressure in the specified direction. A low rating for both members of the pair indicates that the designated area is unimportant in the training of adolescents.

The inculcation of traits refers primarily to indoctrination by the society, including categories of authority figures and teachers, with emphasis on the most important authority figures, indicated by the codes for subordination. The adolescent's behavior is a secondary but important criterion and in some cases is the principal evidence available.

FORTI (273). Fortitude measures suppressions of visible reactions to pain, exertion, frightening situations, discomfort, e.g., the hardening of boys who are forced to display their stoicism while being plunged into cold water. A low rating indicates not only absence of painful procedures but also efforts to protect the adolescent from pain and discomfort.

IMPUL (274). Impulsiveness is defined by encouragement of emotional expressions, such as spontaneous crying or display of affection. It is the opposite of self-restraint and thus more generalized than fortitude.

AGGRE (275). Aggressiveness is defined as aggressive behavior toward other society members, especially peers or animals, that may be implicitly inculcated or condoned by adults, e.g., parental urging to stand up for oneself or retaliate against aggression. Exhortations or frequent retelling of heroic myths may also instill aggressiveness; overt and covert inculcation are both included. If aggressiveness is encouraged only toward alien societies or other communities, however, the rating should be based on the same society or community and the discrepancy noted separately.

OBEDI (276). Obedience is primarily a measure of the degree to which adolescents are expected to obey specific requests by the parents or others in authority. In addition to consistency of obeying, promptness of obeying should be taken into account, e.g., unquestioning response to maternal uncle's demand for assistance. Some degree of obedience is necessarily encouraged in all societies, so that a high score should be given only if there is an unusual insistence on this trait.

SEXEX (277). Sexual Expression refers to encouragement of sexual behavior, taking into account the frequency, emotional intensity, importance, and variety of this type of behavior in adolescence and the range of partners permitted. Heterosexual intercourse is usually the principal criterion, but other types of sexual behavior, such as heterosexual foreplay, masturbation, homosexual acts, sexual jokes, and exposing the genitals, also should be taken into account.

SEXRE (278). Sexual Restraint is a measure of taboo or restrictions in adolescents on heterosexual intercourse and on other erotic behavior, including heterosexual play, masturbation, and homosexual acts. A high degree of modesty, such as the requirement to keep the genitals constantly covered in public, indicates moderately high restraint. Incest taboos are taken into account, especially if highly emphasized or widely extended, but are compatible with a fairly low rating.

SELFR (279). Self-Reliance or Initiative is based on encouragement of adolescents to act without supervision, e.g., playing or performing tasks by themselves. Extremely high ratings require a substantial amount of time spent in solitude or only with younger children or infants. Companionship with the peer group or with adults, in the absence of parents or other authority figures, may be the basis for moderately high ratings.

CONFO (280). Conformity to group refers to encouragement for the adolescent to share tasks, recreational activities, and opinions with a group of companions, such as the family, neighborhood, or peer group. A high but not extreme rating should be given if the adolescent conforms closely to a group, such as a peer group, that is deviant from the adolescent's family or other important group membership.

TRUST (281). Trust refers to confidence in social relationships, especially toward community members outside the family, e.g., adolescents are welcome in any home in the village, possessions are left unguarded. Sorcery and witchcraft generally indicate a low rating of trust. Where trust differs widely between out-group, such as community, and in-group, such as nuclear or extended family, the rating should be based mainly on the out-group.

COMPE (282). Competitiveness refers specifically to achievement of superiority over other people, especially peers, through attaining superiority in a craft or in school, in leadership, or in competitive games. The mere existence of competitive games denotes some competitiveness but not a high degree unless there is a very strong value on winning the game.

RESPO (283). Responsibility mainly refers to regular performance of duties or economic activities without continual supervision. If these are usually performed on command, they are examples of obedience. Typical examples of responsibility are older siblings' care of younger children, schoolwork, or any other expected activity done independently (spontaneously). Other instances are observance of taboos or ritual performances, but not etiquette or general deferential behavior.

ACHIE (284). Achievement (individual skill) measures emphasis on acquisition by adolescents of skills and proficient performance, including informal training or formal education in school or by apprenticeship. A high degree of this trait is generally indicated by proficient performance of adult skills or general admiration of work well done or strong emphasis on teaching of skills. Industry does not necessarily denote high achievement. The quality rather than the amount of performance is the main criterion. Competition for superiority over other individuals in status or performance is not included in this measure.

ANBEA (296). Proportion of adolescents compared with proportion of adults of the same sex who show antisocial behavior. Three codes: Less in adolescents, Same in adolescents, More in adolescents. Antisocial behavior includes all types of violent or illegal behavior, such as crime, delinquency, or cursing and also violations of taboos, such as food, drug use, sexual behavior, and incest.

SELIS (300). Proportion of adults of the same sex who show sexual license, rated on a scale of 0–10. Sexual license refers to any frequency or type of sexual expression that exceeds the cultural ideal, even though the sexual expression may be prevalent and unpunished.

FREQS (309). General frequency of any type of antisocial activities by adults of the same sex, rated on a scale of 0–10.

PERMI (334). Intensity of consistency of the attitude of permissiveness toward adolescents, rated on a scale of 0–10. This refers primarily to absence or mildness of punishment by relevant social agents, such as parents and other authority figures.

AFFEC (335). Intensity or consistency of the attitude of affection toward adolescents, rated on a scale of 0–10. This refers primarily to attention and positive interest expressed by relevant social agents, such as parents and other authority figures.

VALUE (336). Valuation, rated on a scale of 0–10. This refers to the degree to which adolescents are desired and valued by the society as a whole, including both emotional and economic criteria.

DIFCH (338). Differentiation of adolescents from childhood, rated on a scale of 0–10. This refers to activities, status, and all other attributes of behavior and self-concept in which the adolescent may be compared with the child of the same sex.

DIFAD (339). Differentiation from adulthood, rated on a scale of 0–10. This refers to the comparison with young but mature adults of the same sex. If there is a postadolescent stage of youth without full adult status and activities, this stage of youth is ignored, thereby avoiding a spurious lowering of the ratings.

---

# Techniques for Analyzing
# the Coded Information

---

Statistical tests were done with the widely used SPSSX statistical package (SPSS 1988). In tests of statistical significance, we reproduced the probability value rounded to three decimal places. We adhered to the conventional criterion for statistical significance, $p = .050$ or less, but we showed the $p$ value if it was .099 or less. A dash was substituted for probability values of .100 or higher.

We always used the two-tailed criterion, even when testing a hypothesis of a single direction of relationship between two variables. This criterion minimizes the occurrence of $p$ values that are spuriously classified as statistically significant.

Cross-tabulation of the relationship between two variables, both divided into two categories, was tested by the chi square method. We used the correction for continuity, which increases the $p$ level and thereby diminishes the probability of reporting a spurious statistically significant relationship between the two variables.

In addition to the chi square estimate, the SPSSX prints the $p$ value calculated by Fisher's Exact Test when there are fewer than 20 cases in a relationship between two variables, both divided into two categories. We always used this Exact Test when it was available instead of the chi square estimate.

Many of the variables are quantitative scores ranging from 0 to 10. In some statistical tests we divided this quantitative scale into two categories, above and below the median. Societies in the same category thereby have the same code. This loss of quantitative information was accepted in order to obtain the advantage of the simpler and clearer report of the number of societies in the two categories when showing in tables the association of this variable with another variable.

The division of societies into two categories was done separately for boys and girls on each variable, thus sometimes resulting in different dividing points for the two sexes. When two different dividing points equally approached an exactly equal number of cases in the two categories, we selected the one closer to the median score of 5 in the scale of 0–10 or the one that included a more nearly equal number of categories containing one or more societies below and above the dividing point. The same dividing point between the two categories was used in all tests with the same variable.

When one or both of the variables in a cross-tabulation were divided into three or more categories, the categories usually formed an ordinal sequence, such as low, medium, and high size of peer group or quantitative scores ranging from 0 to 10 for inculcation of obedience. The statistical significance test in these cases was the Mantel-Haenszel chi square (Mantel 1963). This chi square test is applicable to an ordinal sequence of categories. It corresponds to the product-moment correlation between the quantitative scale values of the scores represented by the categories. It is a two-tailed test because it does not predict whether the categories that represent progressively increasing magnitudes of one variable are associated with progressively increasing or decreasing magnitudes of the other variable.

When reporting a descriptive measure of the magnitude of association between two variables, we used the product-moment correlation coefficient ($r$). When both variables are divided into two categories, this measure is the same as the phi coefficient. The determinations of statistical significance are based on the chi square test or on Fisher's Exact Test.

In a few cases, a variable was divided into three or more categories that were not specified as an ordinal sequence. An example is several types of customs for property exchange in marriage. Statistical significance of the relationship with another variable was tested by Pearson chi square rather than by the Mantel-Haenszel chi square. These cases are identified by stating the number of degrees of freedom for the Pearson chi square value.

In many of the cross-tabulations, one of the variables was a score on a quantitative scale of 0–10. The statistical significance of these associations was usually tested by the Mantel-Haenszel chi square. In a few cases, we reported the mean of the quantitatively scaled variable for each category of the other variable. The statistical significance test used in these cases was the parametric analysis of variance, reporting the $F$ ratio and its associated $p$ value. These are closely similar to the Mantel-Haenszel chi square and its $p$ value when the same quantitative scores are divided into a different category for each score that contains one or more societies.

When the analysis of variance compares the means of two groups, this is equivalent to the cross-tabulation of a quantitatively scaled variable with a variable divided into two categories. In this case the $F$ ratio is based on one degree of freedom. The square root of $F$ is the $t$ ratio for testing the statistical significance of the difference between two means. The $p$ value is the same whether the measure is the $F$ ratio or its square root, the $t$ ratio.

When the analysis of variance compared the means of three or more groups, which were arranged in an ordinal sequence, we tested statistical significance of the ordinal trend, with one degree of freedom. This corresponds to the Mantel-Haenszel chi square for the relationship between two variables, one of which has three or more categories in an ordinal sequence. If the analysis of variance compared three or more means without specification of an ordinal sequence, the report on the $F$ value included the statement of the number of degrees of freedom. This indicated that the test was based on the difference among the three or more means without a test of the linear trend.

# Index